The World-System of Capitalism

POLITICAL ECONOMY OF THE WORLD-SYSTEM ANNUALS

Series Editor: IMMANUEL WALLERSTEIN

Published in cooperation with the Section on the Political Economy of the World-System of the American Sociological Association.

About the Series

The intent of this series of annuals is to reflect and inform the intense theoretical and empirical debates about the "political economy of the world-system." These debates assume that the phenomena of the real world cannot be separated into three (or more) categories—political, economic, and social—which can be studied by different methods and in closed spheres. The economy is "institutionally" rooted; the polity is the expression of socioeconomic forces; and "societal" structures are a consequence of politico-economic pressures. The phrase "world-system" also tells us that we believe there is a working social system larger than any state whose operations are themselves a focus of social analysis. How states and parties, firms and classes, status groups and social institutions operate within the framework and constraints of the world-system is precisely what is debated.

These theme-focused annuals will be the outlet for original theoretical and empirical findings of social scientists coming from all the traditional "disciplines." The series will draw upon papers presented at meetings and conferences, as well as papers from those who share in these concerns.

Volumes in this series:

Volume 1: *Social Change in the Capitalist World Economy* (1978)
Barbara Hockey Kaplan, *Editor*

Volume 2: *The World-System of Capitalism: Past and Present* (1979)
Walter L. Goldfrank, *Editor*

The World-System of Capitalism: Past and Present

Edited by
Walter L. Goldfrank

Volume 2, **Political Economy of the World-System Annuals**
Series Editor: Immanuel Wallerstein

 SAGE Publications　　Beverly Hills / London

For information address:

SAGE PUBLICATIONS, INC.
275 South Beverly Drive
Beverly Hills, California 90212

SAGE PUBLICATIONS LTD
28 Banner Street
London ECIY 8QE

Printed in the United States of America

Library of Congress Cataloging in Publication Data

Main entry under title:

The World-system of capitalism.

(Political economy of the world-system annuals ; v. 2)
Includes bibliographical references.
1. Capitalism—History—Congresses. 2. Economic
history—Congresses. I. Goldfrank, Walter L.
II. American Sociological Association. Section on
Political Economy of the World System. III. Series.
HC13.W67   330.12'2   78-26935
ISBN 0-8039-1105-X
ISBN 0-8039-1106-8 pbk.

FIRST PRINTING

CONTENTS

PREFACE

With one exception, the papers collected in this volume were presented at the second annual Political Economy of the World-System (PEWS) spring conference at the University of California, Santa Cruz, March 29-31, 1978. The sponsoring agency, PEWS, which is a section of the American Sociological Association, is a recently organized group that, due to the rigidities of the disciplinary organization of the social sciences in the United States, has a formal home and official members *within* the sociology profession, and unofficial network ties to anthropologists, economists, historians, and political scientists. It is perhaps a measure of how far we have yet to go toward our cross-disciplinary aim that only three of the papers herein are the work of nonsociologists; but note that this represents a full 200% gain over last year's annual.

Many persons helped to make the 1978 Conference a success, and it is a pleasure to thank them for their time and effort. Fred Block, Doug Dowd, and Kay Trimberger joined with me to form the organizing committee. Dowd, along with Barbara Hockey Kaplan, Alan Richards, and Theda Skocpol served excellently as discussants; I have benefitted from their comments in formulating parts of the introductory chapter. John Boli-Bennett ably substituted for a tardy colleague.

While the PEWS section of the ASA was the spiritual patron of these works, various sections of the University of California, Santa Cruz, provided indispensable material support: the Divisions of Humanities and of Social Sciences, and the Interdisciplinary Graduate Program in Sociology. In this regard, thanks are particularly due Edmund Burke III, Robert Adams, and Robert Alford. In addition, I remain indebted to many of the marvelous undergraduate and graduate students at UCSC for their assistance and attentiveness. In the last weeks, Kay House did yeoperson-like typing.

Finally, it is appropriate to note here the homage of the volume's title to the British historical journal *Past & Present*, a model for us all in its standards, its taste, its disciplined passion.

Walter L. Goldfrank
October 1978

INTRODUCTION: BRINGING HISTORY BACK IN

Walter L. Goldfrank

Fifteen years ago, George Homans (1964) delivered what may prove to have been one of the last gasps of a dying liberal utilitarianism with his unheeded and quaintly sexist call for "bringing men back in." One of the less noted features of that program for the derivation of sociological laws from an atomistic and behaviorist psychology was its utter ahistoricism. This trait was, of course, not unique to Homans' scheme, as it also marked the other leading paradigms of the day: structural-functionalism, middle-range role theory, conflict theory, symbolic interactionism, positivist human ecology, even newborn ethnomethodology. For so many social scientists to have convinced one another that social reality has no history in spite of their great differences on other important matters was quite a feat. Arguably, such an accomplishment required as its setting the prosperous hegemony of the U.S. in the world-system, which was also, not accidentally, a prosperous time for universities and for the social sciences within them. In those times—the "end of ideology" and its quasi-Marxist opposite, "one-dimensional man"—a few lone academic voices were not convinced. For example, Paul Baran and C. Wright Mills both saw the oppositional forces then emerging and incorporated, as did Barrington Moore, Jr., an historical dimension into their analyses. But the basic fact of the matter is that the social sciences of the time were massively ahistorical. At best, the past was "background" to the present.

Moreover, what was generally true of the leading sociological paradigms was even the case in studies of long-term, large-scale social change: there too, history was absent. Instead, an abstract irreversible

9

process called "modernization" was said to govern each society. Time only entered this "modernization" perspective as it appears in an airline schedule, denoting the presumptive "take-off" of one society after another, with some latter-day Protestant ethic or perhaps a dose of "achievement motivation" as the fuel. After that it would be smooth flying to the comfort and self-satisfaction of "high mass consumption" and "civic culture" and "elections: the democratic class struggle," *if only* "the disease of the transition" could be avoided. And of course, standing ready with all manner of vaccines against the disease was the imperial apparatus of the United States.

By bringing history back in, the papers collected in this volume represent quite a different point of view, called the "world-systems perspective." This viewpoint draws on diverse analytic strands in the history of social science: Braudel and the *Annales* school in French historiography; the historical economics of Weber, Schumpeter, and Polanyi; the Marxism of Lenin and Mao-Tse-tung; the anticolonial sociology of Balandier; the "Third World" perspectives of Fanon and the so-called "dependency" theorists. It thus owes little to the legacy of conventional U.S. social science, though clearly indebted to the directions pointed out by the lonely dissenters during the American celebration. The *locus classicus* of the world-systems perspective is Wallerstein's (1974) application of it to the enduring theoretical problem of the transition from feudalism to capitalism. Its analytic bare bones, in so far as the study of modern social change is concerned, are outlined in the first contribution which follows by Terence Hopkins. The antinomies of core and periphery, capital and labor, strong states and weak polities find useful summary exposition here. Note particularly the emphasis on process and on movement through time: for "accumula*tion*" one must read "accumula*ting*," for state "forma*tion*" state "form*ing*" (and reforming). Note also Hopkins' attempt to codify the methodological senses in which we struggle to recapture the necessarily historical constitution both of our subject matter and of ourselves as its students in a particular time and place.

Edwin Winckler's contribution (China's World System: Social Theory and Political Practice in the 1970s") analyzes a contrasting view of the contemporary world system, the "theory of three worlds" first advanced by Mao Tse-tung and subsequently elaborated by his successors in power. The would-be hegemonic superpowers, the U.S. and the U.S.S.R., comprise the first world; the other industrial countries of Europe plus Canada and Japan make up the second; and the third world is constituted by the familiar tricontinental grouping.

This conception is perhaps more an ad hoc response to changing world political alignments as the Chinese confront them, than an historically grounded perspective on world transformation. Empirically it seems to overrate the hegemonic capacity of the U.S.S.R. (but then we do not share a long border with that power). Yet theoretically, as Winckler suggests, it ironically raises the issue of a rather more Weberian world-system standpoint than Wallerstein's totalizing, essentially Marxian vision. This issue has been raised before (e.g., Skocpol, 1977) and will doubtless be debated for a long time. In my view, while it is crucial to be sensitive to the independent determinants and independent effects of the military/geopolitical world state system—and to avoid counter-factual reductionism, it seems preferable to stress through such a term as "political economy" the necessary interconnections between world politics and world economy. It is precisely the "relative autonomy" of the political, to use an elastic and scarcely precise term, that gives a world-*economy* its remarkable dynamism as compared with a world-*empire*—relative, not absolute, autonomy. Perhaps even more importantly, the economy (like "the personal") is political.

Parts II and III treat aspects of development in the core of the modern world-system, the former primarily in seventeenth-century Northwest Europe, the latter in the twentieth-century United States. Immanuel Wallerstein provides a tantalizing synopsis of the eagerly awaited second volume of *The Modern World-System*, in "Underdevelopment and Phase-B: Effect of the Seventeenth-Century Stagnation on Core and Periphery of the European World-Economy." Briskly he carries us through the contraction half of the long economic cycle whose expansion half (c.1450 - c.1620) was the subject of volume one. He discusses the consequences of contraction/stagnation for core, semi-periphery, and periphery; among them, the concentration of capital in the core through improved production of cereals and textiles, the build-up of strong state machineries there, and the enforcement of mercantilist policies enabling England and France to compete increasingly successfully with the (relatively) declining Dutch after mid-century. However, contraction approximates a zero-sum situation: the relative success of these core states was contingent on decline in the periphery and older semi-periphery; hence misery and involution in most of Eastern Europe and Spanish America, and deindustrialization in Spain and Northern Italy. The treatment of first Sweden and then Prussia as rising semi-peripheral states, taking advantage of rivalries among the core powers, will perhaps begin to satisfy some of the critics of Wallerstein's first volume, who found the analysis of those areas puzzling if not contradictory. In any case, this overview of volume two suggests the great value of seriously studying long cycles as well as the more familiar secular trends in accounting for the contours of the modern world.

Wallerstein argues that one of the indications of the strength of the Dutch state was the absence of major turbulence; Michael Kimmel's contribution, "Absolutism in Crisis: The English Civil War and the Fronde," is a partial account of the major turbulence that beset and temporarily weakened the other core states. Focusing on the state structures of England and France, Kimmel applies the contemporary term "fiscal crisis" to the burdens of competitive and/or imperial warmaking, and examines as well the political strength of the class groupings opposed to the monarchs. He clarifies some of the confusions in the analysis of the "absolutist" state by drawing a sharp distinction between the power of the *monarchy* and the power of the *state*. In England, the victory of the Parliamentarians weakened the king but strengthened the state; in France, the defeat of the *frondeurs* strengthened the king but weakened the state by leaving it, as Toqueville would later describe it, lacking in firm connections to its "natural" defenders, the nobility.

The two essays in Part III address quite different aspects of transformation in the core. In the most general sense, they deal with questions of ethnic stratification and what has come to be called labor segmentation, the specialization of particular groups (including gender and age groupings) in particular economic activities and unequal occupational niches. Against the predominant tendency in Marxism to portray a progressive homogenization of the proletariat, several recent lines of analysis are converging around the idea that differentiation rather than homogenization is the hallmark of modern capitalism. Feminists have rightly pointed to the historic specialization of women in household and reproductive labor as well as in particular service and light industrial jobs; some neo-Marxists have argued that sectoral splits in the economies of the advanced countries are reproduced rather than disappearing, with heavy concentrations of oppressed and/or migrant ethnic groups in the insecure "competitive" sector; and the core-periphery scheme in world-systems analysis portrays a richly layered array of workers with distinct and often conflicting interests.

To be sure, the two contributions here only scratch the surface of the issue of labor segmentation in the twentieth-century United States, let alone in the world economy as a whole. But they scratch that surface in interesting ways. Michael Hechter's chapter ("The Position of Eastern

European Immigrants to the United States in the Cultural Division of Labor: Some Trends and Prospects") documents and accounts for the rise of the East European migrants from the bottom of the class structure at the time of their recruitment into unskilled industrial jobs in the nineteenth century, to the middle of that structure today. He notes the periphery's subsidy to the core in the form of ready-to-work laborers who are, further, willing to work for lower wages than the previously resident population. Less assimilated than groups clustered above them, yet more assimilated in occupational and residential patterns than those below, the descendents of East Europeans are likely to persist in their ethnic identification for some time to come, especially since the growth of the U.S. economy appears sluggish for the foreseeable future. While the implications of this sort of analysis for the more general paradigm of world-system theory remain to be worked out, its discouraging implications for class-based politics have been clear for a century.

David Montejano's contribution ("Frustrated Apartheid: Race, Repression, and Capitalist Agriculture in South Texas, 1920-1930") also touches on the periphery's labor subsidy to the core. But it accomplishes much more than this. In his detailed account of the patterns of labor control in South Texas cotton farming, Montejano shows how class and race interacted to produce a distinctive local social order. He demonstrates how the existence of the political boundary between the United States and Mexico disabled the Mexican laborers, while at the same time the lack of such a border between South Texas and the rest of the U.S. prevented the Anglo cotton farmers from constructing an airtight apartheid system. His discussion of the *combination* of sharecropping (for a stable year-around work force) and migrant labor (for large crews at peak harvest times) is particularly instructive. A final lesson to be derived from his chapter is that one fundamental element in the transformation of core countries is the intensive exploitation of their *internal* peripheries. Cheap Texas cotton helped the U.S. textile industry to be competitive at a time of intense pressures in the then-stagnant world market.

In Parts IV and V, attention shifts largely to the peripheral zones of the capitalist world-economy. The three chapters on incorporation and resistance begin to address the questions on Hopkins' agenda regarding both the modes of appropriating surplus through varieties of "primitive accumulation," and the modes of integrating surplus through varieties of "primitive accumulation," and the modes of integrating this surplus to further expanded reproduction. Dilip Basu's contribution ("The Peripheralization of China: Notes on the Opium Connection") touches on several fascinating aspects of the transformation of China from "external arena" to periphery, and the causes and consequences thereof: the shift of tea from a luxury to a staple; the role of opium production in the peripheralization of Bengal (which, he implies, might have become a powerful semi-peripheral state had its political structure been different); the role of U.S. merchants as intermediaries and the investment in North American railroads of not only *U.S.* profits from the opium and tea trades, but also *Chinese* profits from those trades, over a century before multinational corporations discovered the benefits of seeking peripheral capital.

Paul Lubeck's "Islam and Resistance in Northern Nigeria" stresses the importance, for the fate of that region, of its remaining external to the expanding capitalist world-economy throughout the nineteenth century. First the North inadvertantly benefitted from the peripheralization of Southern Nigeria through the ending of the West African slave trade and the settling of captured peoples on surplus-generating estates. Lubeck further discusses several consequences of the growth of a distinctive "tributary" social form in the North: the role of Islam both for integrating a ruling class that would later strike a hard bargain with the (declining) British conquerors and for providing an ideology of antiimperial revolt for the population as a whole; also, the deleterious effects of the "gentrification" of the Northern ruling class on subsequent economic development. Note the implications of the analysis: counter to the predictions of the "modernization" perspective, the role of Islam increases over time, and the "traditional" ruling class's position is enhanced and solidified by modern colonialism.

A contrasting West African periphery is examined in Timothy Weiskel's chapter on the Baule of the Ivory Coast ("Labor in the Emergent Periphery: From Slavery to Migrant Labor among the Baule Peoples, c. 1880-1925"). The transformation in Baule relations of production is linked, in a manner at once clear and dialectical, to the intrusions of French colonialism. First the Baule system of household production with slave labor was expanded and reinforced by the French presence in nearby territories, where resistance wars had the unintended effects of increasing both the supply of slaves to the Baule and the demand for their products. Initial, successful Baule resistance was motivated by the desire to maintain this system intact when the French threatened to use Baule slaves for their own purposes. Then followed a transitional period of peripheralization in which the Baule began gathering wild rubber for the world market using the same system of labor controls. But when the price dropped in 1907 and incentives to produce thus slackened, the French used Senegalese troops to conquer the Baule and proceeded to institute higher taxes and forced labor to maintain rubber supplies and indeed to produce other tropical crops. Finally, a new system of cash crop production (mostly cocoa) emerged in the 1920s through the competition of three African groups: collaborating chiefs, resident aliens, and returned Baule emigrants. In order to supply labor for these new farms, for settler plantations, and for its own purposes, the colonial state organized a migratory labor system with workers from the North. In his concluding comparison of the situation of the precolonial slaves and their Baule masters with that of the colonial migrant workers and their employers, Weiskel argues that for most people, peripheralization was accompanied not only by a decline in political and social standing, but also by a decline in the level of living—the accumulation of capital at one pole, and of misery at the other.

The papers in Part V treat transformations and struggles in the twentieth-century periphery and semi-periphery, dealing with three of the most vital arenas of our time: China, Viet Nam, and South Africa. Richard Curt Kraus' chapter ("Withdrawing from the World System: Self-Reliance and Class Structure in China") analyzes the consequences of the Cold War isolation of China and the subsequent Sino-Soviet split for the Chinese class structure. If peripheralization is associated with increasing inequality, as the Lubeck and Weiskel papers suggest, so temporary withdrawal from the world-system creates conditions under which radically egalitarian policies can be pursued. Using what might be called a "shooting gallery" model of the class transformations of China, Kraus shows how an initial structure of six broad class groupings was reduced to three (bureaucrats, workers, and peasants) by the elimination first of landlords, then of the indigenous bourgeoisie, and finally of foreign—in this case Soviet—interests. He then proceeds to analyze the constraints on bureaucrats when they have neither foreign nor national capitalists with whom to ally, calling the Cultural Revolution an "ironic harvest" of their previous triumph over potential rivals. He completes his picture of class struggles in China with an account of unity and division among workers and between workers and peasants, closing with an appraisal of the possible obstacles to continued radicalism in Chinese social policy, radicalism made possible in part by the withdrawal called "self-reliance."

Ruth Milkman's contribution ("Contradictions of Semi-Peripheral Development: The South African Case") deals with two major questions: first, how can one account for the movement of South Africa from periphery to semi-periphery, when so few peripheral areas have managed such a transition; and second, what are the obstacles to deepening the accumulation process in the present conjuncture. In addressing the first question, Milkman lays a major emphasis on two factors: the unusual properties of gold as a primary export commodity (its price did not collapse, and actually rose, during the depression), and the role of the British and Afrikaner settlers in pushing for import-substituting industrialization through their growing hold on the state, and in providing an internal market for manufactures. The transformations wrought by gold and settlers then set the stage for the massive foreign investments in South Africa after World War II, and the contradictions of the current period of world-economic stagnation. Here she discerns several severe constraints: a chronic payments deficit due to a rising import bill for oil and capital goods; the inability of South African manufactures to compete outside Africa (and, one might add, perhaps in the middle run, given Nigerian advances, inside much of Africa as well); and the way in which the apartheid system limits the internal market even as it supplies very cheap labor. Finally, she notes the parallels between South African transformations and those of certain other nonsocialist semi-peripheral countries (Brazil, Iran, South Korea) with heavy repressive apparati and rapidly increasing inequalities. Again we find the accumulation of capital at one pole, the accumulation of misery at the other.

The final paper is Martin Murray's account of the heroic struggles of the Vietnamese rubber plantation workers in the period between the two world wars ("The Rubber Plantations of Colonial Indochina: The Colonial State and the Class Struggle between Wage-Labor and Capital, 1910-1940"). Here one finds a detailed analysis of the brutal exploitation of peripheral proletarians, of its increase due to the pressures of the slumping rubber market during the depression, and of the panoply of resistance tactics devised in response. Murray's data force one both to reconsider the easy application of the category "peasant" to the Vietnamese revolution, and to take full cognizance of the role of the colonial state in the construction and enforcement of the plantation labor system (cf. Somers and Goldfrank, 1979). Yet again, the harsh polarization essential to the accumulation of capital emerges with clarity, nowhere more so than in the second of Murray's well-chosen epigraphs.

To sum up the contents of this volume, one can discern two distinct if overlapping directions that world-system studies are taking. The first entails the inclusion of some key ideas from Wallerstein's model in analyses undertaken along rather more conventional lines. Exemplars of such analyses here are Kimmel's comparative-historical work, Hechter's and Montejano's treatments of ethnic stratification, Milkman's account of South African development, and Murray's study of class conflict. This mixing in of "world-system" variables not only enriches the particular works in question, but also suggests ways in which the conceptual framework needs extension, revision, or specification.

The second direction starts from this latter premise, basic, after all, to any scientific inquiry, and comprises a variety of attempts to refine, elaborate, and/or apply the world-system perspective. Here one can point to Hopkins' theoretical and methodological ruminations, to Winckler's review of Chinese world-system notions, to Wallerstein's own grappling with the seventeenth-century stagnation, and to the remainder of the chapters on peripheral incorporation, resistance, and transformation. Alas, it is probably not accidental that students of the core disproportionately resist the world-systems perspective, for it challenges the comfortable illusion that we core-dwellers "advanced" so far through our own efforts. That illusion is, however, myth rather than history, and it is history we wish to retrieve.

REFERENCES

HOMANS, G. (1964). "Bringing men back in." American Sociological Review, 29 (December):809-818.

SKOCPOL, T. (1977). "Wallerstein's world capitalist system: A theoretical and historical critique." American Journal of Sociology, 82(5):1075-1090.

SOMERS, M., and GOLDFRANK, W. (1979). "The limits of agronomic determinism: A critique of Paige's Agrarian Revolution." Comparative Studies in Society and History (forthcoming).

WALLERSTEIN, I. (1974). The modern world-system: Capitalist agriculture and the origins of the European world-economy in the sixteenth century. New York: Academic Press.

PART I

ISSUES IN THEORY AND METHOD

Chapter 1

THE STUDY OF THE CAPITALIST WORLD-ECONOMY: SOME INTRODUCTORY CONSIDERATIONS

Terence K. Hopkins

I address these opening remarks to four topics. The first is the construct of "the modern world system;" the second is capital-accumulation on a world scale; the third, state-formation; and the fourth, some problems of method. The remarks are at every point abbreviated, in keeping with the notion that they are only "introductory considerations."

ON THE CONSTRUCT, "THE MODERN WORLD-SYSTEM"[1]

The kind of inquiry, and the field of inquiry, which are becoming known these days as "world-system studies"—or world-historical studies, or capitalist world-economy studies, or the study of modern social change—develop, in our generation, in a fairly straightforward way. Such studies derive directly from immediately preceding approaches to the study of long-term, large-scale social change of the past, present, and forthcoming future (in this sense "historical" change). There is nothing mysterious or exotic about it, as I shall try to suggest sketchily at the outset here.

Inquiry into long-term, large-scale social change, in the form it commonly takes today, has its beginnings in American universities in the late 1940s and early 1950s. The Cold War produced area-studies programs, and decolonization expanded them. Economists resumed (or invented) studying economic development, sociologists social development, and political scientists political development, while anthropologists (deprived of "their" peoples by independence movements) rediscovered evolution, and historians belatedly recognized that North Atlantic societies had not merely "histories," but actual "patterns of development." These "modernization" studies, as they came to be called, were always "comparative" in approach, at first implicitly, later quite explicitly, usually with Great Britain and/or the United States serving as the anchoring point for the comparisons. In due course, in the 1960s, a procedure (sometimes then called a "logic") for conducting comparative studies of modernization or of national societies became explicitly formulated and fairly widely accepted.

Almost simultaneously with the growth of "modernization" studies, however, their view of social change came under attack. "Modernization" studies focus on "national" units and presume usually tacitly, that as people form "independent" national states, these "new" states start on a course of development that will eventually traverse the same stages of development which the reigning North Atlantic national societies, notably first Great Britain and then the United States, have apparently traversed historically. Those initially challenging this view (the "dependency" theorists) argued that no, the present well-being of advanced states was owing in no small measure to the advantageous relations they have had with less-developed states, which thereby were in a structurally new kind of international setting and so would in all probability have to traverse a different route of development and probably pass through different "stages." The controversy grew and became increasingly "historical." The further claim was made increasingly that not merely the present well-being of the advanced states but their very development as "advanced" states had required and been dependent on their having exploitative relations with other parts of the world. This latter thesis (advanced by the "imperialism" theorists) implied still more, however. It implied that a single basic set of general economic processes underlies the world's uneven development. It was these processes, in conjunction with national-scale and imperial-scale political processes, that had produced, and were continuing to produce, the historical development of the North Atlantic states and the historical underdevelopment of the African, Latin American, and

(excepting Japan) Asian states. Two heretofore unrelated fields of
scholarly inquiry, European economic history and Third-World
political studies, thus became joined—to the dismay for the most part
of specialists in each. It remained, though, to make the argument
explicit. This was done by those advancing the thesis that a single
capitalist world-economy has been developing since the sixteenth
century and that its development has been the driving force of modern
social change. Proposed by several current scholars, this thesis has
been propounded most fully and most forcefully by Wallerstein
(1974a, 1974b).

If, now, one were to try to give the main ideas informing the
construct of "the modern world-system" in a highly abbreviated form,
they might run as follows. First, there is the "structure" of this social
system, consisting of: (a) one expanding economy; (b) expanding
multiple states; and (c) the capital-labor relation. Second, there is this
social system's "development." But before turning to that, let me
briefly comment on these three "structural" features.

(a) There is one expanding economy. This conventionally appears
to us, however, in the form of various "national" (and "colonial")
economies related through "international" trade. This one world-
scale economy, which is progressively more global in scope, has a
single or *axial* division and integration of labor processes ("division of
labor"), which is both organized and paralleled by a single set of
accumulation-processes, between its always more advanced, historically enlarging, and geographically shifting *core* and its always less
advanced, disproportionately enlarging, and geographically shifting
periphery. The terms "core" and "periphery" thus designate complementary portions of the world-economy and only derivatively pertain
to its political divisions (e.g., as in the expression, "core-states)
(Hopkins, 1978:207-208).

(b) There are expanding multiple states in the double sense that
particular states are expanding their jurisdictions and that the number
of states forming units of the interstate system is expanding. They
continually form (and are terminated) in a definite political arena, the
interstate-system, through relations of rivalry and alliance with one
another and externally, and they continually attempt to extend their
dominion (1) in relation to one another, and (2) with considerable
success overall, over external peoples and areas ("imperium"). This
latter movement, however, at once sets in motion processes ("antiimperial movements") that recurrently result in an expansion both of

the number of states and of the number of real (not merely logical) interstate relations forming the interstate-system.

(c) There is also the capital-labor relation, which the accumulation process not only operates through but continually reproduces, and on an expanding scale. This is the social-political framework, itself developing through various forms, that progressively organizes (1) production interrelations, and (2) intra- and interstate politics, so that formally rational considerations, in specific contrast to substantively rational considerations (vide Weber; in Marx, "exchange" versus "use" considerations), thus come increasingly to govern the courses of action pursued by individuals (households), communities, organizations, and "states."

As to the "development" of the capitalist world-economy, two general points may be briefly made. (1) The extensions of (a) the interrelations of production, (b) the state-system, and (c) the capital-labor relation converge to form definite, alternating periods ("social times") of the system's overall expansion-stagnation; probably, too, the chronological lengths of the periods compress as the system's growth eliminates competing forces of social organization and social change (e.g., localism, cultural forces) (Research Working Group, 1978). (2) The inherent contradiction between the development of the "one economy" and the development of the "multiple states" continually paces, and shows itself in specific forms in the course of, the social system's long-term development (which equals modern social change). With respect to this last point—about the "inherent contradictions" between a single world-scale economy and multiple state-jurisdictions—perhaps the fundamental theoretical claim is this: It is the articulation of the *processes* of the world-scale division and integration of labor and the *processes* of state-formation and deformation (the latter in the twin context of interstate relations and relations of imperium) that constitute the system's formation and provide an account, at the most general level, for the patterns and features of its development (hence, of the patterns and features of modern social change). The articulation of the two sets of processes necessarily results, in the theory, in the network of relations among political formations (states, colonies, etc.) being patterned like the network of relations among production-accumulation zones (core-periphery, *and vice versa*. The following elliptically enlarge on this last point. the network of relations among production-accumulation zones (core-periphery), *and vice versa*. The following elliptically enlarge on this last point.

Centrality in the axial economic network and centrality in the political network thus tend to coincide. Strong states, in relation to others, develop in core *areas*; weak states, in relation to others, develop or rather are developed in peripheral areas. Not less important, *strong* states, in relation both to their internal regions and to other states, develop *core* processes; weak states (weak in both directions: relative to internal regions and to contending states) develop, or rather have developed for them, peripheral processes. It is important to have in mind that "peripheral" does not mean marginal in the sense of dispensable: without peripheries, no cores: without both, no capitalist development.

The two sets of processes thus primarily reinforce one another over the reach of the evolving system as a whole. However, they do not do so for long in any one place, owing to several contradictory tendencies. Two important ones illustrates this general point: (1) the growing competition among states (owing to their increasing number and their increasingly competitive policies) to house centers of the production-accumulation network versus the strengthening tendency of that network toward centralization of the accumulation process (fewer centers); (2) the increasing influence of class-organized politics (resulting from capitalist development) on state-policies versus the increasingly competitive search by larger and larger units of capital for larger and larger pools of low-cost labor.

The double level of competition, among states and among capitalists, coupled with their articulation, entails the expansion of the system as a whole. Capitalists further accumulation by seeking low-cost production operations for supplies and/or high-return markets for products. States seek allies and/or resources to further or to attain competitive advantage. The result is the political process we call "imperium" and the economic process we call "peripheralization." The extent of each is a result partly of the opposition encountered or provoked, a *datum*, and partly of the competition among and centralization of the states engaged in the expansion. By the overall movement, the system thus both creates and as it develops eliminates an "external arena"—one which, in the event, has turned out to be everywhere that was outside the system's original arena.

From this preliminary sketch of the construct, several theoretical concerns can be derived. I rapidly review two here, accumulation of capital and formation of states.

ACCUMULATION OF CAPITAL

Marx's theory of *capitalist* accumulation of capital (hence the term "self-expansion of capital") is a useful point of departure for us for two reasons. One is the centrality of the subject matter in the development of the modern world-system. The other is his angle of vision: his is virtually the only major theory of the subject not implicitly or explicitly about national (or international) development, but about capitalist development in general, i.e., as we choose to interpret it, about capitalist development on a world-scale.

The theory being well-known, a sketch of its major points seems sufficient for present purposes. Its focus is the growing extent and complexity of productive forces in the form of increasing mechanization (roughly indicated by increasing capital-labor ratios) owing to pressures on "capitalists" (owners of means of production and employers of wage-labor) to lower overall costs of production. The pressures come from two directions: from among themselves through their competition to buy cheaply and to sell dearly (their given concern being to maximize the difference in all time periods between revenues and costs); and from among workers through their demands for less dehumanizing ("improved") working and living conditions (higher production costs). Central to the formulation are two ideas. One concerns the production (here including distribution) by the work force of commodities "of more value than that of the elements entering into" their production. Specifically of interest (since all produced commodities sell, overall, at relative prices proportionate to their embodied values) are produced commodities whose value, by virtue of the labor power expended to produce them, is greater than the value (as variable capital) of the subsistence goods replenishing (daily, annually, generationally) the labor power expended (and embodied) in their production, the difference being "surplus value." The other concerns the "realization" and appropriation by capitalists of this surplus value in money form through the (successive) sale of the produced commodities and the use of portions of this realized surplus to pay for additions to capital, especially fixed capital.

The accumulation of capital in this way results theoretically and historically in, among other things: the growing concentration of capital; the competitive elimination of small producers and the increasing centralization of capital (the increasing size on the average of the capital owned/controlled by each); the growing proportion of people available to employment by capital, but the decreasing

proportion, ceteris paribus, of those so employed by capital-intensi-
fying branches of industry ("surplus" population); a resulting histori-
cal/political narrowing of social definitions of the employable and/or
of the times of employment, but still increasing unemployment among
the lawfully employable segments of national (colonial) populations; a
resulting overall downward pressure on real wage-levels (costs of
labor), from competition (demand) for employment, but for given (not
examined) social and political reasons, a pressure that is unevenly
distributed among a working population's individuals and groups;
consequently, a tendency for capital to expand labor-intensive production (countering the tendency for capital-intensive production, indicated above) in order to employ the low-wage segment of the
workforce which is continually created by the growing competition for
employment (the effect being to depress wage-specific employment,
but to increase head-count employment); and—finally for here—the
marked tendency through time for these diverse movements to occur in
the form of cycles of expansion and stagnation (Schumpeter's "great
peripeteias of economic life"). This, because of an increasingly
complex array of "proportionalities"—such as capital/labor proportionalities, production-function proportionalities (excluding labor of
course), supply-demand (hence price) proportionalities in various
markets (for money capital, consumer or subsistence goods, producer
or capital goods, labor), proportionalities of competition (size distribution of firms in the same industries), inter-industry proportionalities,
and so forth—these proportionalities change through time at different
rates and, among the set of them either at mutually reinforcing or at
mutually offsetting rates, with "booms" and "busts" the result and
"crises" marking turning points.

As important as the theory is for the study of the modern world-
system's operation and development, in both the detail and the scope
of its arguments, it is not less important for the clarity with which its
author stipulates its limits. For in this way he points in effect to places
where further theoretical work is needed and extensions of the theory
itself may most usefully occur. Two such fundamental points are
specifically of interest here, capital-accumulation itself and the
question of wage-levels.

CAPITAL-ACCUMULATION

The first has to do with the place which the theoretically depicted
process (or complex of processes) of *capitalist* accumulation of

capital occupies in the world-historical or world-systemic accumulation of capital. The residual created by Marx as he constructed his theory was "original" or "primitive" accumulation in *Capital*, Part VIII. By this he specifically meant the historically original creation in Europe of the conditions for the "capitalistic" development of capital (reproduction on an expanding scale), and thus for the kind of development the theory depicts and explains. This is the issue of the "transition" from feudalism to capitalism in northwestern Europe and so lies outside our present purview. But the concept may also be interpreted as referring to the continuing counterpart of that "original" or "primitive" accumulation of capital, namely, the continuing creation (extension) of the conditions for the "capitalistic" development of capital in all branches of production (old and new) in every nook and cranny of the globe outside the geopolitical area of their initial world-historical creation. This requires elaboration.

Marx is reasonably clear about his assumptions, and since in *Capital* he is concerned only with the "self-expansion of capital," and not also with the expansion of capital in other ways (such as the continual conversion of material means of production into capital through the expropriation of direct producers), he assumes for theoretical purposes "that capitalist production (including wage-labor) is everywhere established and has possessed itself of every branch of industry" (Vol. I, chap. 24, sec. 1). There is thus left open: one, the theoretical processes depicting and explaining the ongoing conversion of noncapitalized means of production and subsistence into capital, in the course of the outward expansion of the capitalist-world-economy from its formative locus to, today, virtually the whole of the globe; and two, the integration of these processes with those of capital's self-expansion (so as to form an array of interrelated arguments addressed to the entirety of the accumulation of capital on a progressively wider world-scale).

In particular, the theoretically open matters concern accumulation by capitalists of surpluses from areas of the world-system or branches of production in which (1) non-wage workers of one kind or another (slaves, serfs, indebted tenants, etc.) form the dependent (employed) labor force, and (2) independent producers (family farmers, other small producers) effectively form the labor force. In the context of the capitalist world-economy as a whole, not only do such labor forces include the great majority of workers at any particular time (even today). They may also include those producing the greater part of the total of surplus and surplus-value together which, in realized form and appropriated by capitalists as additions to capital, amounts to capital's total expansion or accumulation.

These observations are, in an important sense, not in the least novel. Before World War I, prompted by theoretical misgivings, Luxemburg wrote a treatise (*The Accumulation of Capital*) on the relations between "capitalist" and "noncapitalist" branches and areas of production. In it she devoted a full third of her study to a review of how previous authors, both pre-Marx and post-Marx, has approached these relations. The subject matter is hardly a new one. In the same period, although prompted more by historical developments than by reservations of a theoretical nature (Marx's treatment of "realization" concerned Luxemburg), other Marxists were also addressing the subject—Hilferding (*Finance Capital*), Lenin (*Imperialism*), and Bukharin (*Imperialism and World-Economy* and *Imperialism and the Accumulation of Capital*) to name three. A generation later Sweezy considered the question (in *The Theory of Capitalist Development*), and most recently Mandel (in *Marxist Economic Theory* and subsequently *Late Capitalism*), to mention only the two best-known contemporaries. And so the theoretically open matter has not exactly been neglected.

Our interests here, however, seem to be seriously different. In the study of the modern world-system the question is not the one posed by Luxemburg, debated by her critics, and reviewed by later theorists, namely, whether imperialism is necessary for an adequate theoretical account of realization (the realization in money form of the surplus value embodied in commodities in material form) or whether, instead, one may remain entirely within a hypothetically closed world of capitalistic accumulation of capital and have no difficulty in providing an adequate theoretical account. It is evidently an important question, but it is not ours, which is entirely different. Ours breaks down into two broad queries. One, what *kinds* of processes, theoretically, combine with the "closed" self-expansion process to depict and account for the *overall* accumulation process of the modern world-system in the course of its continuing development (especially since the latter may have played (and may even now still play) a *quantitatively* subordinate part in accumulation, however qualitatively important its directional role in development has undoubtedly been)? And, two, what have been the relational arrangements through which the different kinds of surpluses have been combined, and how should these segments of larger relational networks be conceptualized and theoretically accounted for?

An illustration on the last point: we know that in some way in the nineteenth century some of the surplus in kind produced by Ottoman peasants and appropriated by their landlords (as tribute, rent, etc.) eventually wound up, in the form of francs on deposit, in ledgers of European capitalists as profits; but we do not know theoretically the circuits through which such appropriated surpluses became transformed into money capital, let alone empirically the relational networks involved, the intervening commissions, or the overall estimated amounts.

WAGE-LEVELS

The determination of wage-levels is another fundamental point where Marx expressly limits the scope of his theoretical system. Central to production, as was said, is the notion of replenishing the labor power expended in production (including distribution or circulation). In the form in which the theory is presented, this replenishment occurs through the capitalists' paying workers money (wages) for their commodity (labor power), and the latter paying merchants the money for their commodities, namely, means of subsistence (or consumer goods). It is here that a limit to the theory's scope expressly comes. For one of course wonders about the "level of subsistence" at which workers are assumed to live and which theoretically must be continually reproduced and hence about the wage-level (cost of production) that needs to obtain if, in accordance with the theory, workers are to replenish—daily, annually, and generationally—the labor power they expend.

Again Marx is clear about the assumption he makes (*Capital*, Vol. I, chap.6):

> The number and extent of workers' so-called necessary wants . . . depend . . . to a great extent on the degree of civilization of a country, more particularly on the conditions under which, and consequently on the habits and degree of comfort in which, *the class of free laborers has been formed*. . . . [T]herefore . . . there enters into the determination of the value of labor-power a historical and moral element. Nevertheless, in a

given country, at a given period, the average quantity of the means of subsistence necessary for the laborer is practically known." [Emphasis added.]

Durkheim phrased the last point a bit differently though, and somewhat more inclusively, using it to state not a limit but a premise of a theory (*Suicide,* Book Two, Chap. V):

As a matter of fact, at every moment of history there is a dim perception, in the moral consciousness of societies, of the respective value of different social services, the relative reward due to each, and the consequent degree of comfort appropriate on the average to workers in each occupation.

The question that arises, of course, is what happens in the overall (combined) accumulation process, and to directions of development, when the world-system's expansion creates or "seizes upon" marked differences among its countries (Marx) or societies (Durkheim), in "degrees of civilization," in the "conditions under which the class of free laborers has been formed," in the "degree of comfort deemed morally appropriate . . . to workers in each occupation?" We can put the matters at issue more sharply, however, if we first briefly review theories about the origins and development of the capitalist world-economy's axial division and integration of core-area and peripheral-area labor processes.

The relational pair of core (or center) and periphery was first extensively used in its current connotation by Raul Prebisch and his associates in the early days of the United Nations Economic Commission for Latin America (United Nations, 1950; Prebisch, 1959; Baer, 1962). The focus of their work was on the deteriorating "terms of trade" for agricultural and mineral products in relation to manufactured products in international commerce, and the terms were used to designate the two major kinds of participants in that commerce, the exporters of manufactures (the industrialized countries of the North Atlantic plus Japan) forming the "center" and the exporters of agricultural and extractive products (the rest of the non-Communist world) forming the "periphery." These two poles were taken as given for the period under review, and attention was focused on a particular mechanism (the formulation of which, however, partially anticipated Emmanuel's analysis of "unequal exchange," discussed shortly), whose operation accounted for the deteriorating terms. The presence of this mechanism contradicted a basic assumption of the prevalent Ricardian "theory of international trade" and therefore was said to explain why what should have been happening theoretically was not in fact happening historically. The conception thus provided a stable framework for a process which, not unlike Myrdal's "principle of circular and cumulative causation" or, even, Nurkse's "vicious circle of poverty," showed how the world-scale regional division of labor, *once established,* was maintained (Nurkse, 1953; Myrdal, 1956).

However, the analysis was not directed at the processes of division of labor through which the respective patterns of export-specialization had formed initially, had been deepened as the world-system developed, and had both anchored and been anchored by the social structures and state-formation in which they were located. It was essentially those who later became known as the "dependency" theorists (again, primarily students of Latin American conditions and history) who, drawing on Baran's work, introduced "the long view" into the core-periphery conception and converted it from being a given condition at a particular time into a continually reproduced feature in the historical development of capitalism and, in particular, of the capitalist world-economy.[2] The central theoretical theme in their studies was (in A.G. Frank's phrase) "the development of underdevelopment." In this view "economic backwardness" was not at all a matter of "starting late," but was instead itself a condition produced in the course of and as the result of the rise of capitalism. Core-periphery thus provided these writers with the indispensable dynamic relational setting they needed for their analyses of trends, patterns, events, and conditions in the countries of the periphery, in which they were primarily interested.

As I stressed in the initial sketch, in world-system studies the core-periphery relation itself is central to the operation and development of the capitalist world-economy. It itself is a major focus of attention. Thus, what is "ground" in dependency studies becomes "figure" in world-system studies.

Now, the workings of the core-periphery relation do not depend on any particular arrangements interrelating the various partial production processes. The integration may be effected by colonial trade monopolies (such as The East India Company), by transactions internal to contemporary multinational corporations, by a world-scale market mediated through one or more commodity-exchanges, by bi- or multilateral barter-like agreements among states, and so forth. Whatever the arrangements, they are always and everywhere characterized (at one level of analysis) by the phenomenon of "unequal exchange" and operate (at a more abstract level) as forms of the process of unequal exchange. As process, then, unequal exchange works through an extraordinarily wide array of historical forms and arrangements to reproduce continually the basic core-periphery division and integration—despite massive changes over the centuries in the actual organization of production processes and despite continual shifts in the areas and processes forming the system's core, semiperiphery, and periphery.

Among those agreeing on the persistence and operation of this fundamental process, however, how it operates and why are still matters of considerable ongoing debate.[3] The issues, I think, are neither so obscure nor so technical as some discussions make them seem; but they are fundamental—of that there can be little doubt. To see that this is so, let us resume the discussion of wage-levels.

A fairly straightforward way of specifying the matter theoretically seems possible: one, there is the explicit limit (see above) to the theory of capitalist development, in the version of it Marx lays out and others have subsequently elaborated; and two, there is the premise Durkheim lays down in order to pursue a particular line of reasoning (about "anomie"). Wage-levels—to leave it at that for now—depend on "historical and moral" elements and in particular "on the conditions under which . . . the class of free laborers has been formed." And the processes assuring relatively slow rates of change in markedly divergent wage-levels, whatever part narrowly market considerations might appear to play in particular times and places, are those operating to reinforce or to alter the "dim perception[s], in the moral consciousness of societies," of the "degree of comfort appropriate . . . to workers in *each* occupation" (emphasis added). In short, we come upon the processes of systems of relational rank in the modern world (what is conventionally called stratification). Historically, these processes are more immediately political than (in the narrow conventional sense) economic, however much directions of economic development undoubtedly lead to, and then away from, the political benchmarks ("liberty, equality, fraternity") and the political processes that give shape and substance to systems of relational, and thus relative, social rank (processes such as enactment and enforcement of laws supporting or preventing relations of personal bondage, civil liberties and civil rights, progressive or regressive taxation, open or closed or discriminating immigration). Put another way, rank systems disintegrate in the face of certain economic developments—"Every technological repercussion and economic transformation threatens stratification by status and pushes the class situation into the foreground" (Weber, 1968:938)—but they *form* in the modern world by virtue of either sustained state-policies or sustained opposition to state policies—the "age of the democratic revolution" was not Palmer's invention (1959, 1964).

More generally, here is a definite place where processes of consciousness and ideology enter as integral to the theory of capital-accumulation on a world scale. But it is also here that we come to an almost abrupt halt theoretically. For aside from general observations by Durkheim, some historically specific constructions by Weber, footnotes in Mannheim, Marshall's sketch, and Ossowki's highly original but seriously undeveloped proposals, there are no studies of a conventionally sociological nature on the *theory* of the formation and development of social consciousness and ideologies that bear even in an involuted way on the matters at issue here (Durkheim, 1947; Weber, 1954; Mannheim, 1936; Marshall, 1964; Ossowski, 1963). Discussions of "rising expectations," "occupational prestige," and the like all of course presuppose a theory of social consciousness, but none that I know of qualifies as even an elliptical, partial, or aesopian statement of such a theory. Were there not important studies in other quadrants of today's scholarly compass, we would simply have to break off our discussion at this most unsatisfactory point. There are such studies, however, particularly in two quarters, which overlap theoretically if hardly in personnel.

One might be called the Black intellectual tradition of inquiry into the relationships between, one, kinds of social structures created in the course of the modern world-system's formation and expansion and, two, patterns of consciousness—hence "habits and degrees of comfort" expected by workers in relation to others—integral to them. Even a short review of the arguments being developed in this quarter of the scholarly world is not possible in the confines of this paper, however, and a mere listing of leading names will have to serve as an elliptical reference to the ideas—names such as DuBois, Cox, James, Williams,

Fanon, Freyre, Memmi.[4] As far as current scholarly inquiry goes, the most advanced theoretical work on material conditions and consciousness is being done out of this developing tradition, and its understandings point the way toward the kind of theory of consciousness that appears to be indispensable to an adequate theoretical account of the process of unequal exchange.

The other is the line of analysis, essentially anthropological in character, emerging out of the decolonization debates of the 1950s and 1960s and embodied in such writings as George Balandier's (1966) "The Colonial Situation: A Theoretical Approach," and Bernard Magubane's (1971) "A Critical Look at Indices of Social Change." Here the movement of economic development under given political conditions, the consequently changing material conditions, and the developing consciousness they result in and, in turn, are affected by, are brought out with especial theoretical clarity. Both the specificity of the debates of which these writings were a part, however, and the details of the situations they are about, make generalized picturings of the interrelated processes they depict difficult to draw and tentative in the extreme when drawn. At the same time, their potential contribution to our theoretical understanding of the fundamental process of unequal exchange as it works on the ground seems considerable.

FORMATION OF STATES

Let me now turn to some processes shaping the modern world-system's major political arenas or networks: its historically original interstate system; its political centers, the constituent states that form or are reconstituted as the interrelated units of that system; and its imperial patterns which these states establish, in relation to one another, over peoples elsewhere in the world—patterns which are continually interrupted and transformed by the antiimperial movements they perforce set in motion and the rivalries they define and reflect.

Here there are difficulties. Most students of modern social change tacitly presume the framework of a relatively autonomous abstract state (or economy, or society) as the given locus within which the changes they are explaining take place. Our concern, in contrast, is with the formation and development of the larger and longer-enduring setting. Put another way, today's world of interrelated and massively unequal sovereign jurisdictions cannot be taken as a given in world-system studies—as the point of departure for picking and choosing a site or two of state-formation or nation-building—in order to construct a theory of such developments inductively. It itself is a subject matter in need of examination and explanation. There is thus no theory of the formation of states on a world-scale comparable to (let alone integral to) the theory of the accumulation of capital on a world-scale. Also there are thus no explicit basic assumptions which, when relaxed, provide sharply defined points of departure for further theoretical work on the fundamental processes of modern social change. In this section, therefore, introductory considerations in the study of the capitalist world-economy concern not theoretical issues proper, but only organizing or potentially organizing concepts and at best, some preliminary sketches for possible theoretical formulations.

THE INTERSTATE SYSTEM[5]

The interstate system (often called the international system) has its beginnings with the virtually simultaneous formation of the so-called "new monarchies" in Europe at the end of the fifteenth century—the French (Louis XI), the Spanish (Ferdinand and Isabella), the English (Henry VII), and the "Austrian" (Maximilian I)—and the subsequent novel establishment at each major European court of permanent embassies from each of the other major courts. None proved able by war or marriage to incorporate the others; and with a pair of treaties in the middle of the seventeenth century, what had perforce become practice—balance of power politics—became as well a principle and a "system."

This European state-system formed in the developing-core area of the world division of labor, primarily as the relations among the states-in-formation there, i.e., among political communities, increasingly centralized in order to mount efforts to expand their jurisdictions over core-area processes and thus, necessarily, over and at the expense of one another. The system, in short, primarily constitutes the interstate relations among rival, and in the event stronger and weaker, core-states and their semi-peripheral state allies. It is thus a set of arrangements not so much for deterring war as for waging it. What marks it is this: the alignments or sides are so formed on each occasion ("balance of power") as to reproduce, as the outcome of conflict, the necessary condition for the state-system to continue to operate, namely, an array of interrelated states no one of which can mobilize the force and allies needed to subjugate all the others (thus perserving the development of the modern world as a world-economy by blocking its conversion into a world-empire).[6] The network expands by invitation, outsiders always being brought in to help block a growing power (the Ottoman court in the sixteenth century against Charles V, the Russian in the eighteenth against the French monarchy's moves). With the inclusion of the United States and then Japan at the end of the nineteenth century, it becomes de facto a global system, which in no way, however, impairs its operation as a system of shifting alliances among core-states and their semi-peripheral-state allies for the conduct of war. What *is* impaired, of course, is the relational (and relative) strength of the states in Europe. The decisive locus of interstate politics shifts out of *their* interrelations and into the relations between the U.S. and the U.S.S.R.; and the so-called "new" and "old" state-units of the now global international system form its Third World.

Both cause and consequence of the shifting alignments, the open conflicts and their outcomes would seem to be the underlying and ongoing changes in the location of what we have been calling the modern world-system's axial division of labor, which is what is meant by speaking of the economic reasons for the wars and alignments. In particular, focusing now on the lines of interrelated production processes that converge toward, and thus form, the respective centers of the core-area, some centers—or rather, some politically unified as well as economically interrelated centers—develop more rapidly than others usually by virtue of more rapid capital formation (which in turn usually results more or less directly from state policies). As this occurs, the existing set of political borders—which reflect and shape the directions in which interrelations of production processes develop—increasingly become constraints on the continued growth of the more dynamic core-area centers. The interstate system is the mechanism, so to speak, through which existing political borders are made more or less permeable (open or closed), and on occasion are redrawn altogether (powerless political entities are not invariably preserved), and new borders demarcating previously unincorporated areas are determined. It operates in part, then, as the reflex of the underlying changing relational strengths and weaknesses of the constituent core-states. But its operation also directly contributes to the rise or decline in the relative centrality of the stronger core-state(s); to the permeability of *their* borders; and to the existence of weaker states either as continuing core-states or as progressively semi-peripheral states (through their borders' coming increasingly to enclose peripheral areas of the axial division of labor).

Here, let me briefly mention the "hegemony/rivalry" notion. In the interstate system, the ongoing rivalries between or among existing core-states (especially between those containing the established centers of the accumulation processes and those developing competing centers) have given the interstate system its major form and phases. Two contrasting forms or configurations of these relations are as follows. In one, a core-state (or, in another language, a great power) is "hegemonic," in the sense that "all roads lead to Rome," from which it follows that the political borders demarcating the sovereign jurisdictions within the core and semi-peripheral areas are relatively permeable (labor, money, and materials move relatively freely across them). In the other, the configuration is one of rivalry; there is no center of centers, so to speak, and the political borders enclosing the rival centers are by comparison much less permeable (or open), and the same holds for the borders of the semi-peripheral states housing regional centers that are, in effect (and usually by design), contenders. As the interstate system has developed from its shadowy origins among the unsuccessful contestants for imperium in sixteenth-century Europe, the configuration of hegemony has occurred only on three occasions, and each time briefly—the periods of Dutch hegemony, British hegemony, and U.S. hegemony. The configuration of rivalry has by definition alternated, although lasting far longer each time, and the overall development of the interstate system has thus had the form of three long cycles.

STATE FORMATION AND TRANSFORMATION

We turn now to conceptions of the formation and transformation of states, viewed from the outset as the sovereignties of the interstate system. There is wide agreement among comparative historians and scholars of civilizations on the historical originality of the European state-system. For example, Walter Dorn (1963:1) begins a study by noting that the "competitive character of the state system of modern Europe . . . distinguishes it from the political life of all previous and non-European civilizations of the world." It is thus especially disconcerting that none of the explicit theories of state-formation (nation-building and the like) takes this apparently unique setting as its point of departure.[7] Perhaps the most generally used picturing of the developmental tendencies of political communities that become units (states-in-formation) of the interstate system is something like this. The relational setting sets in motion within each claimed jurisdiction processes of centralization through which the center (the monarch, court, prince, etc.) gains increasing control over more men and resources (in order to expand and so to have access to still more men and resources, or to defend against others' expansions). The incursion into regional bailiwicks which this entails sets up one kind of opposition, resulting in some form of parliament to mediate the center-region relation. The increased taxation it entails sets up another kind of opposition, resulting in some form of apparatus, emanating from the center, to overcome popular resistance, which in turn requires increased organization on the part of the populace, and so forth. The anatomy thus becomes a center (monarch, court), a parliament of initially regional interests (nobles, higher bourgeoisie, churchmen), an apparatus of administration (bureaucracy) and of war-making and repression (army, police), and a populace more or less able to organize for a local opposition to exactions (usually the more so, *ceteris paribus,* the more concentrated people are). The lines are of course seldom clear cut, and they are further blurred by other organizing forces at work (very broadly, the economic and the cultural). But such seems to be the pattern of the relational networks that in due course are formed into a "state" structure.

Historically, the most important structural transformation of such "states" comes through the revolutionary ascendancy of the bourgeoisie (whether also ennobled or not is irrevelent). They displace the regional lords (and often enough the monarchial center as well), and increasingly utilize and develop the administrative and repressive apparatuses to help with expropriating workers from means of production, securing adequate supplies of workers, and keeping workers under control. The internal operations of core-states thus become increasingly supportive of capitalists' interests; worker opposition accordingly becomes increasingly focused on the state; and, with the growth of working-class organization, state policies increasingly become designed to deal with workers' demands for improving working and living conditions—which over a long period of time results in capitalists both employing more and more systems of machinery (to cut labor costs) and searching about for labor forces that are less costly to reproduce.

This rather common general picturing of internal state-formation relations and processes has, of course, a fundamental limit. It is drawn from and only holds at best for the "national" states (and deriving from the state jurisdictions, the "national" societies) that have formed in or have come to enclose *core-areas* of the capitalist world-system. Not only are there no sound reasons for expecting it to hold in even a loose way for political formations elsewhere in that world-system (a fortiori, outside of it altogether), but also there are good theoretical reasons for assuming it cannot. The presumption that it even could is one of the fundamental mistakes of "developmentalists." There is, though, no comparable picturing of the relational networks and processes of political development in peripheral-areas of the world-system, let alone in areas including in them the transforming effects of (a) peripheralization and (b) inclusion as sovereign units in the interstate system remains a major theoretical task.

IMPERIUM OR PATTERNS OF DOMINANCE

In the development of the modern world-system, its very formation entails (1) the interrelation of productive processes between its increasingly core and increasingly peripheral areas, and (2) some form of political relation between the states-in-formation in the core-area and the political formations and peoples in the peripheral areas. It is the latter relations we designate by patterns of imperium. We are thus not specifically concerned here with the theory of imperialism, which is centrally about capital accumulation and capital centralization on a world-scale (and only incidentally about patterns of imperium per se).

What is of concern under this heading is the patterning of imperium (including, intrinsically, the opposition to it) as a feature of the political development of the capitalist world-economy. The relation, abstractly, is as old as recorded history. The term itself derives from Roman usage, and its modern usage from claims in the reign of Napoleon III. Its usage in world-system studies is weaker still. Magdoff (1969) and Nkrumah (1965) seem right: "empire" factually need not imply "colonies" formally. Each may imply the other, but they need not. Accordingly, imperium or imperial patterns are used to refer to the usually complex political networks that have been—and continue to be—coordinated and interwoven with, but distinquishable from, the production networks linking (and delimiting) core and periphery in the course of the modern world-system's continuing development. The conception thus allows phasings of formal colonization and informal empire to be traced for the system as a whole as it develops and the interrelations between these phasings and the presence or absence of various modes or forms of opposition—"primitive rebellion" (Hobsbawm), "wars of independence," "wars of liberation," "nationalist movements," etc.—to be sketched. Monographic work here is quite extensive, but theoretical work from a world-economy perspective is barely in its beginnings.

SOME MATTERS OF METHOD

The theoretical issues in the study of social change have thus moved forward, beginning with the objections of the dependency theorists to modernization notions and proceeding, currently, to the views of the world-system theorists on the overall wholeness and intrinsic unevenness of modern social change. In contrast, the methodological issues that have necessarily arisen in virtue of the theoretical movement, and that implicitly delineate the ground on which overt controversy has taken place, have themselves still largely to be identified, formulated, and debated. Two matters of method in particular seem in need of comment. One concerns the common distinction between statistical and historical explanatory accounts, which I shall suggest is a distinction not between kinds of inquiry but only between complementary portions of a single kind of inquiry. The other concerns the essentially relational nature, in two senses, of the information we work with in empirical inquiries.[8]

THE STATISTICAL AND NARRATIVE PORTIONS OF INQUIRY

In opposing the "evolutionists" of their day, the then novel "functionalists" charged them with, inter alia, constructing imaginary sequences by taking a shard from here, a bone from there, a temple from somewhere else. Ours is an analogous if rather different misgiving. If one wants to construct sequences of historical change or "laws of development" that might account for them, then the place to go, it would seem, is to the actual (in the sense of "described" of course) sequences of the changes in question in some places where they occur and in some where they do not (or do much less so). That may or may not seem reasonable, but in either case it is precisely what is not done in the "method of comparative study" which a few years ago emerged as the dominant method in the study of modern social change (Hopkins and Wallerstein, 1967).

In this method a logic of inquiry, derived from survey design and analysis, organizes research and theoretical reasoning. (With respect to causal inference the logic is inherently weaker than the logic of experimental inquiry, which it formally resembles in some respects and after which it is directly modeled; but if certain key initial conditions are met and subsequently key procedural steps are taken, it can result in highly plausible results.)[9] The cases being countries instead of individuals, the properties predicated of the cases are of course different: e.g., annual household income gives way to economic development, score on the F-scale becomes degree of democracy, and last grade of school completed is replaced by size of middle class. However, the structure of inquiry is exactly the same. Lazarsfeld (1959:118) depicts it in his usual uncommonly clear and straightforward way:

a. [There is] a set of *elements* ("cases," "units of observation").

b. For the research purposes at hand, these elements are considered comparable. This means that the same set of *properties* is used to describe each of the elements.

c. Each element has a certain *value* on each property (these values may be quantitative or qualitative).

d. The *propositions* assert interrelationships between the properties.

The findings ("propositions") of such inquiries thus say whether and to what extent, over the set of cases examined, ordered differences in the value of one property conjoin with ordered differences in the value of another property. What the finds do not and cannot provide is a tracing over time of such relationships as may occur, between the values of the properties, for each of the cases. The method thus omits (actually, its procedures eliminate) what Danto (1965) shows to be the essentially "narrative" logical structure of an historical explanation.

We thus have not two versions but two halves of a full account: a generalized one, statistical in nature, telling a story in the form of joint distributions of values of properties of cases, for the cases collectively, all at once; and a specific one, "historical" in nature, telling a story in the form of narrative relations among events and conditions, for the cases severally, one at a time.

At this point the concept of "cases" comes into question. As Lazarsfeld says, the *cases* in analyses of statistical relations are considered comparable for the research purposes at hand. In the study of modern social change, such presumptively valid comparability (each case is fully describable for the research purposes at hand by the same complex of properties) is exceedingly rare, if not epistemologically ruled out. Instead what one commonly has are *instances* where the same (or, sometimes, the same sort of) processes are apparently operating, but that aside from that they differ in all manner of other relevant respects. (Capital accumulation, class-struggle, and imperium all presumably operate in all manner of different settings—and differently in each.) Put sharply, the *cases* necessary for the statistical portion of inquiry must be presumed essentially homogeneous (members of a sample of a universe); the *instances* necessary for the historical portion must be presumed essentially heterogeneous (members respectively of universes of one).

Unfortunately, the differences between our two portions of inquiry widen. Next comes how we imagine our processes operating. For *cases*, we imagine them in some way to enclose the processes under review, or at least not to be so proximate as to have the processes' operation in one locus ("case") contaminate, as is said, their operation in another. (It is ordinarily safe in national polls, for example, to assume that, among the members of the sample, the opinion-forming processes of one member do not even indirectly interpersonally influence those of another.) The image is of a kind of process that operates within, or essentially within, the kind of unit or element constituting the cases. Individuals form their own opinions, corporations decide their own prices, countries choose their own political forms, and so forth. For *instances*, the imagery is quite different. Here the picture usually is of rather general processes going on and of an instance being just that—a place, within a far larger plane of occurrence, where the working of the processes are directly observable or clearly traceable through their effects. Alternatively, one may imagine the processes as operating not underneath or overhead, producing different effects in different settings (although thereby relating the instances), but directly through identifiable social relations among the settings, which, though, are still only instances where one sees the processes in operation.

Finally, for here is perhaps, the widest difference between the statistical and historical portions of inquiry, but the one also least amenable to a strictly methodological representation. This is in the purpose of the inquiry. Concentrating attention on the statistical side—on the analysis of statistical relations among values of properties of cases—necessarily means a primary interest in the plausibility of the general propositions thereby under study and an incidental interest, if any, in one case. Alternatively, concentrating attention on the historical side—on the narratively organized sequences of events and conditions of a particular place through a particular time—necessarily means an interest, not primarily in the plausibility of the proposition(s) put to use, but primarily in the plausibility of the complex interpretative account offered of *those* changes in *that* place through *that* time period.

We are used to thinking that, in the study of generalized claims which are structurally incapable of experimental examination, the more we can approach the kinds of *comparisons* realized in experimental inquiry, independently of their individual occurrence and of their time-order, which we do by ruling out or otherwise abstracting from the disturbing details of the particular and by collapsing time intervals, the better we have "tested" the plausibility of the generalized claim *as a generalized claim*. It may be, however, that we are wrong to think in this way. At least, it is far from obvious that such generalized claims are better examined through an apparently frontal but inherently indirect investigation (because of the necessary abstracting) of their general plausibility than through their assessed effectiveness, in diverse interpretative contexts, to organize a variety of narrative account, each of which is judged for its soundness on its own terms. Perhaps Danto's implicit claim[10] is correct: the *narrative* character of experimental inquiry is its most general form, in which case the statistical portion of nonexperimental social inquiries would serve, not to govern the structure of design as it now does, but instead, in preliminary work, to help isolate subjects for detailed inquiry or, in summarizing work, to help collate the results of several detailed inquiries.

THE RELATIONAL NATURE OF INFORMATION[11]

I am concerned here with two elementary points. One is that the processes resulting in observational statements are processes of social relations and are themselves part of the social system under study. The other is that the subjects of observational statements are themselves social relations or processes integral to them, however common appearances to the contrary may be (e.g., commodities "having" prices).

As to the first, I shall be brief to the point of being cryptic but I hope not obscure. There are no detached observers in world-system studies. All observers without exception are participants as well, whether the role is that of census-taker, social analyst, customs officer, historian, or bookkeeper. All information of interest is prepared (recorded, transcribed, collated, analyzed, altered, etc.) by people in definite social relations, and produced by virtue of and as an activity of those relations, and thus is integrally *of* those relations. Observers thus are not and cannot be detached from the developing system whose atomic movements they monitor or assess. The weather does not produce the observations of the meteorologist; the operations of states do produce those of the census-taker and customs officer (and also, incidentally, those of most meteorologists), just as the operations of firms produce the observations of bookkeepers. More generally, so do other social processes produce, analogously, an earlier historian's interpretative uses of recorded figures and, by the same token, such interpretative uses of them as we may make.

This claim, taken as a point of departure in a discussion of method, has many interesting implications, one of which is that a "sociology" of social inquiry is needed in the empirical study of modern social change. It is needed, however, not as still another subfield of study (whose "boundaries" would merely legitimate ignorance of what is beyond them), but as an integral part of the method informing our research and, as far as possible, being consciously developed and used in the conduct of our studies and in our commentaries on each others' work. Thus, the whole of the usual discussion of reliability (whether predicated of observers, instruments, or their products) has to be recast and from the outset firmly grounded in understandings of the relational settings in which (really through which) observations are made. Which means all records of interest, whether made tomorrow or 300 years ago, are archival in the trained historian's sense, and their reliability is to be historiographically estimated. What the analytic philosopher would set to one side, then, as "pragmatic aspects" of inquiry, we must consider as essential and hence as impossible to "abstract from" without eliminating our subject (here our method of inquiry).[12] Concerning the relational nature and derived quality of the information we perforce use (but thereby transform), we have far more to learn *methodologically* from the field anthropologist, and even more from the investigative reporter, than we do from the experimental scientist.

As to the other sense in which our information is relational in nature, the point to make is simple enough: our observations in world-system studies are not only *products* of definite social relations, but also *of* definite social relations. This is a conceptual claim, to be sure, but it is, in the study of modern social change, a conceptual notion both so elementary and so often forgotten as to require dogged attention. I shall simply illustrate it here by two examples. We (and everyone else) talk about "wage levels" (see above). Any figure for this is some measure of a central tendency of some distribution (of wages paid, received, or scheduled), a distribution which itself is the totals row or column of some relational matrix of payments from capitalists, however arrayed, to workers, however arrayed. The wages, hence their level, are produced by those specific instances of the capital-labor relation and are reflective of them. They literally have no meaning abstracted from that setting of their occurrence and reality. (One can perform all manner of operations on them, i.e., on the figures of course, without *having* to set aside that meaning; whether one does or does not abstract the figures in that sense is largely, if not entirely, independent of any decisions about technical operations.)

A seeming caveat, however, is in order. The claim is that *all* observations of central relevance in the empirical study of modern social change are analogously relational in principle; but the "in principle" is important. Some very common kinds are radically not—i.e., they cannot be relationally made in practice—the most fundamental being the simple enumerations (head counts, censuses), where the operation itself, counting only heads (of whatever kind), eliminates the relations from the record as it proceeds in order to proceed—a sentence with which no one who has tried to piece together the relations constituting households following their elimination by enumerators will have difficulty.[13] Accordingly, any of the normally disembedded kinds of observations we use need to have the relational settings that produced them imaginatively reconstructed. (What *sort* of a setting could these be of and from?)

The second example concerns the very common class of observations in our work reported as prices. Almost all of us are by training and culture disposed to see these as the data of markets (not only for us, as distant participant observers, but even more importantly for the immediate participants/observers), and of price-making markets to boot (unless we specifically know otherwise, e.g., when we know they are "administered prices"—in which case we are prone to wonder what the "real going prices" were). And we thus semiconsciously assume a very particular kind of interpretative relational setting as mechanism—even though in sociology (less so in economics) the concept is one entailing very definite, circumscribable parties ("crowds" of interchanging buyers/sellers), scope-duration, and active-latent phases. Along with the assumption that such a network was present and functioning goes its corollary that it was in fact generative of its remarkable "forces," the market forces we so ubiquitously, if vaguely, invoke. Obviously, from these comments, I would enter a note of great caution here. At the same time, let me hastily add, nothing in our work would lead me to propose that market forces have not been formed, and themselves formed integral features, in the modern world-system's development—on the contrary. But it is precisely their growth and its everywhere simultaneous opposite, their regulation (or rather efforts at it, by all manner of acting agencies), that are to be studied. Their scope and scale cannot be defensibly inferred merely from prices, which (as we know from Weber and Polanyi among many others) can be produced by, and be working data of, a wide variety of relational networks not otherwise in the least like the competitive, world-scale price-making markets so "anarchic" in Marx's view and so productive of "anomie" in Durkheim's.

A CONCLUDING COMMENT

I began this sketch of introductory considerations by remarking that there was nothing mysterious or exotic about the kind of inquiry and the field of inquiry coming to be known as the study of the capitalist world-economy or world-system studies. I have also tried to suggest, albeit necessarily sketchily, that this way of understanding modern social change derives in a fairly straightforward way from preceding approaches.

At the same time, and this is the concluding remark, once one begins to work from the premises of world-historical studies, it does become necessary to rethink, rather carefully, most of the conceptions and methods we have learned to work with. Put slightly differently, the basic ideas are all quite familiar: they are fairly simple extensions of widely known ideas. But once one reaches the vantage point afforded by these *extensions*, it becomes necessary to reconsider the very concepts used in reaching that vantage point. Let me illustrate this concluding remark with comments on two key terms, "trade" and "wage labor."

One way we get to a notion of a world-scale social economy is by reflecting on the massive presence of "long distance trade." But from the vantage point of that construct (world-economy), "trade" per se may or may not be of importance. Where trade between two points disposes of irregular surpluses or makes up for irregular shortages is one thing. Where it is the continuing link between two serially related production processes is of course something very different. In the latter, the end product of one may be the raw material of the other (and so "consumed" by it); or the finished product of one may be a tool of the other (and so again "consumed" but it); or the product of one may provide not means of production, but staple means of subsistence for the labor of the other (and so "consumed" by it); and so forth. What is decisive is neither transport of goods nor exchange of "values," but instead whether the trade in question is or is not an integral segment of a larger complex of interrelated production processes.

Analogous considerations attend the question of "wage-labor." In thinking about the production of surplus and accumulation of capital on a world scale, "labor" especially "wage-labor" are necessary points of departure. But once working with the idea of "accumulation on a world scale," we need to rethink our ideas. So, one might say: Where money payments are made to workers who do not have means to produce their means of subsistence and who exchange the money payments for means of subsistence, this is integral in the development of capitalism, *if it forms* a phase of the circuits through which *capital accumulates*; but not otherwise. By the same token, other forms of social relations of production are integral to the development of capitalism if they form integral phases of the accumulation process. From the point of view of the student of modern social change, the liturgical-performing *oikos* or the self-provisioning *latifundium* differ fundamentally from the cotton- or sugar-producing plantation, for they are parts of fundamentally different systems of social relations. So also, therefore, are the seemingly "common" master-slave relations structuring each.

In effect, we use certain conceptual schemas—interrelated concepts —to construct the notion of the modern world-system. But then *it* becomes a construct, a conceptual schema; and the relations among the concepts which we used to gain our new vantage point must then be reworked in the light of the increments to our understanding which our newly acquired angle of vision affords us. For our interest of course lies not in maintaining intact definitional connections among categories just for their own sake, but in comprehending ongoing processes at work at a moment in our active participation in those processes.

NOTES

1. For a much fuller sketch of these organizing ideas, see Hopkins and Wallerstein (1977).

2. The writings are extensive. Key works include Baran (1957) and the subsequent writings of, among others, Samir Amin, F.H. Cardoso, Theotonio dos Santos, Andre Gunder Frank, Tamas Szentes.

3. The original formulation is in Emmanuel (1972). For the continuing debate, see among others, Braun (1973); Amin (1973); Somaini et al. (1973). See Samuelson (1975) for an attack on the concept and Emmanuel (1977) for a rejoinder.

4. See for one line of work formative of this tradition, DuBois (1935). For a second, see Cox (1948, 1964); James (1938); Williams (1944). For a third, Fanon (1966); Freyre (1956); Memmi (1967).

Work in progress by Cedric Robinson on Black Marxists elucidates the originality and continuity of many of the ideas defining the Black intellectual tradition within and against Western social thought and demonstrates their theoretical scope and coherence with such creativity that his study will in all likelihood be received as a major theoretical contribution in its own right.

In a *totally* different vein is James Geschwender's (1977) account of Detroit's League of Revolutionary Black Workers (unhappily entitled against his preferences, *Class, Race and Worker Insurgency*) in which one begins to see how monographic interpretative accounts can use such beginnings of a theory of social consciousness as we have to interrelate social structure, organization, and ideology and in that way to contribute to the theory's development and eventual explicit formulation. Commonly cited sources of such theory include Marx and Engels (1947). Lukacs (1971), Gramsci (1971), and Thompson (1966).

5. Introductory accounts include Polanyi, 1944:3-30, 259-266; Dehio 1962; and Barraclough, 1967:chap. 4.

6. The distinction between world-economy and world-empire is theoretically fundamental to Immanuel Wallerstein's interpretative account of why there ever was a "transition" from "feudalism" to "capitalism" in Europe. See Wallerstein, 1974a: chap. 7, 1974b.

7. Similar dismay, about where "theories" of state-formation start from, is expressed by Tilly (1975), in a work he contributed to as well as edited. However, the line of inquiry being pursued by Stein Rokkan (in too many scattered pieces to cite here) suggests that it may be necessary to qualify this observation in the near future.

8. Both are also taken up, though more briefly, in Hopkins (1978). It is important to be clear here. There is now a growing number of good articles on method which show how, in the author's views, a given method may be made use of in world-system studies as they understand them. I make no attempt to take up any of these here but pursue instead a different line of attack: given the directions which world-system studies are taking, what basic problems of method do they seem to raise? I imagine the two lines of attack will in due course meet and prove complementary, but they are still very far apart now.

9. The list of discussants is long. Three very disparate ones are Nagel, 1961:chap. 14; Campbell 1963; and Zelditch and Hopkins, 1961.

10. "I should be perfectly content if I had shown both that there is no intrinsic difference between historical and causal explanations, and that causal explanations do in fact all have the form of stories" (Danto, 1965:237). Analytical philosophers are of little or no help in suggesting how a researcher may or may not proceed and why. But they are extremely helpful in suggesting what one has probably done or failed to do.

11. The following remarks touch on only two matters of method implied in the profound polemic concluding chapter 1 of *Capital*, entitled "The Fetishism of Commodities and the Secret Thereof" (sect. 4). I call attention to this section of *Capital* here because far too few commentators on method, especially on "Marxist method," seem to have even shuddered at, let alone grasped, the extraordinary implications for the conduct of inquiry (and definition of science) entailed by the reflexive epistemology that informs and organizes this polemic. Categories like surplus value, proletariat, and capital are way-stations on the road to transforming our world, not shrines to be prayed at every time the route our writing takes brings us to one.

12. As Hempel (1965:425) puts it, "Thus construed, the word 'explanation' and its cognates are pragmatic terms: their use requires references to the persons involved in the process of explaining." What is needed, however, is the construction of "a nonpragmatic concept of scientific explanation—a concept which is abstracted, as it were, from the pragmatic one" (1965:426).

13. On that specific point, see, e.g., Hindess (1973).

REFERENCES

AMIN, S. (1973). L'échange inégal et la loi de la valeur. Paris: Ed. Anthropos—IDEP.
BAER, W. (1962). "The economics of Prebisch and ECLA." Economic Development and Cultural Change, 10, (2):196-182.
BALANDIER, G. (1966). "The colonial situation: A theoretical approach." Pp. 34-61 in I. Wallerstein (ed.), Social Change: The colonial situation. New York: Wiley.

BARAN, P. (1957). The political economy of growth. New York: Monthly Review Press.

BRAUN, O. (1973). Comercio internacional e imperialismo. Buenos Aires: Siglo XXI.

CAMPBELL, D.T. (1963). "From description to explanation: Interpreting trends as quasi-experiments." Chap. 12 in C.W. Harris (ed.), Problems in measuring change. Madison: University of Wisconsin Press.

COX, O.C. (1948). Caste, class, and race. New York: Doubleday.

_____(1964). Capitalism as a system. New York: Monthly Review Press.

DANTO, A.C. (1965). Analytical philosophy of history. Cambridge: University Press.

DEHIO, L. (1962). The precarious balance. New York: Alfred A. Knopf.

DORN, W. (1963). Competition for empire, 1740-1763. New York: Harper Torchbooks.

DuBOIS, W.E.B. (1935). Black reconstruction in America. New York: Harcourt Brace.

DURKHEIM, E. (1947). Division of labor in society. Glencoe, Ill.: Free Press.

EMMANUEL, A. (1972). Unequal exchange. New York: Monthly Review Press.

_____(1977). "Gains and losses from the international division of labor." Review 1 (2):87-108.

FANON, F. (1966). The wretched of the earth. New York: Grove Press.

FREYRE, G. (1956). The masters and the slaves. New York: Alfred A. Knopf.

GESCHWENDER, J.A. (1977). Class, race, and worker insurgency. Cambridge, Mass.: Cambridge University Press.

GRAMSCI, A. (1971). Selections from the prison notebooks. New York: International Publishers.

HEMPEL, C.G. (1965). Aspects of scientific explanation. New York: Free Press.

HINDESS, B. (1973). The use of official statistics in sociology. London: Macmillan.

HOPKINS, T.K. (1978). "World-system analysis: Methodological issues." Chap. 8 in B.H. Kaplan (ed.), Social change in the capitalist world economy. Beverly Hills: Sage.

_____and WALLERSTEIN, I. (1967). "The comparative study of national societies." Social Science Information, 5 (1):25-58.

_____(1977). "Patterns of development of the modern world-system." Review, 1 (2):111-145.

JAMES, C.L.R. (1938). The Black Jacobins. New York: Dial Press.

LAZARSFELD, P.F. (1959). "Evidence and inference in social research." In D. Lerner (ed.), Evidence and inference. Glencoe, Ill.: Free Press.

LUKACS, G. (1971). History and class consciousness. London: Merlin Press.

MAGDOFF, H. (1969). The age of imperialism. New York: Monthly Review Press.

MAGUBANE, B. (1971). "A critical look at indices of social change." Current Anthropology, October.

MANNHEIM, K. (1936). Ideology and utopia. London: Routledge and Kegan Paul.

MARSHALL, T.H. (1964). Class, citizenship, and social development. New York: Doubleday.

MARX, K. and ENGELS, F. (1947). The German ideology. New York: International Publishers.

MEMMI, A. (1967). The colonizer and the colonized. Boston: Beacon Press.

MYRDAL, G. (1956). Development and underdevelopment: A note on the mechanism of national and international economic inequality. Cairo: National Bank of Egypt.

NAGEL, E. (1961). The structure of science. New York: Harcourt, Brace and World.

NKRUMAH, K. (1965). Neo-colonialism: The last stage of imperialism. London: Thomas Nelson.

NURKSE, R. (1953). Problems of capital formation in underdeveloped countries. Oxford: Basil Blackwell.

OSSOWSKI, S. (1963). Class structure in the social consciousness. London: Routledge and Kegan Paul.

PALMER, R. R. (1959). The age of the democratic revolution. Princeton, N.J.: Princeton University Press.

POLANYI, K. (1944). The great transformation. New York: Rinehart.

PREBISCH, R. (1959). "Commercial policy in the underdeveloped countries." American Economic Review, Papers and Proceedings.

Research Working Group (1978). "Cyclical rhythms and secular trends of the capitalist world-economy." SUNY-Binghamton: Fernand Braudel Center for the Study of Economics, Historical Systems, and Civilizations.

SAMUELSON, P. (1977). "Trade-pattern reversals in time-phased Ricardian systems and international efficiency." Journal of International Economics, 5 (4):309-365.

SOMAINI, E. et al. (1973). Salari, sottosviluppo, imperialismo. Torino: Guilio Einardi ed.

THOMPSON, E.P. (1966). The making of the English working class. New York: Vintage.

TILLY, C. (ed.) (1975). The formation of national states in Western Europe. Princeton, N.J.: Princeton University Press.

United Nations (1950). The economic development of Latin America and its principal problems. New York: Author.

WALLERSTEIN, I. (1974a). The modern world system. New York: Academic Press.

_____(1974b). "The rise and future demise of the world capitalist system." Comparative Studies in Society and History, 16 (4):387-415.

WEBER, M. (1954). Law in economy and society. Cambridge, Mass.: Harvard University Press.

_____(1968). "The distribution of power in political communities: Class, status, party." In Economy and society. New York: Bedminster Press.

WILLIAMS, E. (1944). Capitalism and slavery. Chapel Hill, N.C.: University of North Carolina Press.

ZELDITCH, M. Jr., and HOPKINS, T.K. (1961). "Laboratory experiments with organizations." In A. Etzioni (ed.), Complex organizations, A Sociological reader. New York: Holt, Rinehart and Winston.

Chapter 2

CHINA'S WORLD-SYSTEM: SOCIAL THEORY AND POLITICAL PRACTICE IN THE 1970s

Edwin A. Winckler

As more applications of the world-system paradigm are published, it becomes obvious that the unstated, conflicting, and sometimes debatable assumptions of different authors have resulted in significantly different models within that paradigm, particularly as applied to contemporary development.[1] Few authors have been explicit about the relative weights, causal interrelations, and temporal phasing of the politico-military, technico-economic, and cultural ideological dimensions of international stratification.[2] Most writers discuss "political economy" without disentangling politics and economics (Wallerstein, 1974b; Chirot, 1977). Recognizing that over time different bases of power reinforce each other, they have found it a convenient and effective shortcut to characterize the states in the world system primarily in terms of long-term economic relations.[3] Not only does this tend to obscure the partial "autonomy of the state" and the quasi-independence of ideology in both the domestic and international system, but it also tends to ignore interdependence within the world system that is other than economic. In particular it is not obvious why systems of relationships created by military interaction—even when short-run or not accompanied by economic exploitation—should be of less theoretic interest or practical significance than systems of relationships created by the long-run international economic division of labor (Goode, 1972). This is especially true for the last half of the twentieth century when the catastrophic nature, geographic scale, and resource demands of relations of force are unprecedentedly large and rapidly growing.

This paper uses Chinese models of the contemporary world-system both to highlight differences among existing western models—particularly the book-length analyses of Wallerstein and Chirot—and to illustrate additional possibilities. Although phrased in terms of the same Marxist-Leninist intellectual heritage underlying most recent western world-system theories, the three-world model which has prevailed in Chinese foreign policy in the 1970s sees the monopoly and threat of force as a primary fact creating global interdependence and national outcomes. In many respects the model represents the transposition to the world-system of a practical theory of military conflict evolved by the Chinese communist movement—with spectacularly successful results—in the course of the Chinese civil war (Winckler, 1976). The result is an analysis basically similar in structure to the recent western academic Leninist models, but provocatively different in significant details.

Briefly, the current Chinese three-world model divides the globe horizontally into three categories of nation-states. The First World includes the two superpowers, the U.S. and U.S.S.R., contending with each other for global hegemony. The Second World includes the less powerful but still imperialistic developed countries, essentially Europe and Japan. The Third World consists of the developing countries of Asia, Africa, and Latin America historically exploited by both the first and second worlds, but gradually asserting themselves within the global political economy. This model completes a transition in Chinese foreign policy away from China's "cold-war" model of the 1950s which, like western models at the time, divided the world vertically into capitalist and socialist blocs led by the implacably contending U.S. and U.S.S.R. More immediately, it replaces a transitional model of the 1960s in which China portrayed the U.S. and U.S.S.R. as colluding against their own followers in their respective blocs. Implicit in many Chinese statements in the late 1960s and early 1970s, the three-world model received formal exposition in speeches in Teng Hsiao-p'ing and Chou En-lai in the mid-1970s (Chou, 1973; Teng, 1974). Its most recent and most elaborate statement was an article which occupied the entire October 31, 1977, edition of the *People's Daily* (hereafter PD, 1977).

The practical purpose of the current Chinese three-world model is to identify the Soviet Union as the principal threat to world peace, to provide an ideological rationale for China's increasingly close relations with the U.S. and second world, and to encourage the formation of a united front against the Soviet Union. This requires temporarily downplaying in practice—though never permanently denying in theory —three classic themes in Chinese foreign policy: the threat posed by the United States to China and other countries, the conflicts of interest between developed and developing countries, and the class conflicts within nation-states.[4] It should be emphasized that each Chinese exposition of the three-world model represents a studied balance among conflicting themes, and that the balance among these themes changes subtly over time. To what extent this represents the changing assessment of a changing world by a consensual Chinese elite, and to what extent it reflects disagreement within that elite, it is difficult to say. The effort here is to sidestep these complexities and their political origins in order to highlight the heuristic usefulness of the basic model for western social scientists.[5]

Let us briefly contrast the current Chinese three-world model with the most extended recent western specification of a contemporary world-system model, Chirot's (1977) analysis, *Social Change in the Twentieth Century*. In effect, Chirot concludes that, when applied to the contemporary world, Wallerstein's (1974b) *Modern World System* is no longer modern, worldwide, or systemic. It is no longer *modern* because according to Chirot the distinctions between core, semi-periphery and periphery in Wallerstein's model are losing their relevance as fewer and fewer countries are available which resemble the historically peripheral areas (Chirot, 1977:179-181). In contrast, the Chinese three-world model suggests that Wallerstein's categories remain relevant if suitably respecified in terms of contemporary relations of military power. The result is to distinguish sharply between the role in the world system of the militarily dominant superpowers and that of other developed countries, defining the three-level system of contemporary and future relevance (PD, 1977:A2-A10).

Chirot's version of Wallerstein's model is not *worldwide* because the interdependencies it identifies between capitalist and socialist countries, or among socialist countries themselves, are insufficient to constitute a system (Chirot, 1977:229-245). The current Chinese model would deplore this failure to grapple systematically with the role of the Soviet Union and Eastern Europe in the world system, and argue that the crucial global interdependencies—politico-military relationships—are not only amply systematic, but also rapidly intensifying. The result is to integrate North-South and East-West relations into a single global system.[6]

Finally, Chirot's version of Wallerstein's model is not *systemic* because it does not identify rational interests sufficient to account for the behavior of individual actors and the dynamics of the system as a whole. Chirot argues that the developed countries behave "as if" they believed that they must compete to maintain access to the economic resources of the periphery, but seems skeptical that they need to do so (Chirot, 1977:48-54). In contrast, the Chinese three-world model claims to identify rational interests of military security and to predict the behavior of the actors in the system under norms of rationality, given the state of the system as a whole. The crucial behaviors are the formation of military-strategic coalitions both within and across categories of countries. The result is to highlight the potential effect on outcomes of opportunities for diplomatic stratagem created by the dynamics of the system as a whole (PD, 1977:A9-A10). The Chinese do not assume the automatic conversion of the military power of individual states into international outcomes, much less the automatic conversion of economic capacity into military power (Aron, 1966).

COMPARISON OF CURRENT CHINESE AND WESTERN MODELS

What are the similarities and differences between current western and Chinese world system models? Table 1 summarizes their categories and contents. Overall, the schemes are quite similar. All focus on differentiating the roles played by nation-states in a system of global scale. All group countries into three "tiers" by level of development rather than ideological affiliation. All posit a basically antagonistic relationship between the first and third tiers, with the second tier in the ambivalent position of exploiting the third tier but being exploited by the first. However, when each tier is examined in detail, significances emerge in the basis, membership, and dynamics of the models.

THE FIRST WORLD

Wallerstein includes Europe and Japan in the core along with the U.S. and U.S.S.R., presumably on the ground that they are all highly

Table 1. Alternative Specifications of the World-System Paradigm for the 1970s

CHIROT	WALLERSTEIN	CHINESE
U.S.S.R. China E. Europe	U.S.S.R	U.S. U.S.S.R.
U.S. W. Europe Japan Canada Australia	U.S. E.E.C. Japan	E.E.C. Japan E. Europe
Iran Saudi Arabia Brazil Mexico Turkey Egypt Indonesia India et cetera	China Czechoslovakia N. Korea N. Vietnam Poland Hungary	
	Israel S. Africa Chile Greece Mexico Brazil Argentina	
Guatemala Niger	Albania Bulgaria Cuba	Third World
very few countries	Most of Third World countries	Virtually all of Asia, Africa, and Latin America

industrialized mobilizers of other countries' resources (Wallerstein, 1974a:16, 19; 1974c:412; Chirot, 1977:229-245). Chirot (1977:181) remarks once that "There is properly speaking only one core power, the United States," but does not explain what he means; everywhere else in his exposition he includes the U.S., NATO, Japan, Canada, Australia, and even Israel in the capitalist core. The Chinese three-world model reserves the core role in the global system for the U.S. and U.S.S.R. alone, on the grounds of their dramatically greater military power and their aggressively hegemonistic intentions. It is the relationship between the superpowers which both poses the greatest threat to the rest of the world and provides a weather vane indicating the appropriate revolutionary strategy in the present era (PD, 1977:A11-A16).

In effect, the Chinese have extended to the Soviet Union Lenin's model of intensifying competition among a progressively smaller number of imperialist powers (Lenin, 1939). The contenders for imperialist global hegemony are now down to two, and one of them is a formerly socialist country which has degenerated into "social imperialism." Because in Marxist-Leninist vocabularly a socialist democracy could not become an imperialist superpower, the Chinese have simply declared that the Soviet Union now has a "monopoly capitalist" economy and a "fascist" political system (PD, 1977:A14-A16). Whether or not this terminological reclassification generates persuasive analysis of domestic Soviet society, it does succeed in placing the U.S.S.R. within a model of global political and economic conflict.

Although it is military interaction which most concerns the Chinese and which defines the U.S. and U.S.S.R. as interdependent within a single system, the question remains of whether this military relation is one of collusion, contention, or both. In the mid-1960s Chinese global assessments emphasized the collusion between the U.S. and U.S.S.R. in pursuit of their joint interests through their joint military power, and Chinese foreign policy resigned itself to attempting to cope with these and lesser imperialists through "self-reliance." In the early 1970s, China asserted that the superpowers were both colluding and contending, but that the collusion was only partial and temporary whereas the contention was fundamental and permanent. By the late 1970s, China has placed exclusive emphasis on the contention between the U.S. and U.S.S.R., predicting an eventual showdown between them, and meanwhile exploiting their rivalry to bring the United States into de facto protection of the P.R.C. (Pillsbury, 1975). The balance between common and conflicting interests among core countries has not yet become an issue between alternative western world-system models, but deserves more explicit attention. For example, although both Wallerstein and Chirot assume conflict among capitalist countries at the core of the world capitalist system, one of Chirot's grounds for concluding that the communist countries do not constitute a system is that there is political rivalry among them (Chirot, 1977:231).

Westerners who build world-system models to influence rather than to describe events may wish to note that the Chinese shifted their analytical emphasis from the collusion to the contention of the superpowers during a period when it could plausibly be argued that the actual balance in the relationship between the U.S. and U.S.S.R. was shifting from contention to collusion. The Chinese may have been sincere in arguing that detente between the U.S. and U.S.S.R. was a sham, and in the long run they may prove to be correct. Even many American doves are concerned today at the evidence of a Soviet drive for military superiority. On the other hand, the Chinese may have privately decided that the collusion between the U.S. and U.S.S.R. was becoming so serious that, instead of reinforcing it, they should publicly capitalize on the remaining areas of contention in order to retard it.

The Chinese three-world model posits the long-term rise of the U.S.S.R. and decline of the U.S., and suggests four reasons why, for the foreseeable future, the U.S.S.R. is more dangerous to world peace than is the U.S. (PD, 1977:A14-A16). First, since the Soviet Union must catch up with the United States, it must be more aggressive. Second, the fact that the U.S.S.R. remains economically weaker than the U.S. means it must achieve and exploit an advantage in military power. Third, the fact that the Soviet Union has a centrally planned, government-controlled economy means that its ability to mobilize resources for military purposes greatly exceeds that of even highly developed "monopoly capitalism." Fourth, the fact that the U.S.S.R. poses as a progressive socialist country misleads many socialist and third-world countries into underestimating the U.S.S.R.'s aggressive intentions and therefore into lowering their defenses. These are interesting claims which deserve modelling. Chirot, for example, mentions points one and three, but not two and four.

THE SECOND WORLD

In its analysis of developed societies—capitalist and socialist—which are not superpowers, the Chinese three-world model again emphasizes military power as the definer of position and military threat as the creator of interdependence. Western Europe loses its core role with the rise of American—and later also Soviet—military power. Moreover, a significant change has occurred in the past 30 years in the balance of military forces affecting the Second World. Whereas immediately after the Second World War both Western Europe and Japan were completely under U.S. domination and protection, they have since established partial autonomy from the U.S., though now increasingly threatened by the U.S.S.R. This account of sudden downward mobility followed by partial comeback is a more complex assessment of the changing role of Western Europe in the world-system than is implied by leaving them in the historic core, as does Chirot; Wallerstein's idea of hegemony within the core is more nuanced.

The Second World exploits the Third World but is in turn exploited by the First. It thus has the dual role, which is one of the diagnostic characteristics of Wallerstein's semi-periphery. The Chinese agree with Wallerstein that the immediate tier of societies serves a bascially political rather than economic function (Wallerstein, 1974c:405). However, whereas Wallerstein has emphasized the role of the semi-periphery as agent of the core in controlling the periphery, the more recent formulations of the Chinese three-world model emphasize the potential role of the Second World as a key ally for the Third World in overthrowing the hegemony of the First (PD, 1977:A23).

The Chinese assert that the Soviet Union regards the Second World, particularly Western Europe, as the strategic focal point in its struggle with the United States. The U.S.S.R. has devoted great resources to encircling U.S. and European positions in northern and southern Europe, and U.S. and Japanese positions in East Asia (PD, 1977:A23-A24). The Chinese model thus accords well with "realist" American strategic thinking such as the 1947 Kennan containment doctrine which identified industrialized countries as the key areas to be denied the U.S.S.R., leaving many areas of the periphery expendable. It is interesting that "radical" world-system theorists have intellectually ignored the competing world-system model of "establishment" economists and diplomats. If this is because in the Vietnam era radicals opposed establishment foreign policies, it should be noted that according to "realist" thinking, which gives priority to the Second World, the United States should not have intervened in Vietnam.

The current Chinese three-world model tentatively includes the Eastern European countries as active participants in the Second World, as does Wallerstein, rather than setting them in isolation, as does Chirot (Wallerstein, 1974d:16; Chirot, 1977:229-245). Again the basic dynamics are military. Eastern Europe is just as threatened by the Soviet drive for hegemony over the United States as is Western Europe; the basic sense in which it is exploited by the U.S.S.R. is that the U.S.S.R. is using it as a forward military position, strategic buffer, and potential battleground. Consequently, the Chinese are pleased to posit that the Eastern European countries "have never ceased waging struggles against Soviet control"; the October 1977 article views this control as "increasingly intolerable" to them (PD, 1977:A24). Although the Chinese placement of Eastern Europe within the world-system is suggestive, it is also deliberately vague. It avoids discussing whether particular countries belong in the Second or Third Worlds in order to avoid the issue of whether placement should be according to level of development, or according to how genuinely "socialist" they have remained despite Soviet domination.

Although Chirot faces the issue of Eastern Europe's role in the world-system more directly, the judgments he offers are too summary to resolve it persuasively (Chirot, 1977:229-245). He concedes that it is Soviet military power which has partially reoriented the East European economies toward the Soviet Union and prevented their integration into the world capitalist system. However, he denies that the resulting economic relationships represent core-periphery exploitation within the socialist camp (because on balance the U.S.S.R. provides Eastern Europe with raw materials rather than the other way around), and he denies that the socialist countries are part of a global system (because of their relative economic autarky). A more detailed report of facts and a less mechanical application of historical criteria should derive the complexly changing role of Eastern Europe from the logic of global conflict rather than regarding it as an isolated anomaly. The success of Poland, Czechoslovakia, Romania, and Yugoslavia in loosening Soviet control results precisely from its countervailing transactions with the United States, Western Europe, and Communist China (Simon, 1977).

In terms of practical foreign policy, the main point of the October 1977 article is that the Second World is "a force that can be united within the struggle against hegemonism" (PD, 1977:A23). The article rationalizes the acquisition of Second World military technology and the negotiation of long-term trade agreements with both the European Economic Community and Japan, a type of agreement which China has had previously only with other communist countries. It is likely that these involvements were opposed by some Chinese leaders who would prefer less contact with either the First or Second Worlds. The October 1977 editorial bears some signs of compromise with the principled reservations of this opposition, and takes great pains to explain that it is only a specific conjunction of circumstances that makes such contact prudent. Contrary to the fears of some Chinese that imperialists make unreliable allies, the Second World countries can be counted on to contend rather than collude with the superpowers. They fear the Soviet Union, and "so long as the United States continues its policy of control, they will not cease in their struggle against such control and for equal partnership" (PD, 1977:A23). In the course of the 1970s, the Chinese have become increasingly blunt in advocating that the Second World should strengthen its defense ties with the United States, as would seem obviously to be implied by an overwhelming Soviet threat.

THE THIRD WORLD

The Chinese model also emphasizes military force in defining the Third World and its role in the world system (PD, 1977:A16-A23). Although clearly less developed, it is more important that the countries of the Third World are the victims of oppression by the imperialist First and Second Worlds, and do not themselves exploit other countries. It is this oppression which dictates their objective interests and gives them their special moral quality. They largely replace the international proletariat—which stretches across the First, Second and Third World—as the "main force" combatting "imperialism, colonialism and hegemonism." At the global scale, struggle by Third World nations with armies, rather than struggle by groups within nation-states, becomes the most important manifestation of class-struggle under current historical conditions. The October 1977 article dismisses the proletariat in industrialized societies as weak and divided, though still obliged to struggle for revolution (PD, 1977:A20).

In any case, according to the Chinese, the oppressed people of the Third World are now vastly stronger than they were when Lenin wrote in the 1920s. The entire periphery is now in revolt, organized into nation-states, many of which now have their own armies. By regaining control of their national resources, they can gradually restore equitable terms of trade and in the long run undermine the entire capitalist world-system. So far the Chinese would agree with Chirot that the periphery is no longer as powerless and penetrated as it was earlier in the century.

However, they would emphasize that despite formal political independence, Third World countries remain politically oppressed and economically exploited, and must continue their struggle against the First and Second Worlds. Struggle is the basic tendency in the Third World taken as a whole, despite the fact that because "their social and political systems differ, the level of their economic development is not uniform, and there are constant changes in the political situation in each country. Hence it is often the case that the authorities of these countries adopt different attitudes toward imperialism and the superpowers and towards their own people" (PD, 1977:A21). Thus, despite the generality and elegance of the three-world formula, the Chinese leave themselves plenty of room for considering national idiosyncracies in their actual policies toward particular countries. Their position is similar to that of Skocpol and Trimberger (1978), who emphasize the impossibility of predicting exact outcomes in particular countries from a generalized world-system model without considering facts of social composition, location, and timing specific to each country.

Although the Third World countries are gradually acquiring power and gradually undermining imperialism, their basic strategy should be to remain in the periphery and exploit the weak points and contradictions among their oppressors. There are limits to the capacity of the imperialist countries for suppression in the vast areas of Asia, Africa, Latin America, and Oceania where the 120 or more countries of the Third World are located. With much of the strength of the superpowers tied down in Europe, "they are not likely to maintain tight control over many Third World countries, for it is very often the case that they cannot grab at one without losing hold of another" (DP, 1977:A20). Again, these are features seldom modelled in existing academic western world-system models, which pay little attention to the practical logistics of bringing power to bear at a distance to suppress revolt in the Third World or to protect lines of supply from other imperialists (Kemp, 1977).

Furthermore, the interests of the imperialist countries of the First and Second World in the Third World often clash. "The countries and people of the Third World. . .have begun to. . .exploit the contradiction between the hegemonist powers themselves" (PD, 1977:P20). Here the Chinese are describing not only what China herself is currently attempting to do in the world arena, but also what the Chinese communist movement successfully did within China during its civil war with the Chinese Nationalists: they retreated to the geographic periphery of China safely distant from Kuomintang power, and waited for the warlords, Nationalists, Japanese, and Americans to knock each other off, after which they returned to the core and filled the resulting power vacuum (Winckler, 1976).

In terms of practical foreign policy, the principal implication of the model's treatment of the Third World is China's need to defend itself against Soviet accusations that it is abandoning Marxism-Leninism by substituting the Third World for the international proletariat, while at the same time obscuring the relatively small capacity of the P.R.C. to aid other Third World countries, militarily or economically. As regards orthodoxy, the October 1977 article begins with a detailed intellectual history of how both Lenin and Stalin redrew the political map whenever changing circumstances required it for practical political results. The principal point of this actually quite interesting history is that although on different occasions Lenin and Stalin emphasized different kinds of contradictions and came up with different numbers and configurations of "worlds," their analysis was always at a global scale and never neglected the role of Third World nation-states (PD, 1977:A3-A7). As regards aid, given her own pressing needs, China has maintained relatively large programs of economic and military assistance to Third World countries. However, such aid has usually been calculated to win diplomatic support and access to resources for the P.R.C. while undermining that of the U.S. and U.S.S.R. (Szuprowicz, 1978). On balance, even during periods of more radical foreign policy rhetoric, China has been remarkably rational about allocating its energies where the military calculus of its three-world model dictates—toward strengthening itself against the First World, and strengthening relations with the Second World to that end.

CONCLUSION

In summary, the current Chinese three-world model displays a number of attractive characteristics which no existing western academic world-system model combines. First, rather than dwelling retrospectively on the relevance of specifications of past world-systems to the present, it groups the world's nation-states *prospectively* into political-economic blocs of contemporary and future relevance. Second, rather than omit major areas and aspects of the world, it treats all significant countries and processes as part of a single *inclusive* system. Third, rather than base its dynamics on actors' perceptions, it claims to identify the *rational interests* of those actors and to predict their behavior from the state of the system as a whole. Fourth, rather than emphasizing exclusively technico-economic facts while leaving politico-military processes unconceptualized, it persistently emphasizes relations of *military force*. Fifth, rather than assume the automatic conversion of military power into international outcomes—much less the automatic conversion of economic capacity into military power— it explores the opportunities for diplomatic *stratagem* created by ideological perceptions of the complex dynamics of coalition formation within the world system as a whole.

Needless to say there are other desiderata which the current Chinese three-world model fails to meet. Like most western models, it is woefully inexplicit about the relationships among variables, particularly the relationships among military, economic, and ideological bases of power. Although it concedes that the international characteristics and international behavior of societies are not completely dictated by their international position, it does not explore under what states of the world-system which domestic variables *exogenous* to the world-system must be taken into account. Although it assumes interaction between domestic and foreign processes, it does not explore seriously through what linkages this occurs. In general, of course, both its strengths and weaknesses derive from the fact that the model is intended to persuade political practitioners rather than to elaborate social theory.

The emphasis of this paper on military force is intended not to denigrate other bases of power, but rather to illustrate the need for more serious attention to different kinds of interdependencies within the world-system. The ideal model would posit politico-military power, technico-economic capacity, and cultural-ideological prestige as independent components of both the internal and external processes of nation-states. It would recognize that the political resources and strategies on which a politician or group relies in domestic politics have implications for the political resources and strategies which they can advocate in foreign policy, and vice versa (Rosenau, 1973). It would recognize that while all three of these dimensions are generally present in all domestic and foreign politics, the mix actually prevailing in particular historical situations varies with the resources and preferences of the winning policy coalition (Almond et al., 1977).

Such a model of contenders for power in China is implicit in the application to the Chinese case by Skinner and Winckler (1969) of Etzioni's analysis of the consequences of reliance on normative, remunerative, or coercive power. The party, government, and army institutionalize distinctive emphases on these three forms of power, respectively. Although prospective policy coalitions often cross-cut these institutions, differential reliance on these three forms of power leads to a characteristic three-way contest among radicals (professional ideologues operating from the propaganda organs of the party), moderates (modernizing bureaucrats basically concerned to speed economic development), and the military (those in the elite with professional responsibility for assuming the nation's security). Much of Chinese domestic politics over the past quarter-century has revolved around the rise and fall in the salience of these three contrasting functional specializations to the pressing domestic or foreign policy problems of the moment.[7]

As elaborated for foreign policy alternatives by Roger Brown (1976), Kenneth Lieberthal (1977), and Thomas Gottlieb (1977), these functional proclivities have led to three alternative strategic recommendations for coping with China's major adversaries over the past 10 years. Briefly, the *radicals* saw the ideological challenge of Soviet revisionism as the most damaging threat in the long run, but the American military threat as the most immediate; they recommend maintenance of China's revolutionary principles, reliance on defensive "people's war," and avoidance of being drawn into a conventional arms race which China could not win. The *moderates* saw the U.S.S.R. as the greatest and most immediate threat, and proposed using diplomacy to bring the U.S. into the strategic balance against the U.S.S.R. while driving for economic modernization to increase China's defense capabilities in the long run. The *military* saw the U.S. as the greatest and most immediate threat, and proposed a quick fix of China's military establishment while avoiding any increase in tensions with the U.S.S.R. The moderates prevailed and the three-world model we have been discussing provides the rationale for their preferred strategy.

The relative weights, causal interrelations, and temporal phasing of the normative, remunerative, and coercive components of Chinese foreign policy and their relation to changes in the international environment over time must be the subject of another paper. The point here is simply that alternative world-system models have been advanced in China, just as they have in the West. Elaboration of the world-system paradigm requires explicit comparison of variant specifications. Among these, the current Chinese three-world model is contemporary, global, systemic—and persuasive.

NOTES

1. I accept any model as a specification of the world-system paradigm if it replaces the country-by-country approach of previous modernization theory with a global geographic scale of analysis, and it if posits a systematic dynamic which creates interdependence among subglobal units (nations, classes, organizations, or whatever) on a global scale. For the sense in which I am using the concept of paradigm—more specific than a "perspective but not as specific as a model"—see Etzioni (1965:2).

2. I accept the "Weberian" position that these three dimensions of stratification are analytically independent though empirically interrelated. See Weber (1966) for the locus classicus, and Etzioni (1965) for an ingenious application to international relations.

3. See, for example, Finer (1975) for an account of the evolving relationship between military and economic power in the development of western states more precise than Wallerstein's.

4. The best short history of these and other themes in Chinese foreign policy remains Hinton (1970).

5. For more "political" approaches, see Ra'anan (1968); Harding and Gurtov (1971); and Gottlieb (1977).

6. For a western theorist whose emphasis on global relations of force converges with that of China, see Gray (1977).

7. However, for the argument that these competing positions sometimes cross-cut the party, government, and army, see Ra'anan (1968).

REFERENCES

ALMOND, G.A. et al. (1973). Crisis, choice and change: Historical studies of political development. Boston: Little, Brown.

ARON, R. (1966). Peace and war: A theory of international relations. New York: Doubleday.

BROWN, R.G. (1976). "Chinese politics and American policy." Foreign Policy, 23 (Summer):3-23.

CHIROT, D. (1977). Social change in the twentieth century. New York: Harcourt, Brace Jovanovich.

CHOU EN-LAI (1973). "Report to the Tenth National Congress of the Communist Party of China." Peking Review, 35-36 (7 September):22-24.

ETZIONI, A. (1965). Political unification. New York: Holt, Rinehart and Winston.

FINER, S.E. (1975). "State and nation-building in Europe: The role of the military." Pp. 84-163 in C. Tilly (ed.), The formation of national states in Western Europe, Princeton, N.J.: Princeton University Press.

GOODE, W.J. (1972). "The place of force in human society." American Sociological Review, 37 (5):507-519.

GOTTLIEB, T.M. (1977). Chinese foreign policy factionalism and the origins of the strategic triangle. Santa Monica: RAND (R-1902-NA).

GRAY, C. (1977). The geopolitics of the nuclear era: Heartland, rimlands and the technological revolution. New York: Crane, Russak.

HARDING, H., and GURTOV, M. (1971). The purge of Lo Jui-ch'ing: The politics of Chinese strategic planning. Santa Monica: RAND (R-548-PR).

HINTON, H.C. (1970). China's turbulent quest: An analysis of China's foreign relations since 1949. Bloomington: Indiana University Press.

KEMP, J. (1977). "The new strategic map." Survival, 19 (2):50-59.

LENIN, V.I. (1939). Imperialism, the highest stage of capitalism. New York: International Publishers.

LIEBERTHAL, K. (1977). "The foreign policy debate in Peking as seen through allegorical articles, 1973-1976." China Quarterly, 71 (September):528-554.

People's Daily Editorial Department (1977). "Chairman Mao's theory on the differentiation of the three worlds as a major contribution to Marxism-Leninism." People's Daily (1 November). Translated in Foreign Broadcast Information Series CH-77-210, pp. A1-A37. Springield, Va.: National Technical Information Service, U.S. Department of Commerce.

PILLSBURY, M. (1975). Salt on the dragon: Chinese views of the Soviet-American strategic balance. Santa Monica: RAND (5457).

RA'ANAN, U. (1968). "Peking's foreign policy debate, 1965-1966." Pp. 23-72 in Tang Tsou (ed.), China in Crisis, Vol. II. Chicago: University of Chicago Press.

ROSENAU, J. (1973). "Theorizing across systems: Linkage politics revisited." Pp. 25-56 in J. Wilkenfeld (ed.), Conflict behavior and linkage politics. New York: David McKay.

SIMON, J. (1977). Comparative communist foreign policy, 1965-1976. Santa Monica: RAND (P-6067).

SKINNER, G.W., and WINCKLER, E.A. (1969). "Compliance succession in rural communist China: A cyclical theory." Pp. 410-438 in A. Etzioni (ed.), A sociological reader on complex organizations (2nd. ed.). New York: Holt, Rinehart and Winston.

SKOCPOL. T., and TRIMBERGER, E.K. (1978). "Revolutions and the world-historical development of capitalism." Pp. 121-138 in B.H. Kaplan (ed.), Social change in the capitalist world economy. Beverly Hills: Sage.

SZUPROWICZ, B.O. (1978). The Sino-Comecon connection. Contemporary China, 2 (3).

TENG HSIAO-P'ING (1974). Speech to the special session of the UN General Assembly on raw materials and development, 10 April. Peking Review, 16 (19 April):6-11.

WALLERSTEIN, I. (1974a). "Dependence in an interdependent world: The limited possibilities of transformation within the capitalist world economy." African Studies Review, 17 (April):1-26.

_____(1974b). The modern world-system: Capitalist agriculture and the origins of the European world-economy in the sixteenth century. New York: Academic.

_____(1974c). "The rise and future demise of the world capitalist system: Concepts for comparative analysis." Comparative Studies in Society and History, 16 (4):387-415.

_____(1974d). "Trends in world capitalism." Monthly Review, 26 (May):12-18.

WEBER, M. (1966). "Class, status and party." In R. Bendix and S.M. Lipset (eds.), Class, status and power: Social stratification in comparative perspective (2nd. ed.). New York: Free Press.

WINCKLER, E.A. (1976). "Military outcomes in the Chinese civil war: Organizational and spatial models." Paper presented at the annual meeting of the American Political Science Association, Chicago.

PART 2

THE DEVELOPING CORE IN THE SEVENTEENTH CENTURY

UNDERDEVELOPMENT AND PHASE-B: EFFECT OF THE SEVENTEENTH-CENTURY STAGNATION ON CORE AND PERIPHERY OF THE EUROPEAN WORLD-ECONOMY

Immanuel Wallerstein

Il est évident que dans le champ élargi, depuis le siècle, précédent, de l'économie mondiale, le XVIIème voit un nouveau partage des richesses, sous le signe d'une concurrence multiple, déloyale, féroce, préméditée, car régression et stagnation sont mauvaises conseillères: on ne cède rien, on prend tout ce que l'on peut à son voisin ou à son rival lointain. [F. Braudel, P. Jeannin, J. Meuvret, R. Romano, 1961:81]

I start with a world-system perspective on underdevelopment. What does that mean? Essentially two things. (1) Economic processes in the modern world take place within the framework of a system we may call the capitalist world-economy, and "underdevelopment" is therefore merely a descriptive term for that part of the *processes* (processes, not states of being) found in peripheral areas of this world-economy. (2) Neither the "development' nor the "underdevelopment" of any specific territorial unit can be analyzed or interpreted without fitting it into the cyclical rhythms and secular trends of the world-economy as a whole (Wallerstein, 1979).

AUTHOR'S NOTE: The empirical data to justify the statements in this article will be found in Wallerstein (forthcoming).

I will explore in this chapter the particular consequences of a Phase-B. At the outset, I must indicate there is an ambiguity in the expression, Phase-B. There are in fact two different A-B cycles. There are the Kondratieff cycles (Kondratieff, 1935) now returning to popularity, which in my opinion do indeed exist. One Kondratieff cycle, with an A-expansion phase and a B-contraction phase, presumably lasts 40-55 years. There are, however, in addition longer cycles, to which Rondo Cameron (1973) has recently given the name "logistics."[1] These presumably last 150-300 years. They are called logistics because they taken the shape of a statistical logistic curve, in that although the A-phase is an expansion, the B-phase is not a contraction but a stagnation. When we speak of the "long" sixteenth century as an A-phase, and the period 1600-1750 as a B-phase, we are referring to one of these "logistics." And it is of this B-phase of the logistics that I shall be speaking: the so-called "crisis of the seventeenth century."

These logistics are important theoretically not only because they describe a social reality, but because they are themselves evidence for the existence of a capitalist world-economy. Let me explain myself. The late Middle Ages is generally considered to have shown an A- and a B-phase. Although scholars debate the exact dates, the years 1100-1250/1300 as the A-phase and 1300-1450 as the B-phase are fairly standard in the literature. Thus, we have two successive long cycles, each about 300 years: 1100-1450, 1450-1750.

There are striking differences between the two cycles. In the period 1100-1450, the A-phase saw expansion of population, trade, and land under cultivation, the strengthening of political apparatuses, and the expansion of feudal obligations of rural laborers to their lords. The B-phase saw the exact opposite of each of these trends: the decline of population, trade, and land under cultivation (*Wustungen*), the weakening of central political apparatuses, and the decline of feudal obligations. The expansions and contractions took place more or less uniformly throughout Europe.

In the period 1450-1750, the A-phase saw expansion of population, trade, and land under cultivation as happened earlier. However, in terms of the political apparatuses, they were strengthened in some areas (primarily western Europe) and weakened in others (primarily eastern Europe). In terms of "feudal" obligations, they were strengthened in some areas (the "second serfdom" of eastern Europe), but weakened still further in other areas (primarily northwestern Europe).

The B-phase of the 1450-1750 logistic is even more different from the 1100-1450 logistic than is the A-phase. Instead of a *decline* in population, trade, and land under cultivation, there was *stagnation*, as calculated Europe-wide, and this overall *stagnation* was a vector of several curves: some zones expanding, others staying level, and still others declining. In terms of both the political apparatuses and the obligations of the rural laborers to their lords, instead of reversing the tendencies of the A-phase (as had occurred in the B-phase of 1100-1450), the tendencies of the A-phase of 1450-1750 were *reinforced* in the B-phase. The obligations of "serfdom" became even greater in eastern Europe, the states even weaker, and so forth.

The implications of these variances are in my view clear. The period 1100-1450 was a period in which the feudal mode of production dominated Europe. One of the characteristics of this mode of production is the relatively high segmentation of adjacent areas. The factors that explain expansion and contraction, whatever they are, applied relatively uniformly over the whole area. The period 1450-1750 was a period in which a capitalist world-economy had come into existence in Europe. One of the characteristics of this mode of production is the relatively high degree to which the economic processes in different areas are interrelated, such that the workings of the systems lead to ever-increased spatial hierarchization. Instead of uniformity, we find differentiation. Instead of a B-phase being the mirror image of an A-phase, we find an asymmetrical pattern of development.

Let me now try to sketch quite briefly the asymmetrical developments in the three spatial zones we can identify: the core, the periphery, the semi-periphery, and then add a comment on the impact of the B-phase on the external arena.

A downturn in the world-economy poses the same problem for all of its zones. Demand is sluggish and profits decline. To maintain the same level of profit, one must either reduce costs somehow or increase one's share of the total market precisely at a moment when the market is not expanding. One can reduce costs by increasing efficiency or by extracting a higher rate of surplus-value from the labor force. One can increase one's share of the market by underselling, by monopolizing, or by being the beneficiary of the failures of competitors. Any and all of these means are attempted by virtually everyone, but only a few actors can succeed in maintaining or expanding their advantage in the face of general economic adversity. It is for the reason that downturns are always a moment of increased concentration of capital. This is done at the level of the firm, but it is also done at the level of the world-economy as a whole.

The "crisis of the seventeenth century" was specifically associated historically with the rise of "mercantilism" as an ideology. But mercantilism generically is simply the response of all actors (except the very strongest) in a tight economy to maintain the level of profit by cornering markets in the short run, and by increasing overall efficiencies of production in the middle run.

In the B-phase of a logistic, core countries have certain strengths they can utilize. They can utilize their disproportionate hold on technological expertise to improve techniques of producing competitively products which in the A-phase had been located in the periphery. They thus reduce their overall zonal product specialization. They thereby force peripheral areas also to seek to reduce specialization. But if the core areas can manage, during the B-phase, to hold onto as large or almost as large a share of world production of the products in which they previously specialized, they can in effect increase concentration of capital in the core at the expense of the periphery. Specifically, in the seventeenth century, if we look at the world market for two key products, cereals and textiles, we can see this is exactly what happened. There was increased efficiency of cereals production in the United Provinces, England, and northern France, which production effectively displaced production from eastern and southern Europe. At the same time, textile production rose only marginally in peripheral areas. Hence, in crude summary, by 1700, northwestern Europe made the profits both from textiles *and* from cereals, and eastern Europe from neither.

At the onset of the long economic downturn, the United Provinces was, among core powers, the most efficient agro-industrial producer by far. It was this productive efficiency which led to its commercial primacy, which in turn made possible its financial centrality. The triple superiority was successive but overlapped in the period 1625-1672, which might be designated as the period of Dutch hegemony. Dutch hegemony was marked by a *strong* state. Its strength internally can be measured by the relatively low rate of internal turbulence, the high degree of efficacy of state decisions (however cumbersome the machinery appeared to be on the surface), and its ability to serve as a world center of political refuge as well as of internal social welfare. Externally, its strength was of course in its navy, but in its army as well (after the reforms of Maurice of Nassau). It was in short, in Renier's (1944) phrase, a "social dictatorship of the middle class."

It was initially in opposition to this hegemony that England and France enunciated mercantilist policies. The English Navigation Act of 1651 might be considered the opening gun of a serious attack. It then took only 20 years to unseat the Dutch from their hegemonic position. 1672, the so-called "Year of Disaster," marks the turning point. It was less that the Dutch had lost so much than that the English and French had advanced so far and could now consider their battle with each other for the succession as more vital than the battle of either with the Dutch, now clearly in "decline."

In both the period before and the period after 1672, English and French tactics centered around (a) increasing the efficiencies of their own production and (b) creating protected markets. The increase of efficiencies in agriculture took the form both of agronomic improvements (in England but in northern France as well), and of increased concentration of ownership—in particular, the sharp decline of the small and medium-sized owner-occupier (known in England as the yeoman farmer and in northen France as the *laboureur* with a *charrue*). As for industrial production, the moment of great increase in efficiencies is generally considered to be after 1750. But insofar as there were improvements in the period 1600-1750, they appear to be roughly parallel in England and France.

The new colonization of the "extended" Caribbean must be seen as part of this same movement of concentration of capital in the core. (The "extended" Caribbean is defined as the tropical and semi-tropical zone that lies between the Chesapeake Valley of North America and Brazil.) This zone was *in part* already colonized by Spain and Portugal. Economic downturn in the world-economy led the core powers of northwestern Europe in the early seventeenth century to explore the economic advantages of creating *new* areas of primary production under their direct control. In the case of wheat, they could obtain the transfer of the locus of production merely by agronomic improvements; but sugar, for climatic reasons, could never be grown in northwestern Europe. An alternative, which had similar consequences for capital accumulation, was the creation of "sugar colonies" in the Caribbean. Where areas were uncolonized, the three core powers engaged in a competitive "scramble" for territory. Where Spain and Portugal already occupied territory, it proved economically feasible and politically easier to obtain the same benefits through the creation of a trade system, partly legitimate and partly contraband, which turned Spain and Portugal into economic conveyor-belts between Iberian America and northwestern Europe.

But there was a second colonization at this time in the Americas—in the temperate zones, most importantly in the New England and Middle Atlantic areas of North America. Here the motive was not primarily the concentration of staple production under direct core-country control, but rather the creation of protected markets for core-country manufacturers. And here, unlike in the extended Caribbean, we find a difference among the core powers—only England colonized. To see why this should have been so, let us return to the comparison of England and *northern* France as the competing core economic zones (rather than England and France). In this case, England's outlet for surplus wheat and surplus manufactures was located in *foreign* trade; but France's outlet for the same surpluses could be, at least in part, *southern* France. One could describe the Colbertian attempts to create a more politically and economically integrated France as, in part, an alternative to English colonization of temperate zones in North America. This would be consonant with both the absence of French parallel attempts to colonize temperate zones and the absence of English parallel buildings of bureaucratic superstructure at this time. "L'état, c'est moi" was not the slogan of a strong state, but the battle-cry of a weak one seeking to become as strong as the English.

If increased concentration of capital in the core is a consequence of a B-phase, it follows that the periphery must suffer economically *even more* in B-phases than in A-phases. This attendant economic behavior may take on the appearance of involution and lowered participation in world trade; but the reality is in fact further "underdevelopment." Let us shift our perspective to that of major owner-producers in the periphery who, in the A-phase, had specialized in export staples for the world market. How can they maneuver in the face of the onset of a weakened world market for their products, a weakening caused by world overproduction in relation to world demand, and evidenced by a decline in world prices (both nominal and real)? They can react like everyone else: by seeking to lower costs and to gain an increased share of the world market.

The large owner-producers can lower costs primarily by using their combined political and economic power over the rural laborers to obtain an increase in the amount of corvée-labor (which happened everywhere in eastern Europe at this time) *and* by ending (licitly or illicitly) quit-rent tenancies and forcing former tenants into the role either of serfs *or* of wage-labor (which happened in eastern, northern and southern Europe at this time).

The large owner-producers can expand their *share* of the market merely by increasing corvée-labor (thus leaving the serfs less time for independent production for the market). In addition they can purchase the lands put up for sale by tenants who have suffered economic reverse. Such (often forced) purchase occurred throughout Europe. But in peripheral areas such land was often left uncultivated (reduction of overall land-use), whereas in core areas such land was precisely made fruitful by new improved techniques.

There were two clear consequences of such tatics. The initial *increased* production by large owner-producers led to the exhaustion of both land and labor, and was reflected in subsequent famines, epidemics, etc., resulting in the long run in decreased overall production. The land was increasingly concentrated in the hands of the large owner-producers. Both in the periphery *and* in the core, and indeed in the semi-periphery as well, the leitmotif of phase-B was the massive decline of the yeoman farmer. That he survived in wine-growing regions stands out all the more clearly as an exception, but even there, did he not decline relatively?

In the periphery, two things went along with these shifts in agricultural structure. Whereas the agronomic improvements in the core were eliminating for this period the market for staples from peripheral areas, the decline of the small owner-producer and/or tenant-producer meant that there was an *increased* market in peripheral areas for the products of the large owner-producers, who thus continued to produce for the market. The market now, however, was no longer the "world" market, but became "regional."

Because the regional markets provided less total income for the large owner-producers than had the world market in phase-A, the large owner-producers sought to supplement their income by recreating local industrial production for the regional market. Such production had drastically declined in phase-A, as textiles and metal wares were imported from core countries. Now in any case there was not the bullion with which to import these goods. Local nonluxury textile and metalware production revived, either directly on the domains of large owner-producers or as putting-out industries (*Verlagssystem*). To this process of what today we would call "import substitution" was added a creative innovation: the alcohol industry. The production of vodka and the extension of wine-growing for a mass market was propelled by large owner-producers in peripheral areas who legally monopolized this production and actively encouraged the new taste patterns of the lower strata. This new industry was economically of very great importance in furthering the concentration of capital in the hands of the large peripheral owner-producers.

The increased concentration of capital in the hands of the large owner-producers went hand in hand with the increase of their political rights and legal jurisdiction. The strength of the state either steadily declined (as in Poland) or became entirely subordinate to foreign states (Hungary, Livonia, Naples, etc.) whose proconsuls came to terms with the local aristocracy by extending the latter's juridical domains and their tax-exemptions.

What of the semi-peripheral areas? Did they share the relative advantages of the core areas or the relative decline of the peripheral zones? Here we must distinguish between those areas that were semi-peripheral as part of a "decline" and areas that were or became "semi-peripheral" as part of a rise. The allocation of roles in a capitalist world is not static. Indeed, it is particularly in phase-B that positional movement occurs. In general, the semi-peripheral areas in decline looked more like the peripheral zones, whereas the rising semi-peripheral areas shared some of the advantages and characteristics of the core areas. In particular, mercantilist tactics were more likely to be associated with the latter than the former. Examples of declining areas were Spain, Portugal, and the states located in the old dorsal spine of Europe (northern Italy, the southern and western Germanies including Saxony, the Spanish Netherlands). Examples of rising areas were notably Sweden, Brandenburg-Prussia, and the temperate-zone colonies of British North America, and to some extent Austria. (Denmark, Norway, and Finland should be thought of as part of the peripheral zone.)

We immediately notice that the "declining" semi-peripheral zones all suffered population declines in this era, as did peripheral zones, whereas the "rising" semi-peripheral zones were all zones of relative population expansion. The power of the state in these "declining" semi-peripheral zones can be said clearly to decline vis-a-vis other states (so much so that there was even an attempt to "partition" Spain at one point, albeit an abortive one). The power of these states relative to internal regional and aristocratic forces was ambiguous: the least that can be said is that it was a domain of constant struggle. The aristocracy did continue to dominate the state administration.

From the point of view of the core powers, these states were prey, and the core powers felt free to intervene in the internal affairs of these states. Their armies all grew weaker. If their power did not decline still further, it was precisely because of the protection afforded by the acute competition *among* the core powers. Still, *grosso modo*, it can be said that over the seventeenth century, Portugal became economically a satellite of, and transmission belt for, first Dutch, then English interests, while Spain played this role for France. In consequence, the states of northwestern Europe significantly expanded their trade not only with the Iberian peninsula itself, but also with Iberian America as well.

This is the era of the relative "deindustrialization" of northern Italy, and central Spain, and even of the Spanish Netherlands and the Rhineland. Insofar as world industrial production was cut back, these were the areas where the cuts were made. Within these areas, there was a transfer of capital to investment in agriculture, and there as elsewhere the seigniorial domain grew at the expense of the peasant economy. The state administrations were not generally successful at implementing mercantilist policies. From the perspective of these states, the seventeenth century was a somber era.

The picture was rather different in Sweden and Brandenburg-Prussia. Both are instances of state machineries which deliberately sought to take advantage of a B-phase, and the subsequent sharp rivalries among core powers, to carve out a new place for themselves. Sweden at first seemed to do very well indeed until its aspirations were crushed in the Great Northern War. Brandenburg-Prussia started from an infinitely weaker base point, but was able by the early eighteenth century to pass Sweden by and emerge at the end of phase-B as the one great semi-peripheral beneficiary of the era.

Without treating here the historical specificities of what made it possible for these two states to attempt this "bootstrap" operation when others could not and did not, and for Prussia to succeed where Sweden eventually did not, let me make a few general points. In the nature of things, the "Prussian" path was not a path everyone could take. Many could try, but a world-economy in stagnation with increasing concentration of capital was not compatible with the emergence of *many* new centers of capital accumulation.

Secondly, the key weapon that both Sweden and Prussia used was the creation of a strong military force which alone made possible the mercantilist measures central to the strategy. Of course, the strong military required a strong tax base which necessitated an efficient administration, one relatively open to talents.

Thirdly, it should be observed that both Sweden and Prussia actively sought to manipulate core-power rivalries both to aid their advance and even more importantly to block negative moves against their advance. They did this by alternating alliance and economic sweeteners (for example, opening their "protected" economies at crucial junctures to core-country investment and core-country personnel in their administration apparatuses). In twentieth century language, they played the "neocolonial" role very well. They were aided in the game by the fact they were *not* the rich prizes per se that Spain, Portugal, and northern Italy were.

The case of the New England and Middle Atlantic states is a very particular one, and it is only by stretching our language that we can call these areas semi-peripheral in the seventeenth century. But the groundwork for later developments was laid then in the development of a major shipbuilding industry and of other minor industries. Their advantage is that they were settlers in a nontropical area of the power that was to win the competition and that the mercantilist strategy of England inadvertently benefitted them. When the English realized this toward the end of the seventeenth century, they tried to reverse matters but it was historically too late.

I shall conclude with a brief word on the external arena. Already in the long sixteenth century, Russia, the Ottoman Empire, India, and West Africa were all linked by trade to the European world-economy, but externally and not essentially. What happened in phase-B? The attempts of the core powers to hold their own in these times of economic adversity led them to try to find new sources of profit by importing new staples from these countries. But the weakness of these same core states, primarily concerned with their struggle with each other, made it impossible for the core states to undermine sufficiently the state apparatuses in these external arenas, so as to "peripheralize" them. This would only occur after 1750. Phase-B represented therefore a period of "economic" corrosion for these external arenas that no doubt prepared the ground for what came later. But it was not sufficient in my view to support the argument that these states had already by that time been "incorporated" into the world-economy.

A phase-B is, as we can see, a time of great positional movement. It represents stagnation over all to be sure, but stagnation as the sum of increased concentration of capital and therefore of increased polarization and differentiation. It does *not* slow down the workings of capitalism; it is rather an integral part of them.

NOTE

1. In the French literature, what Cameron (1973) calls "logistics" are often called "trends séculaires." But this is confusing, because they are precisely *not* secular trends, that is unidirectional tendencies. Since unidirectional tendencies *also* seem to exist, I shall reserve the term "secular trends" for them.

REFERENCES

BRAUDEL, F., JEANNIN, P., MEUVRET, J., and ROMANO, R. (1961). "Le déclin de Venise au XVIIe siècle." In Aspetti e cause della decandenza economica Veneziana nel secolo XVII. Venezia-Roma: Instituto per la Collaborazione Culturale.

CAMERON, R. (1973). "The logistics of European economic growth: A note on historical periodization." Journal of European Economic History, II(1):145-158.

KONDRATIEFF, N. (1935). "The long waves in economic life." Review of Economic Statistics, XVII(6):105-115.

RENIER, G.J. (1944). The Dutch nation: An historical study. London: Allen and Unwin.

WALLERSTEIN, I. (1979). The capitalist world-economy. New York and London: Cambridge University Press.

_____(forthcoming). The modern world-system, Vol. II: Mercantilism and the consolidation of the European world-economy, 1600-1750. New York: Academic Press.

Chapter 4

ABSOLUTISM IN CRISIS: THE ENGLISH
CIVIL WAR AND THE FRONDE

Michael S. Kimmel

For many years, historians considered the seventeenth century a "splendid century," *le grand siècle* (Lewis, 1964; Ashley, 1970). But history is commonly rewritten by each generation; today there is general agreement among historians and social scientists that the seventeenth century was, instead, a century of crisis.

In the middle of the century, the opulent facade of courtly brilliance was punctured by the outbreak of revolt across Europe. The English Revolution is perhaps the best known and most studied, for it was the single success of the era. In part, the English Revolution was triggered by revolts in Scotland and Ireland. In 1640, Catalonia and Portugal rebelled against Castillian domination; in 1647, Naples and Palermo likewise revolted. In France, the members of the *Parlements* and the high nobility attempted to thwart royal encroachments during the Revolts of the Fronde from 1648-1653. In 1650, a palace revolt in the Netherlands displaced the *stadholderate*, and there were uprisings in the Ukraine from 1648-1654. In addition, countless peasant uprisings marked the century.

AUTHOR'S NOTE: A number of people have provided helpful comments on this paper, among them: Vicki Bonnell, Edward Fox, Jerome Himmelstein, Lynn Hunt, Tim McDaniel, Lloyd Moote, J.H.M. Salmon, Neil Smelser, Charles Tilly, and Laurie Wermuth. Discussion with the San Francisco Bay Area KAPITALISTATE collective has been very fruitful. Finally, the careful criticisms of Wally Goldfrank have been especially valuable.

The crisis of the seventeenth century was expressed on a number of different levels. Hobsbawm (1958) writes that the crisis was spurred by a series of Malthusian conjunctures, noting that the early part of the century was a desperate time of epidemics, famines, and plagues. These he subsumes, however, under a more general economic heading, and argues that the crisis was expressed at the levels of both production and distribution in a developing world-economy. In addition, old ideas lost many adherents and both sacred and secular thought was in a period of rapid change.

The crisis of the seventeenth century was also a profound political crisis, a crisis of the state. Koenigsberger called it a "genuine crisis of societies and the political constitutions" (1971:276), while Salmon claims it was a "general crisis in government and society caused by the challenge of the crown to the holders of venal offices" (1967:27). Trevor-Roper's original critique of Hobsbawm's economic orientation argued that it was a crisis "not of the constitution nor of the system of production, but of the State, or rather, of the relation of the State to society" (Trevor-Roper, 1966:101).

This political dimension can most easily be seen in the strategic alignments and the unfolding of events in the Thirty Years War and the mid-century revolts. A pan-European confict involving almost every nation, the Thirty Years War manifests elements of both feudal and capitalist war; it is part dynastic struggle, and part the first "world war." In part, the Thirty Years War was precipitated by increased financial pressure on the continental states; the bureaucracy that had been developed to meet the administrative needs of a wartime state further exacerbated that financial pressure.

The structural preconditions of the mid-century revolts lay deeply embedded in the social foundations of the absolutist state and the relationship of the state to the political nation. Through an empirical comparison of two of these revolts, the English Revolution and the Fronde, it is hoped that the distinctly political dimension of the crisis can be seen.[1] Further, the focus on the state and its fiscal crisis may allow a theoretical mediation between those perspectives that focus on productive class relations and those that stress the capitalist world-economy as the theoretical lens by which to view the transition from feudalism to capitalism. Only through an interweaving of these levels of analysis—world economy, class struggle, and the state—can an adequate understanding of the revolts of the seventeenth century be achieved (Goldfrank, 1975).

THE CHARACTER OF THE CRISIS

What was the character of the crisis of the state that we are claiming is crucial to the understanding of the period of transition of the seventeenth century? In 1562, Etienne Pasquier (1966:100) wrote with remarkable insight,

> There are three things of which one should be infinitely afraid in every principality: immense debts, the minority of the King, and religious turmoil; for there is not any of these three that is not capable alone to bring mutation to a state.

Let us briefly examine each of these possible challenges to the political power of the absolutist state to better understand the character of the crisis.

During the sixteenth century both England and France were plagued by religious dissatisfaction and factionalism. The Henrician Reformation had, by the reign of Mary Tudor, decided little, and loyalty of Charles I to the Church of England (and, in the eyes of his adversaries, Laudian principles of Church organization) did not ease religious tensions. In France, the Edict of Nantes had secured a legitimate position for the Huguenots, and Henry IV's conversion promised royal adherence to the Roman Church, which struck a balance between the Catholic League and the Protestants. However, the political legacy of an autonomous Huguenot force remained a sensitive issue to the King and his ministers in their quest for political centralization.

However, these religious problems were, for France, secondary by the seventeenth century; early in the century Richelieu had successfully neutralized the Huguenots politically during the famous Day of Dupes (April 13, 1629) and doctrinally through the peace of Alais (June 1629). In England, religious factionalism remained a significant motivating force for the unity of political alliances; but it was not the deciding factor—the events of the 1640s were a civil war, more than they were a Puritan Revolution.

Religion had been neutralized in France and remained significant though not primary in England. Pasquier also indicates the potential disruption of a royal minority, which frequently allowed significant groups the opportunity for rebellion. Louis XIII died in 1643, just a year after this most trusted minister. Anne of Austria and her newly appointed minister, Jules Mazarin, were left (with a balanced treasury) to rule as Regent during the minority of Louis XIV.

In France, however, a Regency was always a time for the nobility to rebel. During the first Regency of the century, in which Marie de Medici ruled for her son (Louis XIII), there was a rebellion of significant proportions by a segment of the most important nobles, which culminated in the summoning of the *Estates-General* in 1614. At that time, the nobles composed a satirical ditty, which expressed their sentiments about such Regencies:

> You see then how we are
> To serve the King forbidden,
> Are worthy men in our quarter
> Where the law is given by women [Hayden, 1974].

A Regency government was apparent sanction for the rising of the upper nobles, and frequently intra-class struggle of courtiers for a more favored position relative to the minor king took place. But the Fronde was not simply a revolt of the upper nobles. The First Fronde was the revolt of an important and previously loyal segment of the class of venal officeholders who had assumed positions in the provincial parlements (and especially the Parlement of Paris). To understand their rebellion, one must not overemphasize the significance of the king's minority. The Frondeurs exploited the minority of the king, but the minority did not cause the revolt.

Religious factionalism and the minority of the king loomed in the background of the mid-century revolts, but neither was sufficient to bring the state to the brink of collapse. On the other hand, the last of Pasquier's fears, enormous state debts, was sufficient to paralyze the state, and, I will argue, in both England and France, these debts were the result of profound fiscal crises.

The absolute monarchies constructed in Bourbon France and Stuart England were characterized by an increasingly desperate position: they must not only survive, but increase their purview and consolidate political power. The ante had been raised for the state; it must grow or die. Rabb (1975:60) notes that

> Common to every kingdom, principality and republic were certain essential changes in the institutions and aims of politics, many of which aroused fierce opposition. The all pervasive issue was the increase in central governmental power, exemplified by the growth of bureaucracies.

Yet in order to grow, the state inevitably set some social groups in opposition to it. The contradictions of the crisis of the seventeenth century were expressed at the political level:

> Political contradictions centered in the structure and situation of states caught in cross pressures between, on the one hand military competitors on the international scene and, on the other hand, the constraints of the existing domestic economy and (in some cases) resistance by the internal politically powerful class forces in efforts by the state to mobilize resources to meet international competition. [Skocpol and Trimberger, 1978:104]

The character of this crisis was largely fiscal, a "tendency for government expenditures to outrace revenues" (O'Connor, 1973:2). The state was squeezed by the larger economic demands of a mobile and developing Europe; any state that did not keep pace was faced with the uncertain and unhappy future of clientage to a more powerful state. On the other hand, internal class relations that characterized the traditional social structure constrained the activities a state could undertake to increase its share. J.H. Elliott (1969:54) writes that by the 1640s

> The main thrust of state power was fiscal. . . . The financial demands of the state brought it into direct conflict with important sections of the political nation, which expressed its discontent through its representative institutions, where these still existed, and through the tacit withdrawal of allegiance.

The fiscal crisis of the absolutist state was located in the state's insufficient fiscal resources to pursue the economic and political objectives that seemed integral to its continued growth. Attempted resolution of the fiscal crisis inevitably engendered legitimacy crises as traditional social arrangements were abridged in order to garner more revenues. This fiscal crisis then is both the empirical and theoretical conjuncture of the cross pressures of the developing capitalist world-economy and the constraints of internal class relations. The demands of the world-economy encouraged states to centralize their powers. Centripetal reorganization, however, directly conflicted with the entrenched centrifugal tendencies of the older nobilities and early modern towns.

It was embedded in the character of the absolutist state that it be faced with endemic fiscal crisis. Increased expenditures necessary to meet the needs of venal officers (themselves a creation of earlier fiscal crises), to participate in the longer and more draining wars, and to maintain the luxurious lifestyle that characterized the Renaissance court pushed the state to attempt to increase its revenues. On the other hand, the state was seriously limited in its ability to increase those revenues. Bouwsma (1961:233) remarks that

> Nothing so clearly indicates the limits of royal power . . . as the fact that governments were perennially in financial trouble, unable to tap the wealth of those most able to pay, and likely to stir up a costly revolt, whenever they attempted to develop an adequate income.

Traditional political arrangements exempted the nobility from taxation for any causes other than immediate procurement for war. This often propelled a state toward war. The nobility staunchly resisted any encroachments on their local prerogatives to retain tax exemptions and to serve as the king's agents in tax collection. Of course, the non-noble population was limited in the amount of taxation it could be expected to bear; often the exactions demanded by the Crown went unpaid because the population was simply unable to pay. This often did not deter the state and, as a result, "most of the rebellions in European states from the fourteenth century to the seventeenth century were tax revolts" (Ardant, 1975:194). Without the development of an alternative source of revenues, the state would be unable to participate in the lucrative trade opening up with wider markets or retain its political position relative to other dynasties.

The English and French states faced severe fiscal crisis in the early part of the seventeenth century. The exacerbation of this crisis through the first half of the century led each state to attempt to resolve it. Each state took a different route toward resolution, and did so for different reasons. Yet in each case, the actions of the state provoked a serious strain in its relationship to the political nation.

What is necessary then is an examination of the causes and the consequences of the response of the state to persistent fiscal crisis. To perform such a comparative historical analysis, we shall look at two general dimensions of the structure of political relationships in England and France. What fiscal resources did each state maintain? How credible was the state in its taxation policies? How visible were the burdens on the larger population as emanating directly from the state? How centralized were these states? How bureaucratized? What was the structure of that centralization and bureaucratization?

Second, we need to examine the structure of the opposition to the state. What was the power and organizational strength of the institutions that contended for political power with the state at the local, regional, and national levels? What was the structure of the class opposition to the state's program of fiscal resolution? Did these classes have an independent economic base for political action? In the remaining sections I shall attempt a schematic sketch of these two general areas for both France and England. Following that, the essay will conclude with a brief summary of these questions.

FISCAL CRISIS AND THE FRONDE

In the capitalist world-economy, Marx's epigram that "France limps slowly behind England" (Marx, 1967:300) was as accurate for the seventeenth century as for the nineteenth. But when it came to state-building, France outpaced her island rival. The French state appeared strong and resilient, highly centralized, and highly bureaucratized. However, it was the monarchy that was strong and bureaucratized, and this at the expense of traditionally representative political institutions. For a long time, the monarchy had been encroaching on the autonomous power of the high nobility lodged in the provincial parlements and previously secure in their fortresses as provincial gouverneurs. The chief mechanism for this royal encroachment was venality, the sale of offices, by which a merchant, burgher, or even some wealthy artisans were able to purchase noble title and consequently receive tax exemptions and increased social status.

This venality of offices expressed the fundamental contradiction of French absolutism as the monarchy encroached on the autonomous powers of the class upon which the state had been based. As Anderson (1974:109) writes,

> The objective contradiction of Absolutism: the monarchy sought to tax the wealth of the nobility, while the nobility demanded controls on the policies of the monarchy: the aristocracy, in effect, refused to alienate its economic privileges without gaining political rights over the conduct of the royal state.

The expanding bureaucracy needed to place its servants; at both the national and local level royal bureaucrats began to usurp the traditional functions of the hereditary nobility, undercutting both their political jurisdiction and their economic integrity. In the parlements, a paid political class of locally drawn officers administered, while *élus* were charged with the collection of local taxation.

These groups were able to undermine the power of the high nobility to a large extent. However, ironically, they also tended to limit the power of the monarchy. First, they represented a general trend which placed "constraints on the power of the state arising from measures taken by the king to evade the difficulties which insufficient fiscal resources had imposed on his needs or ambitions" (Ardant, 1975:188). Further, because they were locally drawn bureaucrats, they tended themselves to become guardians of local privilege.

Late in Richelieu's tenure a policy was initiated which was later pursued vigorously by Mazarin. New political groups were developed that served the dual purpose of increasing state revenues through the creation of more offices, and of undercutting further the powers of the *élus* and the *officiers*. At the local level, *intendants* (who were not permitted to serve in their home region) were charged with administration of tax collection, while in Paris a new set of *financiers* invested in the state through tax-farming and challenged the regional powers of the *parlementaires*. The monarchy continued its venerable tradition in which it "superimposed one administrative layer upon another without much consideration for the shape of the structure as a whole" (Salmon, 1967:33).

In addition, both Richelieu and Mazarin attempted to curtail the autonomous power of the towns, particularly in the *pays d'état*. In these outlying provinces, where Protestantism was legitimate, the Huguenots had developed strong links to the developing capitalist world-economy and had strengthened the towns at the expense of the monarchy. The monarchy demanded regular revenues from these towns, confiscated town *octrois* (internal tariffs), and manipulated elections. In addition, the monarchy promoted a tariff structure that increased its revenues at the expense of curtailing capitalist trade and constraining commercialization of agriculture.

These taxation policies also set town against countryside. As Mousnier (1970:328) writes,

> Royal taxation also had the consequence of causing antagonism
> between countryfolk and townsfolk, for it was in the towns that the

finance officials lived, men who were unpopular because they were obliged in the end to carry out royal edicts and commissions, because some of them were hand in glove with the tax-farmers, or were tax farmers themselves, and also because the village communities and the peasants individually had to incur debts in order to pay their taxes, and the expense arising from the *mortalités*, and their chief creditors were these finance officials in the towns.

The fiscal structure of the French state was based on its ordinary revenues, collected by its ordinary fiscal machine. Direct taxes (the *taille*) were collected to pay the royal armies. There were three regularly assessed indirect taxes: the *aides*, a sales tax that frequently impeded the flow of commodities; the *gabelles*, a tax on salt that forced localities to buy minimum quantities of salt at highly inflated prices; and *traites,* the internal customs and tariffs that served to reduce interprovincial trade and encourage local consumption. Finally, the provincial parlements and even the Estates-General would frequently be called on to grant an occasional tax.

These ordinary revenues were spent as quickly as they came in; frequently the monies had been spent before the taxes were collected. The wages of the royal officials had to be paid, armies and increasing numbers of mercenaries had to be paid, and the interest on the *rentes sur l'Hôtel de ville de Paris* (an early form of municipal bonds which will be more fully discussed below) had to be paid as well. Dent (1974:41) claims, in his detailed study of the fiscal system, that these ordinary revenues were "never enough," that is, the state was faced with fiscal crisis.

Given this situation, the state had also developed an extraordinary fiscal machine designed to extract larger and larger sums from the nation and still maintain a semblance of fiscal legitimacy. Although more interest would have to be paid, the state created a larger number of *rentes*, which were usually purchased by merchants and officials in the parlements. These rentes were barely disguised loans to the state, beneficial to the purchaser because the politically controlled market in the state was potentially more lucrative than the world-economy, largely because the state had developed such a large series of barriers to successful entry into the world market. Many individual burghers and officiers signed *traites* promising large loans to the state in return for political privileges and the farming out of taxes. Others preferred shorter term loans. Finally, the state was never above a series of frauds, as it found "deception essential . . . to the credit of the state" (Dent, 1974:73).

In the early seventeenth century, military expenditures, wages for officials, and the interest payments of the rentes all rose sharply. The state farmed out the interest-payment on the rentes to the financiers, creating some hostility toward them by the officers. In 1620, the Maréchal d'Effiat estimated a state debt of 5 million livres; in 1661, Colbert believed the debt was closer to 450 million livres.

The entrance of France into the Thirty Years War in 1635 provided the most serious drain on royal finances. The Crown attempted to increase all its ordinary taxes, especially the indirect taxes of aides and gabelles. Unfortunately for the monarchy, however, the productivity of these indirect taxes "was much less impressive than the burdens on the community which they represented, since their collection was farmed out and a great deal of the actual income from them remained in the pockets of the tax farmers" (Beloff, 1961:75). Nevertheless, the state attempted to increase them. In the year of French entry into the war, the people of Agen rose in rebellion against these increased impositions shouting, "Death to the gabeleurs! Kill the gabeleurs! Long live the King without gabelles!" (Mousnier, 1970:46). In these slogans, the population of Agen (and many other towns) reaffirmed their loyalty to the monarchy at the same time declaring their opposition to the gabelles. Further, these slogans offer ample evidence of the personalization by the population of the taxation policies of the monarchy; frequently, the collectors of the taxes were attacked and sometimes killed by the angry crowds.

Mazarin believed that he required extraordinary fiscal measures to continue France's participation in the war with Spain. He revived some old edicts and sold an increasing number of offices. Perhaps most significantly to this essay, he manipulated the rentes. As we have mentioned, these rentes were purchased often by Parisian merchants and parlementaires as a means of realizing some return on an economic investment, investing in the state where it seemed safer. Suddenly, though, Mazarin announced that the state would be unable to meet the interest payment on the rentes. In the ensuing price decline, many of these officers sold their holdings. The state furtively bought up as many as it could, at a fraction of the original price, and just as suddenly announced that the interest would be paid. The price soared, and even eclipsed its original price; Mazarin ordered the rentes resold at these inflated prices. The result was a windfall profit for the state.

However, there were also deleterious consequences. The officers who had originally held these rentes were furious and declared that they would not invest in the state again. The new purchasers of the rentes were no longer officiers, but the new financiers, who were now viewed by the officiers as the king's agents against their power.

The merchants and the officiers in the parlements were allied against the monarchy and the newly arrived financiers. It was the class alliance that originally characterized the "elemental challenge to sovereign monarchy" (Coveney, 1977:39) known as the Fronde. The suspension of the payment on the interest of the rentes, the deprivation of new salaries owed to the officiers, and the failure of the monarchy to renew the *paulette* (an annual payment made by venal officeholders that allowed the office to be inheritable by the officer's son) had thrown the bourgeoisie and the magistrates together. Its original motivations were fiscal, the demands of the judges were often for the reform of the fiscal administration, including the suppression of the intendancies, the renewal of the paulette, and the immediate payment of interest on the rentes.

Part of the state bureaucracy had split off from the monarchy and presented its most fundamental challenge. Kossman (1969:61) argues that it was a "conflict between part of the bureaucracy and the court" and Mousnier sees it as "a revolt of the public services."[2]

However, the segment of the state bureaucracy that first rebelled in the Fronde had no basis for social action other than through their political office. The only representative institution in France, the Estates-General, was not in contention with the monarchy. When last called in 1614, they drew up a set of cahiers that evidenced strong support for centralization by the monarchy. Hayden writes that,"the deputies of the *Estates-General* of 1614 wanted a better organized state, a centralized state with clearly defined organs of government led by a strong monarchy" (1974:197).

Opposition to the monarchy was left to the parlements, and the officials who sat in these parlements had abandoned their class base for political position. The officers were creatures of the monarchy, and this greatly limited their potential action against it. The parlement,

> while it thought of itself as the overseer of all provincial life in the absence of the king, it was continually frustrated in the realization of its pretensions by its limited means of political control and its constant need for support from the monarchy. [Beik, 1974:589]

As a result,

> The *parlementaires* . . . were faced with the dilemma that if they wanted
> to maintain their authority against their rivals and retain their influence
> vis-a-vis the local population, they could not jeopardize their royal
> connections or rely too strongly on local allies. [Beik, 1974:607]

Unable to extricate themselves from their dependence on the Crown,
the officers who revolted in the first Fronde were unable to sustain a
challenge to it.

So the Fronde failed, twice as it turned out. The first Fronde ended
as the officers realigned themselves *with* the monarchy in the face of
opposition by the upper nobility. The second Fronde, the Fronde of the
Notables, failed because these nobles were unable to rouse popular
sentiments against the monarchy, and it generated into inter-noble
squabbles. The defeat of Condé led to the eventual political exclusion
of the high nobility from the continued development of the ancien
régime. The nobility was excluded from the *Conseil de Roi* in 1661.

As a result of the Fronde, the French monarchy emerged strengthened. For the Fronde "did not challenge the basic assumptions upon
which their (the *officiers*) livelihood, the *Parlement* and the monarchy rested" (Beik, 1974:594). The Parlement of Paris was deprived of
rights gained since its rebellion in 1648; the Treaty of Reuil (which had
ended the first Fronde with an apparant royal capitulation in 1649)
was ignored and Louis forced the humbled parlements to register an
edict which prohibited their consideration of affairs of state unless
specifically requested to do so by the king.

Louis XIV, le roi soleil, was able then to construct the absolutist
state upon the two tiered foundation of the subordination of representative provincial assemblies and the undermining of the autonomous
political power of the nobility. This edifice stood unchallenged for
another 150 years, at which time it was finally razed.

FISCAL CRISIS AND THE ENGLISH CIVIL WAR

Structured differently, the English state took a strikingly different
route to the solution of its fiscal crisis, and with very different results
from those obtained by the French. It is a commonplace, but

nonetheless important to remember that England maintained neither a paid political bureaucracy nor a standing army. The extension of royal sinecurists was foreclosed and the development of a royal army unnecessary and illegitimate.

While the nobilities in both France and England were experiencing a grave social crisis, the structure of local political administration differed markedly between the two nations. The English countryside was administered by various courts of competing jurisdictions and landlords of various political persuasions, to be sure, but the workhorses of local administration continued to be the justices of the peace. The justice "was a native not only of the county but usually of the division for which he sat" (Kenyon, 1974:86). Thus, in attempting any encroachment on local liberties, the state faced a "centrifugal tendency of the Commission of the Peace; the danger that its members would come to regard themselves as representatives of the localities against the government" (Kenyon, 1974:492).

Bureaucratic centralism might have circumvented the outbreak of civil war, but only if it succeeded in controlling local government; that is, in asserting control from the royal center over those gentlemen and merchants who ran local government and who were represented in the House of Commons (Hill, 1978). But such centralization was impossible for Charles I. "The Stuarts were too wary of antagonizing powerful subjects to gamble on centralizing measures that would have provided greater fiscal strength as well as a broader base of social support" (Moote, 1973:227). Charles I had inherited a weak and ineffective monarchy in which religious intrigues overlaid foreign policy and fiscal deficiencies. Stone (1973:67) writes that

> whether one looks at its political support, financial resources, military and administrative power, social cohesion, legal subordination, religious unity or control of propaganda, the Elizabethan polity appears to have been shot through with contradictions and weaknesses.

Weak and decentralized, lacking an adequate military and bureaucracy, the English Crown faced persistent fiscal crisis (Stone, 1973:62):

> By 1603, the propertied classes had become accustomed to avoiding taxation, and efforts by the Stuarts to tighten things up and to tax the rich at a realistic level by means of impositions, fines for wardships, forced loans or ship money inevitably ran into serious legal and political obstacles.

Thus, Stone concludes,

> The early Stuart monarchy was financially boxed in at all points, since it could only achieve fiscal solvency and the equitable distribution of the tax burden at the cost of a political crisis.

Charles' administrative mismanagement may have triggered this crisis, but he had inherited much of its potential explosiveness.

When James I died in April 1625, he left his son Charles a troubled legacy of a treasury near bankruptcy and a severe erosion of confidence in the monarchy. By 1617, the credit of the royal administration was so poor that the Crown could obtain revenues only by demanding that the city of London guarantee its loans. In 1618, the royal debt was estimated at close to £900,000. This financial difficulty was coupled with serious political opposition against the free hand given to Buckingham in foreign affairs.

Parliament played its only political card to trump in June 1628 when it withdrew its confidence in the government over a fiscal measure. They voted the Petition of Right, which prohibited additional taxation without the consent of the Parliament. Charles' acceptance of the Petition was the condition of Parliament's voting him needed funds. Such overt constitutionalism was too much for Charles, and he exercised his prerogatives and dismissed the Parliament in March 1629. This act ushered in a contentious 11-year period of prerogative government, in which the fiscal crisis of the English state built slowly and decisively to its political climax in 1640.

Fiscal expedients that had been successfully employed by continental monarchs were either unsuccessful or structurally precluded in England. For example, continental kings and the Holy Roman Emperor had declared royal monopoly over any essential minerals to raise additional revenues. Stone notes, however, that the English monarchy, "tried to exploit first copper and then salt and alum, but failed to make a profit from any of them" (1973:61).

Many continental monarchs (especially in France) had procured short-term fiscal windfalls through the sale of offices. But the structure of local government in England precluded potential profitability, because the sale of offices more often benefitted the officeholder than it did the Crown. Further, venality was unpopular with the traditional nobility; frequently, the administration "put political goodwill before fiscal efficiency" (Stone, 1973:61).

Without the legitimation of Parlimentary consent, Charles was forced to develop extra-legal methods of obtaining revenues. In a "heavy-handed centralizing movement by the monarchy" (Moote, 1973:227), he

> resorted to every possible feudal and non-feudal device in the quest for tax revenues capable of sustaining an enlarged State machine beyond Parlimentary control: revival of wardship, fines for knighthood, use of purveyance, multiplication of monopolies, inflation of honours . . . and sale of offices. [Anderson, 1974:141]

In the 1620s Charles' attempts to generate revenues through forced loans generated instead widespread opposition and frequently the refusal to pay the loans. Zagorin (1971) documents this defiant stance by wealthy merchants and gentry in Somerset, Northamptonshire, Yorkshire, Gloucestershire, Cornwell, Norfolk, and other counties. In addition, Charles attempted to expand the collection of ship money. Originally, ship money was an occasional tax on particular port cities, a tax that those cities paid in lieu of providing a ship for the royal navy. In 1635, ship money was extended to include inland towns, and in the ensuing years "it looked like becoming a regular tax not voted by Parliament" (Hill, 1973:13). In 1637, John Hamden, a Member of Commons, refused to pay his alloted ship money; this act indicted that a number of significant creditors of the state were withdrawing their support of the Crown.

Each of the fiscal expedients that Charles instituted was less successful financially then he had hoped. Further, their combined weight had set in motion serious political opposition. Stone (1973:123) writes that,

> The fiscal policies of the 1630s caused formidable opposition not because royal taxation was particularly oppressive to any class of society . . . but because the money was levied in an unconstitutional and arbitrary manner, and was used for purposes which many taxpayers regarded as immoral.

Ultimately, however, it was the military plans that Charles had formulated that brought the fiscal crisis to a head. In France, the decision to enter the Thirty Years War gravely exacerbated the fiscal crisis; in England, it was the King's preparation to invade Ireland and

Scotland that brought final withdrawal of Parliamentary support for the monarchy.

Desperately short of funds, Charles called a Parliament in April 1640, which immediately registered disapproval of his management of English government. He dismissed this short Parliament in May, but without securing the needed funds to wage war. Scotland, seizing its opportunity to catch the English state at a political stalemate, invaded England, and occupied unopposed both Northumberland and Durham. They demanded £850 per day in reparations until a treaty could be arranged; but Charles was indisputably bankrupt and this new demand pushed him to call another Parliament. On November 13, 1640, this Parliament assembled. Immediately they voted a measure that ensured that they could not be dismissed without their own consent. Charles was trapped, the state paralyzed. He accepted their resolution, and the Long Parliament was convened. It would, in various incarnations, sit until the restoration of Charles II in March 1660.

The English Revolution had begun in 1640 with the subordination of Charles to the will of Parliament. The first phase of the Revolution was characterized by a breakdown within the state caused by a split in the political nation, a struggle between Parliament and the King. As one Leveller leader later put it to Commons, "the grounds of the late war between the King and you was a contention whether he or you should exercise supreme power over us" (Wolfe, 1944:237).

The Parliamentarians saw themselves with two missions in the assertion of their primacy in political matters. First, they sought to deliver the people of England from the tyranny of the Anglican bishops through the establishment of popular churches and a small degree of religious toleration, destroying episcopacy "root and branch." (It is not clear whether these Parliamentarians merely wished to substitute Presbyterianism or establish a genuine religious toleration.) Second, the Parliamentarians sought to deliver England from the arbitrary tyranny of the Crown by forever subordinating it to the sovereignty of Commons.

But what had brought the House of Commons, or at least a significant portion of it, to this rebellious position? Some of the answer is to be found in the class structure of English society, some in the position of England in the capitalist world-economy. In addition, it appears that the measures employed by the state to resolve its fiscal crisis had a critical role in setting various elements of society against the Crown, and for uniting these somewhat disparate elements in common cause.

As we have earlier noted, "The state needed more money. It had to get it, among others, from an aristocracy unwilling to pay because its own finances had been affected by the price revolution" (Stone, 1958:66). In the end, however, the aristocracy did not have to pay that much more because their declining revenues meant that the Crown could do little to increase their share of the tax burden. Stone (1970) has documented this "crisis of the aristocracy" caused by, among other factors, the relative decline in income, the shrinkage of their holdings, supersession in military affairs, inflation of honors, their residential patterns, religious preferences, and court indulgences. The Crown moved against the peerage in another way than increasing the tax burden. Instead, the "Tudors deliberately built up the authority of the gentry as a means of destroying the local power bases of their overmighty subjects"[3] (Bowden, 1962).

The political rise of the gentry, then, is attendant upon the political decline of the peerage. After the execution of the Duke of Norfolk in 1572, the balance of class forces within the ruling class appears to have changed. Thereafter, "the peers were no longer the chief threats to central power but the gentry, increasingly active in politics and openly trespassing on royal prerogatives through the House of Commons, maintained pressure on the government" (Stone, 1973:62).

It would be a serious error, however, to see the crisis of the aristocracy as the decimation of the peerage. In fact, part of the opposition by the gentry was precisely because of the new support of the peers the state was now developing. After undermining their autonomous power, the Crown was now involved in subsidizing the peers by farming taxes out to them, granting monopolies and large pensions. These actions served the double effects of undermining the autocratic foundation of the peerage, a foundation that frequently provided the bases for noble revolt. It also exacerbated Parliamentary hostilities; members of Commons saw these state-sponsored peers as social parasites.

The lower middle classes were also profoundly affected by the fiscal expedients attempted by the state. Their antipathy toward Charles, who seemed to be pushing them back into servile status, increased so that, when sides where chosen, "among the small freeholders and yeomen in the countryside, and among apprentices, artisans, and small shopkeepers in the towns there was a definite tendency to side with Parliament" (Stone, 1973:62).

Finally, Stone comments on "the extraordinary lightness of the burden of taxation placed on the poor, most of whom were altogether exempt" (1973:77). As a result, it would appear that from nowhere in the ordinary structure of taxation and impositions could there be squeezed the additional revenues that Charles required, especially if his campaign against the Scots was to be successful.

The state was also seeking to control trade in order to raise additional revenues. The control and sale of monopolies and the extension of privileges to trading companies had the effect of limiting the economic possibilities of the London merchants. The state was forcing many merchants to grant loans to the state, thus siphoning off capital that could have been invested in the more lucrative wool trade. It is not surprising, therefore, to find the wealthy wool manufacturers supporting the opposition to Charles.

Bowden describes a petition submitted to Parliament by these wealthy manufacturers, "some of whom had financed the parliamentary cause" (1962:175). In the petition, the wool manufacturers sought to regain control over the production and distribution of wool, and raised issues that indicated their concern with royal interference.

Even at the local level, the capitalist farmers were encroached on by a Crown that was attempting to limit the extent of enclosures. These economic pressures translated into political positions by the radicals in Parliament that were decisively antimonarchist. The Parliamentarians wanted far less intervention by the state, not more.

In the cities it was the merchants, and in the countryside the gentry who were hardest hit by the encroachments of the state. As Trevor-Roper (1966:87) writes,

in England the cost of the Court fell most heavily on the gentry: they were the taxpaying class: wardships, purveyance and all the indirect taxes which were multiplied by the early Stuarts fell heaviest on them.

Politically, the gentry were also ired because the prerogative government of Charles had excluded them from political power. It is the political position of these disaffected gentry that prompts Wallerstein to label the English Revolution a "rebellion of the 'mere' gentry against a Renaissance court" (Wallerstein, 1972:242), which is similar to Trevor-Roper's claim that it was the "revolt of the mere and poor gentry against the officed and the rich" (1953:63).

The English monarchy faced a tradition of local autonomy, privileges by the upper classes, and a discontended set of political officers. But these political officers were based on an independent economic foundation; they were not creatures of the English monarchy. There were lodged in legitimate representative institutions without which the King was unable to rule. Ultimately, it may have been this class basis of the Parliamentarians that allowed them to take the decisive step their French counterparts could not: on January 11, 1649, Charles I was tried by the House of Commons for high treason and, three days later, beheaded in the courtyard at Whitehall. Regicide was an act unparalleled anywhere in Europe as a solution to the crisis of the seventeenth century.

It is true that the monarchy was restored in May 1660, and the House of Lords and the Church of England reestablished; but the Restoration did not evidence a regression to the pre-1640 era of unlimited monarchical power that has frequently been suggested. The form of government appeared unchanged; England was still ruled by a King, and the "King was acknowledged to be a necessity in the then State of England" (Acton, 1961:220). But the content of government had been changed decisively, as political power was not the product of the relationship between King and Parliament. Parliament could not rule effectively without the King, as they had discovered, but the King could not rule legitimately without Parliament. The Exclusion crisis which brought William of Orange to the throne in 1688 demonstrated the birth of a *nouveau régime* in England, the fusion of monarchy and representative institutions. What had weakened the English monarchy had strengthened the English state, through the incorporation into the state of the political institutions that had contended for power.

The results of the English Revolution are well known. Obstacles to free production were removed and landowners gained exclusive rights to property. Great changes in trade, colonial, and foreign policies were facilitated; these economic policy changes were the "chief evidence for the special character of the English Revolution" (Hobsbawm, 1958:72). Primogeniture was established, the nation unified, and local landowners consolidated their local power. At the local administrative level, the justices of the peace continued to administer in accordance with their conception of local needs. Parliament emerged strengthened at the expense of the King, and "emerged from the Civil War mainly as an instrument of a commercially minded landed upper class" (Moore, 1966:29).

Finally, Parliament controlled taxation, and therefore, policy. As the French ambassador to the court of Charles II wrote to Louis XIV, "If Aristotle were to come again to the world he could not find words to explain the manner of this government. It has a monarchical appearance, and there is a king, but it is very far from being a monarchy" (Hill, 1967:107).

CONCLUSION

What I have tried to describe in this essay is the following. First, I have contended that a critical dimension of the crisis of the seventeenth century was a political dimension; that in many ways the crisis was a political crisis. As such, it is irreducible to either the totality of the social relations of production or the dynamics of the capitalist world-economy. Second, I have argued that a most significant characteristic of this political crisis was that it was a fiscal crisis, a crisis that led English and French monarchies to attempt to raise revenues through various expedients that in the end set certain groups in opposition to it.

Most importantly, I have argued that the attempted solutions to persistent fiscal crisis differed between the two countries because the structure of each state differed and the structure of that state's opposition differed. The French state attempted to undermine locally entrenched social groups and their institutions through visible, centralized bureaucratic agents. The monarchy could maneuver against the officers in the provincial parlements because they were a political class with no independent economic base. Their investment had been a political market, and their political obligation was to the institution that had spawned them: they saw their mission as saving the monarchy from threats of mismanagement by a Regency and they cast their rebellion in the interests of the King. The French monarchy could also move against the nobility because they could easily be isolated from the rest of society without a serious threat to political legitimacy. The French monarchy, then, was strengthened through the exclusion of those institutions that challenged it. In that exclusion, the French state was weakened.

The English state attempted to encroach on a class that was also lodged in a representative institution, although this time nationally drawn. The Parliamentarians had developed an economic base independent of the state; they had invested in the capitalist market and were tied to the capitalist world-economy. Their political obligation was to a nascent body politic; they sought to advance the interests of the nation. When the state moved against them and allied with the older nobility, the gentry could then take the decisive step of regicide, whereas their French counterparts were unable to move beyond a weak and ineffective challenge to a Regency government.

In the last analysis, no one would deny that long run structural changes in the relationship between lords and peasants in France and England and the forging of capitalist world-economy in Europe provided the parameters for state response to its fiscal crisis and conditioned the types of rebellions such state activity engendered. I have argued here for a more historically specific analysis of each state to supplement our theoretical analyses. Through the theoretical linkage of class relations, world-economy, and the fiscal crisis of the absolutist state, we can, I think, get a much clearer understanding of the processes of capitalist development than any one of these positions could alone provide. We could then, in the words of Marc Bloch, "learn not to attach too much importance to local pseudo-causes; at the same time . . . learn to become sensitive to specific differences" (1967:73).

NOTES

1. I am comparing these two events for a variety of reasons. If we examine the similarities of causes and consequences of these two events, we can perhaps better understand the general nature of the crisis of the mid-seventeenth century. But only the English Revolution was successful in the sense that I am using that term here. And a comparison of the differences between England and France may provide the necessary clues to understand why only in England was the power of the monarchy reduced and subordinated to the national representative institution.

2. Mousnier (1966). It is interesting to note that three pages later Mousnier labels the Fronde as a "struggle of feudal elements against the state." To Mousnier, the officiers, who comprised the public service, were still structurally and ideologically tied to feudal political relations, because their offices were venal and tenure was based on privilege rather than performance. Thus, for Mousnier, a revolt of the public service is synonymous with a reaction of feudal elements against the state. This contrasts interestingly with the English case as presented by G.E. Aylmer (1959).

3. These issues concerned the illicit transportation of wool, corruption and abuses in the winding of wool, the engrossing of wool by middlemen, and the manufacture of cloth by clothiers who had not served an apprenticeship.

REFERENCES

ACTON, LORD (1961). Lectures in modern history. New York: Meridian.

ANDERSON, P. (1974). Lineages of the absolutist state. London: New Left Books.

ARDANT, G. (1975). "Financial policy and economic infrastructure of modern states and nations." Pp. 164-242 in Tilly (ed.), The formation of national states in Western Europe. Princeton University Press.

ASHLEY, M. (1970). Louis XIV and the greatness of France. New York: Free Press.

AYLMER, G.E. (1959). The Kings service. New York: Columbia University Press.

BEIK, W. (1974). "Magistrates and popular uprisings in France before the Fronde: The case of Toulouse." Journal of Modern History, 46:585-608.

BELOFF, M. (1961). The age of absolutism. New York: Harper.

BLOCH, M. (1967). Land and work in medieval Europe, New York: Harpers.

BOUWSMA, W.J. (1961). "Politics in the age of the Renaissance." Pp. 199-244 in Chapters in western civilization, I. New York: Columbia University Press.

BOWDEN, P.J. (1962). The wool trade in Tudor and Stuart England. London: Macmillan.

COVENEY, P.J. (1977). "Introduction." In Coveney (ed.), France in crisis 1620-1670. Totowa, N.J.: Rowman and Littlefield.

DENT, J. (1974). Crisis in finance: Crown, financiers and society in seventeenth century France. New York: St. Martin's.

ELLIOT, J.H. (1969). "Revolution and continuity in early modern Europe." Past and Present, 42:35-56.

GOLDFRANK, W. (1975). "World system, state structure, and the onset of the Mexican Revolution." Politics and Society, 5 (4):417-439.

HAYDEN, J.M. (1974) France and the Estates-General of 1614-1615. New York: Cambridge University Press.

HILL, C. (1967). Reformation to industrial revolution. London: Weidenfield and Nicolson.

_____(1973). Century of revolution. New York: Norton.

_____(1978). "The new history of England." New York Review of Books, April 6.

HOBSBAWM, E.J. (1958). "Seventeenth century revolutions." Past and Present, 13:63-72.

KENYON, J.P. (1974). The Stuart Constitution. Cambridge: Cambridge University Press.

KOENIGSBERGER, H.G. (1971). The Hapsburgs and Europe, 1516-1660. Ithaca: Cornell University Press.

KOSSMAN, E.H. (1960). "Comment." Past and Present, 18:8-11.

LEWIS, W.H. (1964). The splendid century. New York: Anchor.

MARX, K. (1967). Capital, 1. New York: International Publications.

MOORE, B. (1966). The social origins of dictatorship and democracy. Boston: Beacon Press.

MOOTE, A.L. (1973). "Preconditons of revolution in early modern Europe: Did they really exist?" Canadian Journal of History, 8:207-234.

MOUSNIER, R. (1966). "Comment." In T.S. Aston (ed.), Crisis in Europe, 1560-1660. New York: Anchor, 1966.

_____(1970). Peasant uprisings in seventeenth century France, Russia and China. New York: Harper.

O'CONNOR, J. (1973). The fiscl crisis of the state. New York: St. Martin's.

PASQUIER, E. (1966). Lettres historiques (1556-1594). D. Thickett (ed.). Geneva.

RABB, T.K. (1975). The growth of stability in early modern Europe. New York: Oxford.

SALMON. H.H.M. (1967). "Venal office and popular sedition in seventeenth century France." Past and Present, 37:21-43.

SKOCPOL, T., and TRIMBERGER, K. (1978). "Revolutions and the world historical development of capitalism." Berkeley Journal of Sociology, XXII:101-114.

STONE, L. (1958). "Comment." Past and Present, 13:63-72.

_____(1966). "Century of crisis." New York Review of Books, March 3.

_____(1970). The crisis of the aristocracy. New York: Oxford Press.

_____(1973). The causes of the English Revolution. New York: Harper.

TREVOR-ROPER, H.R. (1953). "The gentry 1540-1640." Economic History Review Supplement, 2:1-55.

_____(1966). "The general crisis of the seventeenth century." In T.S. Aston (ed.), Crisis in Europe: 1560-1660. New York: Anchor.

WALLERSTEIN, I. (1972). "Three paths to national development in sixteenth century Europe." Studies in Comparative International Development, 7(2).

WOLFE, D.H. (1944). Leveller manifestoes of the Puritan Revolution. London.

ZAGORIN, P. (1971). The court and the country. New York: Atheneum.

PART 3

THE DEVELOPING CORE IN THE
TWENTIETH CENTURY

Chapter 5

THE POSITION OF EASTERN EUROPEAN IMMIGRANTS TO THE UNITED STATES IN THE CULTURAL DIVISION OF LABOR: SOME TRENDS AND PROSPECTS

Michael Hechter

One of the consequences of the development of the European world-economy since the seventeenth century has been the rise of international migration. As the international division of labor widened, the economic functions of states became increasingly divided between those specializing in diversified manufacturing at one pole, and those specializing in the production of primary products for export at the other (Wallerstein, 1974). This growing economic interdependence at the international level spurred movements of trade and migration. Though the decision to migrate was made by individuals or households for an infinite number of separate reasons, the patterns of these migration flows were determined by uneven development, that is, by the increasingly divergent rates of economic growth in different sectors of the world-economy (Davis, 1974; Thomas, 1973). In general, immigrants left areas of high fertility and low economic growth to go to areas of lower fertility and higher economic growth. The rate of international migration did not, of course, increase steadily; rather, it varied extensively with fluctuations in the level of world and national economic activity (Beijer, 1969). In periods of economic expansion

AUTHOR'S NOTE: This article was first presented at the ACLS Conference on the Dynamics of East European Ethnicity outside of Eastern Europe, held at Villa Serbellonni, Bellagio, Italy, June 28-July 2, 1977.

international migration tended to be high, whereas during depressions it naturally leveled off. Further, differences in the rates of growth among societies at a comparable position in the world-economy were also important in determining the exact patterns of migration.

The functions of migration in this world-economy seem to have been twofold. Migration served the accepting economies (by and large at the core) by providing an unskilled labor force for their growing industries. This new labor force had two very significant economic benefits. In the first place, it represented a straightforward gain in human capital, since the accepting country did not have to bear costs for the reproduction of these new workers (Burawoy, 1976). In the second place, immigrant laborers would in general work for lower wages and in a more reliable fashion than their indigenous counterparts.[1] This is because they were used to a lower standard of living, having largely emigrated from poorer regions of the world-economy (Hechter, 1976; Castells, 1975; Castles and Kosack, 1973). Because rapidly industrializing economies needed large amounts of labor at minimal cost, migration was an efficient means to fulfill this demand. At the same time migration was functional from the point of view of the donor country, because it could reduce population pressure in a flagging economy, thereby increasing income per head as well as short-run prospects for political stability.

Since large-scale international migration requires the cooperation of both sending and receiving states, it can occur only where their economies are in alternating phases: the industrializing economies must be expanding at the same time the peripheries are faced with a surplus of labor. In these circumstances, which have occurred at several times in the nineteenth and twentieth centuries, migration chains arise (MacDonald and MacDonald, 1964). This chapter is not, however, principally concerned with the political economy of international migration (see Zolberg, 1978). Rather, it deals with one of the consequences of international migration for the political integration of the United States, namely the establishment of different systems of ethnic stratification or cultural divisions of labor (Hechter, 1978).

The United States is one of the several countries in the modern world to have been formed almost entirely through immigration, both voluntary and, in the case of its African slaves, involuntary. Immigration is therefore one of the great leitmotifs of American history. It is responsible for the diversity and cosmopolitanism of the American people, as well as for a distinctive and persisting set of social problems.

Because it was a new country, and because it had no institutions of the *ancien régime* (this is true even for the plantation economy of the Old South, which had no real European counterparts), American history diverged in this respect from that of the older European states which it resembled in many other ways. Like many of these other societies at the core of the world-economy, the United States achieved industrialization early, developed a democratic political system, and competed on the world stage for resources and power. At each stage in its development its population could be divided into classes—a bourgeoisie, petit-bourgeosie, and proletariat—in roughly the same proportions as these older societies. Its diversified production came increasingly to be carried out in factories. Growth in its industrial economy was initiated in textiles, moved to iron, steel, chemicals, and other heavy industries, and since the Second World War has expanded into the service and public sectors. American workers combined into trade unions, as did the workers of Britain, France, and Italy. But unlike the old states of Western Europe, the United States faced special problems of national integration.

The very maturity of the Western European states had led to substantial cultural homogenization within their boundaries. However else the people of England might be divided, they knew themselves to be English. To be English meant, in the first instance, to speak a common tongue. In the second it tended to mean being Protestant. There were, to be sure, differences among England's Protestants— between conformist and nonconformist sects, for example. There had been sprinklings of Catholicism dating from the Reformation, and a comparative handful of Jews as well. Nevertheless, Englishmen had little difficulty uniting in antagonism to Catholics in Ireland and on the Continent, let alone to the heathens found in the overseas colonies. This same kind of cultural homogeneity characterized many of the other economically advanced societies, most especially France.[2] It ensured that during the process of industrialization relatively culturally homogeneous classes were formed.

In the United States and the other new countries of immigration the situation was far different. The vast mix of immigrant groups and ex-slaves was held together without benefit of such a nationalist (or statist) ideology. Because the cultural characteristics of the American population have changed so much in the past two centuries, there has always been debate about what precisely the concept "American" meant. Indeed, some of the most important struggles in the history of the United States have been fought over definitions of Americanism. Whatever the immigrants had been in their countries of origin, it was clear they had not been American. At various times they were thought to hold loyalties to foreign powers and churches, to be politically subversive, and to be morally corrupt due to their predilection for hard drink. If they were to stay, if America were to hold together despite this incredible cultural mosaic, the immigrants had to be made into proper Americans.

The problem of immigrant and "racial" assimilation continues to this day. Two positions have often been taken regarding this process. The first presumes that assimilation is a universal process for all immigrant groups—that their assimilation occurs in the same way, at the same pace, via the same processes of the famous metaphorical melting pot. The second assumes that some groups—those which are religiously, linguistically, or "racially" most distant from the original settlers—are more difficult to assimilate than others. These alternative stances have been taken for at least a century; it is a measure of the complexity of the issues and of the lack of definitive data that they continue to be debated today. Opinion on the processes and prospects for ethnic assimilation has shifted considerably in the twentieth century. In the early part of the century an immigration commisision established by the Congress to look into the issue concluded that the newer immigrants from Eastern and Southern Europe were qualitatively inferior to previous Northern and Western European groups, and, on this basis, recommended that further immigration from these areas be restricted. This report has subsequently been subject to the most careful scrutiny and its conclusions have been demonstrated to be false (Handlin, 1957). Nonetheless, legislation in effect ratifying the commission's position by providing preferential quotas to Northern and Western Europeans was passed in 1924 and was not rescinded until the last decade (Dinnerstein and Reimers, 1975).

Some time thereafter the University of Chicago sociologist Robert Park began formulating a different hypothesis. He argued that each immigrant group went through similar stages, which he described as a pattern of ethnic succession, in its eventual progress to assimilation.[3] This became an influential way of looking at the problem, because it discussed group prospects for assimilation in terms of concrete intergroup relations rather than of cultural differences between groups which were in large part unmeasurable and at the same time subject to invidious ethnocentric evaluation. Park (1950:16) concluded that the ultimate source of cultural differentiation between groups lay in "an irrepressible conflict between a society founded on kinship and a society founded on the market place; the conflict between the folk culture of the provinces and the civilization of the metropolis." In essence, he proposed a diffusion theory of ethnic change which predicted that the basis for communal solidarity among immigrant groups would be undercut by the group's participation in industrial society. For this reason Park and his followers expected the assimilation of immigrant groups to occur as a function of their time spent in the industrial setting. Once the group became assimilated, it was anticipated that its ethnic identity would be supplanted by more general loyalties to class.

Elsewhere I have discussed the shortcomings of this perspective (Hechter, 1975). The apparent persistence and perhaps even the resurgence of ethnic sentiments among groups by now long resident in the United States—many of whom are of Eastern European ancestry —has also raised questions about the adequacy of this diffusionist position.[4] One of the greatest difficulties with the expectation that assimilation should occur as a simple function of the time of residence of immigrant groups in the industrial setting is that it fails to give the complexity of the industrial division of labor its due. Leaving aside for the moment the influence of urbanization per se—which rather easily accounts for the persistence of ethnic identity among rural groups such as the Amish in Pennsylvania—it is nevertheless evident that many structural obstacles to assimilation may be found within the urban-industrial setting.

There are two major causes of ethnic group formation in culturally heterogeneous populations. As long as the members of a particular ethnic group are more likely to interact with each other on a basis of equality than they are with members of different groups, their sense of ethnic identity (and differentness) will persist or even develop. Thus, if Lithuanians in a certain locality tend to work together, choose the same types of jobs, and live in the same neighborhood, a collective solidarity organized around Lithuanianness is unlikely to disappear. The assumption that urban residence necessarily leads to greater interethnic contact is unwarranted because such groups may have quite different sectors of segregated activity within cities.

The other cause of ethnic group formation is more reactive in nature. The sociological rule that the greater the interaction between individuals, the more likely they will come to consider themselves to be members of a corporate group holds only when such interaction occurs between equals (Homans, 1950). Interaction between superordinates and subordinates leads precisely to the opposite result, to the intensification of the boundary distinguishing individuals of high status from those of low (Campbell and LeVine, 1972:29).

These considerations suggest that any model of ethnic group formation must seek to examine two different kinds of factors: To what extent does interaction in workplaces, neighborhoods, schools, and voluntary associations of all kinds occur within the boundaries of a single ethnic group? And, to what extent does interaction with outsiders (that is, nonmembers) stimulate distinctions of hierarchy? For instance, if most Poles in a certain area are miners, while most Welshmen are supervisors and mineowners, interaction between Poles and Welshmen in that area is likely to involve both class as well as ethnic antagonism.

This is where the cultural division of labor approach may prove useful. It offers a simplified means of estimating patterns of interaction for societies as a whole in the absence of complete data on the full range of participation in social institutions. The approach emphasizes the division of labor because it is held that intergroup relations within the workplace will determine much about the course of interaction in other spheres of social life as well. This is only partially due to the fact that the waking hours of most people are spent in workplaces of one kind or another. Occupations also directly shape interaction patterns by influencing residential location (Hawley, 1950), and by promoting divergent styles of life and social identities (Kohn, 1969).

The cultural division of labor is composed of two dimensions common to all stratification systems: a hierarchical dimension related to class, and a segmental dimension related to status. The hierarchical dimension is straightforward. Just as an individual's occupation may be used to place him or her in a particular position in a class structure, so the occupations of a group may be used to place that group within a class structure. At the extreme, all Xs could be relegated to proletarian occupations, whereas all Ys could occupy positions within the bourgeoisie.

However, even if Xs and Ys had the same class position, other distinctions emanating from the occupational structure might encourage—or inhibit—the rise of ethnic identity among them. This is because there are many different *kinds* of occupations at each level of the class structure. Miners and textile workers may both be proletarian, but differences in the nature of each task, its ecological setting, and the conditions of labor are all important in determining the degree of solidarity that should emerge in each group. The prospects for ethnic solidarity among a population of miners would doubtless be greater than that among a population *divided equally* between miners and textile workers.

For this reason it is essential to consider the extent to which given groups are clustered in particular niches of an occupational structure. This differential clustering may be termed the occupational specialization of an ethnic group. These two parameters of ethnic groups, their occupational specialization and position in the class structure, should affect the extent of their ethnic solidarity. Each describes a certain kind of isolation that can beset groups within an occupational structure. Taken together these two concepts are critical indications of the cultural division of labor.

A cultural division of labor exists whenever individuals having different cultural markers (religion, language, skin color, and so forth) are distributed through an occupational structure. To the extent a culturally marked group, such as an ethnic group, is clustered in particular occupational niches, and to the extent it is restricted from occupations at the higher levels of the class structure, it will develop a sense of ethnic identity—and thereby tend to resist assimilation to the dominant majority. Recent research has shown that 73% of intergroup differences in rates of endogamy—a critical indicator of ethnic identity—in the United States in 1970 can be explained by the interaction of these two cultural division-of-labor variables (Hechter, 1978). A third variable that independently determines ethnic identity is the extent of residential segregation of groups, but its effect is considerably weaker than either of the previous variables, and is in some measure dependent on them.

Whereas the position an ethnic group takes in the class structure of the United States reflects to some extent its level of skills on entering the cultural division of labor, this is by no means the case with respect to its degree of occupational specialization. This is no doubt affected by factors such as the structure of opportunities at the time of entry, and possibly even the cultural legacies of these groups. The affinity of Eastern European Jews for education is a well-known example.[5]

The American cultural division of labor may be visualized much as a stratified geological formation composed of a series of sediments. This sedimentation is due to the fact that immigration to the United States occurred in fits and starts, more or less in lock-step sequence with the expansion and contraction of the American economy. Because North America had been sparsely settled by an indigenous population resisting labor control, its economic development had required large inputs of labor from elsewhere. The peculiar form of the American cultural division of labor results from the fact that the geographical (and thus the cultural) sources of this labor supply changed markedly from the seventeenth through the twentieth centuries. For the most part the seventeenth-century colonists came from a Great Britian increasingly concerned about overpopulation. Colonization, first in Ireland, later in North America, was held to be an acceptable safety valve with a most profitable commercial spinoff. Following independence, the United States economy continued to move in two separate directions, each of which required fresh inputs of labor. The Southern states imported slaves from West Africa to extend a plantation economy oriented to the new textile factories in Northwest England. But the Northern and Midwestern sectors of the United States were much more interested in competing with England than with merely providing primary products for her factories. Textile factories went up in New England and urbanization proceeded rapidly north of the Mason-Dixon line.

When in the early nineteenth century new labor was needed to work in the factories, to perform services in the expanding cities, and to settle the frontier, it came principally from Britain, Ireland, and Northwestern Europe. Germans, and to a much lesser extent Scandinavians, took up farming in the Midwest, but most Irish—and many Germans as well—remained in the East Coast cities of disembarkation (Thernstrom, 1975). In these cities the Irish filled the most menial roles in the economy whereas the German—in aggregate much more highly skilled—tended to specialize in occupations of intermediate prestige (Ward, 1976). In 1850, then, the cultural division of labor outside of the South had the following form. The native-born population, for the most part of British origins, had access to the full range of occupations—including, of course, a virtual monopoly of those professional and managerial categories at the very top of the class structure. The German immigrants were in aggregate at an intermediate position in the occupational structure, whereas the Irish were heavily concentrated in the proletariat. The first Catholic immigrants to arrive in the United States in large numbers, the Irish were often victims of nativist prejudice (Billington, 1974), and their situation was in most respects quite similar to that of contemporary Blacks and Hispanics in American cities. Native workers resented them because they would work for the lowest wages.

Following the Civil War and depression, the American economy entered a second wave of industrial expansion—this time spurred by the development of its heavy industries (North, 1966). Again new sources of labor were sought. By this time fertility had begun to decline sharply in many of the countries which previously provided surplus labor, and labor came principally from Eastern and Southern Europe —neither region having yet experienced declining fertility. By the year 1900 the relative position of ethnic groups in the cultural division of labor had changed in several respects.

The British and Western European groups (including the Germans) remained at the top of the occupational prestige distribution, followed by the Irish. The only large Eastern European group (the Poles), the Italians, and French Canadians brought up the rear. In these census data for all occupations save the professions, another group of Eastern European origin (most of whom were Jews), the Russians, had the highest position in the class structure of any immigrant group (see Table 1).[6] The range of differences in occupational prestige between groups is rather low in these data, partly because professional occupations were excluded due to the small number of professionals among the immigrants. There is much greater variation, however, in the data on the occupational specialization of these groups. In 1870, Scandinavians, Germans, and Irish—all relative newcomers at this date—were the most occupationally specialized groups, but by 1900 their occupational distributions had become much more similar to that of the native-born males. All of the East European groups (Russians included) were by comparison highly specialized (Table 2). Table 3 presents the five most specialized occupations for the four East European groups for which data are available. Three of the four groups are most concentrated in the garment industry, as tailors, while other specializations were in the steel industry, mining, cigar manufacturing, and—particularly important for the Russians—the self-employed (that is, merchants).

THE WORLD-SYSTEM OF CAPITALISM

Table 1. Characteristics of U.S. Ethnic Groups in 1900

Country of Birth	Total Population[1]	Occupational Specialization[2]	Occupational Prestige[3]
AUSTRIA	130,450	48.5	31.78
BOHEMIA	85,374	41.4	32.76
CANADA			
- ENGLISH	274,530	29.3	31.75
- FRENCH	207,520	43.5	29.30
DENMARK	87,016	37.8	32.34
ENGLAND and			
WALES	661,815	34.0	32.88
FRANCE	73,757	31.2	32.17
GERMANY	2,083,647	30.8	31.98
HUNGARY	75,897	58.0	30.68
IRELAND	1,340,575	37.3	30.70
ITALY	225,885	62.5	77.09
NORWAY	221,007	45.2	32.29
POLAND	169,476	50.0	28.32
RUSSIA	117,466	53.5	36.43
SCOTLAND	176,877	35.5	34.44
SWEDEN	237,242	44.4	32.42
SWITZERLAND	73,920	30.0	32.22

SOURCE: Hutchinson, 1956.

1. Males only.

2. Computed from Hutchinson, 1956: Table 35a, pp. 192-173, and footnote 33.

3. Based on Treiman, 1975.

The second generation of each of these groups (save the Russians) had lower levels of occupational specialization, indicating some movement toward assimilation. There does not seem to be much evidence that the second-generation immigrants had an improved position in the class structure over the first generation as a whole. However, the data in Table 4 are very tentative on account of the very small numbers of second-generation immigrants among many of the groups.

Overall, in 1900 the Eastern Europeans (save for the Russians and Bohemians) tended to be employed in the lower reaches of the occupational structure, particularly in those industries undergoing rapid expansion: steel, iron, and textile manufacturing, and in mining. This suggests that the occupational specializations of these recently arrived groups were in large part determined by the opportunities

Table 2. The Relative Occupational Specialization of Selected Immigrant Groups at Two Points in Time

Country of Birth	1870	1900
GERMANY	43	31
IRELAND	45	37
ENGLAND and WALES	37	34
SWEDEN, NORWAY, and DENMARK	56	36/45/38
BRITISH AMERICA	34	29
POLAND	—	50
RUSSIA	—	54
HUNGARY	—	58
BOHEMIA	—	41

SOURCE: Hutchinson, 1956: Table 22, p. 93, and Table 35a, pp. 172-173.

Table 3. The Five Most Specialized Occupations of Selected East European Immigrants in 1900 (First Generation Males)

BOHEMIA
1. Tailors (917)
2. Tobacco and cigar operatives (867)
3. Boot and shoe makers (187)
4. Iron and steel workers (179)
5. Saloon keepers and bartenders (188)

POLAND
1. Tailors (625)
2. Iron and steel workers (504)
3. Hucksters and peddlers (522)
4. Cotton mill workers (354)
5. Miners (305)

RUSSIA
1. Tailors (2387)
2. Hucksters and peddlers (1926)
3. Tobacco and cigar operatives (569)
4. Merchants (367)
5. Boot and shoe makers (268)

HUNGARY
1. Miners (1195)
2. Tailors (554)
3. Iron and steel workers (405)
4. Tobacco and cigar operatives (333)
5. Hucksters and peddlers (249)

SOURCE: Hutchinson, 1956: 174.

available in an expanding occupational structure. At the same time, differences in income of the immigrant groups were principally due to two factors. Nearly 80% of the variation in weekly earnings among the foreign-born in mining and manufacturing occupations is explained by the respective percentage in each group speaking English, and the percentage literate in any language (Higgs, 1971). These are important skills in any labor market. Thus the relatively high

Table 4. The Relative Occupational Specialization and
         Occupational Prestige Among Selected
         Eastern European Immigrant Groups By
         Generation Resident in the
         United States (1900)

Country of Birth	1st Generation		2nd Generation	
	Occupational Special- ization	Occupational Prestige	Occupational Special- ization	Occupational Prestige
BOHEMIA	41.8	33.4	40.5	31.5
POLAND	50.8	28.8	43.7	24.3
HUNGARY	58.5	30.5	50.8	33.8
RUSSIA	53.1	36.8	57.0	31.9

SOURCE: Hutchinson, 1956: 174.

occupational position of the Russian-born in 1900 was due to the fact
they came to the United States with higher skills than the
predominantly peasant immigrants from Eastern Europe. To
illustrate: among groups of Russian Jews and Poles having lived in the
United States for the same period of time, 93% of the Jewish sample as
against only 80% of the Poles were literate. The discrepancy in
English-speaking was even greater between the two groups: 75% for
the Jews as against only 44% for the Poles (Higgs, 1971).

Thus far the Eastern European groups as a whole did not occupy a
distinctive position within the cultural division of labor in 1900.
Together with the Italians, the Poles were clustered in the lowest
sector of the class structure and—at the same time—were more highly
occupationally specialized than the other white immigrant groups. It
would be most interesting to compare their position with that of
nonwhite groups, such as the Chinese and small number of Blacks in
the northern cities, but comparable data are unavailable. While it is
often assumed that the Eastern European shared a common fate with
all the other "new immigrants," the case of the Russian-born does not
permit this interpretation to be wholly sustained.

All told, groups placed in this position of a cultural division of labor
should be expected to be extensively ghettoized. Table 5 indicates this
was indeed the case, as all of the newer groups (here including the
Russians) have substantially higher rates of residential segregation
than the old groups. In 1900, then, the new immigrants undoubtedly
had great ethnic self-consciousness. But this cannot be much of a

Table 5. Residential Segregation of the Foreign-Born in 10 American Cities[1]

Country of Birth	1910	1920	1930	1950
ENGLAND and WALES	18.0	16.9	16.6	20.9
SCOTLAND	21.6	21.9	29.6	27.5
IRELAND	25.6	25.5	33.1	31.4
FRANCE	19.8	18.5	17.8	25.8
GERMANY	27.7	26.1	30.0	26.8
AUSTRIA	42.8	31.7	35.8	27.0
HUNGARY	52.4	47.0	48.8	43.4
RUSSIA	57.3	52.1	61.6	59.5
RUMANIA	69.9	57.9	55.2	47.7
LITHUANIA	—	—	56.6	49.5
CZECHOSLOVAKIA	—	—	52.6	45.2
YUGOSLAVIA	—	—	62.5	50.6
ITALY	47.5	53.8	54.7	45.7

SOURCE: Lieberson, 1963: App. F. The cities are Boston, Buffalo, Chicago, Cincinnati, Cleveland, Columbus, Philadelphia, Pittsburgh, St. Louis, and Syracuse.

1. Means (indices of dissimilarity) across cities. Not all groups are represented in all cities.

surprise: they had only recently come to the United States. It would be much more interesting to learn about ethnic identity among the Irish, Germans, and Scandinavians of the time. Their relative occupational specialization and position in the class structure was intermediate between the native-born on the one hand, and the new immigrants on the other. This would suggest that these groups as a whole were becoming partially assimilated. The residential segregation data from 1910 are generally corroborative. Yet to have second rank in a three-tiered hierarchy it itself provides some basis for continued solidarity. Though the Irish knew they were better off than the new immigrants, they were also aware that native-born Americans and most other Western European immigrants looked down on them with suspicion and not a little distaste. Al Smith's fortunes in Presidential politics were merely one among many such indications.

However, there is a danger in ascribing Irish ethnic identity at this period solely to anti-Catholic discrimination. There were also several powerful incentives acting to promote ethnic identity in this intermediately placed group. As the first large Catholic immigrant group, the Irish wrested control of two critical institutions for all succeeding Catholic immigrants—the hierarchy of the Roman Catholic Church, including control of its large educational system, and hegemony over many urban political machines. They succeeded in monopolizing these loci of power for some time, bringing them great influence in American life, as well as the antipathy of most non-Irish Catholic groups (Greene, 1975).

To gain insight into more general processess of assimilation, it is crucial to determine how the position of the Eastern European groups in the cultural division of labor has changed in the twentieth century. While the 1900 and 1970 data are not wholly comparable (based as they are on somewhat different measures),[7] nevertheless, Table 6 reveals that by 1970 males having an Eastern European mother tongue are clustered near the top of the cultural division of labor. Yet, they are still not quite at parity with the groups which had traditionally superseded them (once again, excepting the Eastern European Jews— here identified by their Yiddish mother tongue—who remain at the pinnacle of this stratification system).

The Eastern European groups are far more clustered in 1970 than they were in 1900, and in general they may seen to occupy an intermediate position in the cultural division of labor—in fact, much the same kind of position held by the Irish in 1900. The situation of the Poles and Italians in 1900 at the bottom of the cultural division of labor is taken in 1970 by Blacks and Hispanics—many of whom immigrated to Northern and Western cities after the Second World War. In 1970 the Eastern Europeans—again, except for the Jews—are among the least occupationally specialized of all ethnic groups. Their most common specializations remain, however, in heavy industry—as foremen and highly skilled laborers. It is thus evident that many of the descendants of the early immigrants remained employed in heavy industry, and once unionization occurred they proceeded into higher positions partially due to seniority (Kornblum, 1974).

The position of all the Eastern European groups in the cultural division of labor has thus markedly improved in the past 70 years, but it is important to realize that *this mobility has not occurred at the expense of any other ethnic groups in American society*. There was no displacement involved in their mobility. Rather, this mobility is no doubt due to changes in the American occupational structure itself, that is, in the expansion of professional, technical, and managerial jobs at the top of this structure and the simultaneous contraction of unskilled and farm employment at its bottom (Blau and Duncan, 1967).

The current social base of ethnic identity among groups of Eastern European origin rests, in part, on their intermediate position in the

Table 6. Characteristics of U.S. Ethnic Groups in 1970

Ethnic Group	Occupational Specialization	Occupational Prestige		Territorial Concentration	N*	Index of Endogamy	N†
		M	SD				
1. Black	.138	26.74	14.65	2.93	4,756	.987	2,941
2. Asian	.155	35.85	19.63	11.84	415	.803	253
3. British	.129	41.10	17.14	3.86	821	.141	685
4. Irish	.118	38.78	16.47	5.45	470	.224	382
5. Other English Speaking	.149	40.82	16.91	3.38	2,476	.172	1,939
6. French-Canadian	.126	37.16	14.41	4.24	700	.411	567
7. German	.160	38.33	16.60	4.30	2,326	.349	2,028
8. Scandinavian‡	.178	37.85	16.34	4.60	659	.281	551
9. Italian	.126	36.52	15.20	6.28	1,692	.505	1,394
10. Yiddish speaking	.370	47.62	17.94	11.60	689	.655	584
11. Polish	.116	36.18	14.92	4.74	1,025	.412	821
12. Czech	.199	37.34	16.60	3.84	191	.363	179
13. Slovak	.126	37.30	15.79	6.93	209	.318	171
14. Hungarian	.111	37.25	17.62	3.35	181	.324	143
15. Greek	.273	39.56	16.50	4.13	178	.595	129
16. Dutch	.225	39.14	18.08	3.78	134	.405	121
17. Hispanic§	.153	28.92	15.80	4.91	1,795	.766	1,266
Unidentifiable	.101	36.47	16.87	—	36,231	.565	26,106
Other nonwhite	.145	27.99	15.25	—	243	.599	154
Russian-Ukrainian	.130	39.09	17.27	—	192	.365	159
Lithuanian	.193	40.49	16.16	—	90	.407	74
Cuban	.211	34.13	17.24	—	126	.646	98
Non-English-speaking white	.116	38.34	17.34	—	1,001	.307	760
Total	—	35.95	16.95	—	56,600	—	41,505

SOURCE: Hechter, 1978, Table 1.   NOTE. — Data are for males only.

*Refers to the total number of employed (or occupied) males enumerated in each ethnic category. All variables in cols. 1-4 are calculated from this baseline.

† The total number of married males (employed or not) enumerated in each ethnic category. It is used to create the endogamy variable.

‡ Includes Swedish, Danish, Norwegian, and Finnish mother tongues.

§ Excludes Cubans, since a high proportion of Cuban marriages did not take place in the United States.

cultural division of labor. This is reflected in intergroup rates of endogamy: Eastern European groups lie between the highly endogamous Blacks and Hispanics and the highly exogamous Irish, Germans, and Scandinavians. But unlike the Irish before them, the Eastern Europeans have neither the desire nor the opportunity to lead the groups beneath them, the Blacks and Hispanics.

Another basis of ethnic identity is residential segregation. Presently there are no national-level data on the residential segregation of American ethnic groups, but a survey of three cities in 1970 showed the Eastern European groups, with the Italians, remain more highly segregated than others—even at comparable levels of socio-economic status (Guest and Weed, 1976). This seems to indicate that the differences in residential segregation in 1950 (see Table 5) between the same groups persist. Here, as well, the Eastern Europeans remain in an intermediate station, since both Blacks and Hispanics are considerably more residentially segregated (Taeuber and Taeuber, 1969).

What can be said about the future of ethnic identity among the Eastern European groups in America? For this question the census data are of little help, because they do not enumerate the third and fourth generations of Eastern European ancestry. Despite Marius Hansen's (1954) confident expectation of a resurgence of ethnicity in the third generation, the available evidence tends toward the opposite conclusion. Both attitudinal (Borhek, 1970; Sandberg, 1974) and behavioral (Alba, 1976) measures of ethnic identity among individuals of Eastern European descent indicate a steady dropoff in its salience from the first to the third generations. Yet, even among the second and third generations differences remain. The Eastern Europeans, on the average, still appear to be more endogamous than the so-called older immigrant groups (Alba, 1976).

Further complicating the picture is the undeniable fact that ethnic political mobilization among Eastern European groups is more highly visible now than ever before (Novak, 1972). This may well indicate the growing prosperity and confidence of the Eastern European ethnic groups. They are presently both willing and able to challenge other groups for positions of leadership in government, business, organized labor, and in the Roman Catholic Church. Like those Jews who have strong loyalties to Israel, there remain many in these groups with much interest in the political situation in Eastern Europe itself. This kind of concern would simultaneously reflect ethnic identity and tend to reinforce it.

More fundamentally, however, the analysis presented here would suggest that as long as the Eastern Europeans maintain their intermediate position in the cultural division of labor, their sense of ethnic identity will persist. The fact of their rapid upward mobility in this division of labor is clear, but since much of this aggregate mobility is probably due to changes in the occupational structure itself, it is difficult to estimate the prospects for further mobility for these groups in the short-run—and hence, for a continued decrease in their ethnic identity. In the last analysis such prospects would depend principally on the fate of the world-economy. Because continued expansion of the world-economy is in doubt at this juncture (1978), any speculation on this issue would be risky. Nevertheless, the prospects for another period of rapid growth such as that experienced in the United States from 1950 to 1965 seem most remote in the near future. This means that Eastern European ethnicity in the United States will most likely be with us for some time to come.

NOTES

1. "As the Pittsburgh *Leader* bluntly put it, the East European immigrant made 'a better slave than the American' " (Dinnerstein and Reimers, 1975).

2. However, these societies were typically faced with significant disparities of regional development, leading in part to regional separatist movements (see Hechter, 1975).

3. For a discussion of more recent literature on ethnic succession, see Price (1969).

4. It of course assumed that the immigrants brought some notion of ethnic identity with them to America; but this was for many, not in fact true. "Like in Africa, some of their concepts of ethnic identity only emerged in the new urban environment, as the immigrants were not used to identifying themselves in terms of nationalities of origin which were in some cases recently established and rather artificial" (Hannerz, 1974).

5. There is some controversy about the weight of cultural differences in determining occupational choice. For a positive view, see Glazer (1958); for a negative, see Steinberg (1974).

6. It should be noted that these census materials give far from a totally accurate description of the distribution of immigrant groups in the United States. For a useful discussion of their limitations, see Hutchinson, 1956:Appendix B. Within these limits, however, the fundamental patterns do stand out.

7. The greatest problem of comparability with the 1900 and 1970 data is with the indicators of occupational specialization. For 1900, Hutchinson (1956) developed an index of occupational concentration which measured the extent to which a given group deviates from the occupational characteristics of *the populaton as a whole*. This

measure is described on pages 56 and 92-93. The indicator for 1970 measures the degree to which the occupational distribution of each group deviates from *random* assignment to occupational categories (see Hechter, 1978). These two measures are not directly comparable.

The principal variable in the comparison—the mean occupational prestige of each group—also differs in the two years but is much more comparable (see Treiman, 1975).

REFERENCES

ALBA, R.D. (1976). "Social assimilation among American Catholic national-origin groups." American Sociological Review, 41:1030-1046.

BEIJER, G. (1969). "Modern patterns of international migratory movements." Pp. 11-59 in J.A. Jackson (ed.), Migration. Cambridge: Cambridge University Press.

BILLINGTON, R.A. (1974). The origins of nativism in the United States, 1800-1844 (originally published in 1933). New York: Arno Press.

BLAU, P., and DUNCAN, O.D. (1967). The American occupational structure. New York: Wiley.

BORHEK, J.T. (1970). "Ethnic-group cohesion." American Journal of Sociology, 76 (1):33-46.

BURAWOY, M. (1976). "The functions and reproduction of migrant labor: Comparative material from Southern Africa and the United States." American Journal of Sociology, 81 (5):1050-1087.

CAMPBELL, D., and LeVINE, R. (1972). "Realistic group conflict theory." In D. Campbell and R. LeVine (eds.), Ethnocentrism. New York: Wiley.

CASTELLS, M. (1975). "Immigrant workers and class struggles in advanced capitalism: The Western European experience." Politics and Society 5 (1):33-66.

CASTLES, S.,and KOSACK, G. (1973). Immigrant workers and class structure in Western Europe. London: Oxford University Press.

DAVIS, K. (1974). "The migration of human populations." Scientific American, 231:92-107.

DINNERSTEIN, L., and REIMERS, D.M. (1975). Ethnic Americans. New York: Dodd, Mead.

GLAZER, N. (1958). "The American Jew and the attainment of middle class rank: Some trends and explanations." Pp. 138-146 in M. Sklare (ed.), The Jews. Glencoe, Ill.: Free Press.

GREENE, V. (1975). For God and country. Madison: State Historical Society of Wisconsin.

GUEST, A.M., and WEED, J.A. (1976). "Ethnic residential segregation: Patterns of change." American Journal of Sociology, 81 (5):1088-1111.

HANDLIN, O. (1957). Race and nationality in American life. New York: Anchor Books, 74-110.

HANNERZ, U. (1974). "Ethnicity and opportunity in urban America." Pp. 37-76 in A. Cohen (ed.), Urban ethnicity. London: Tavistock.

HANSEN, M.L. (1954). "The problem of the third generation immigrant." In E.N. Saveth (ed.), Understanding the American past. Boston: Little-Brown.

HAWLEY, A.H. (1950). Human ecology. New York: Ronald.

HECHTER, M. (1975). Internal colonialism. London: Routledge and Kegan Paul; Berkeley: University of California Press.

———(1976). "Ethnicity and industrialization: On the proliferation of the cultural division of labor." Ethnicity, 3:214-224.

———(1978). "Group formation and the cultural division of labor." American Journal of Sociology, 84:293-318.

HIGGS, R. (1971). "Race, skills, and earnings: American immigrants in 1909." Journal of Economic History, 31 (2):420-428.

HOMANS, G. (1950). The human group. New York: Harcourt & Brace.

HUTCHINSON, E.P. (1956). Immigrants and their children, 1850-1950. N.Y.: Wiley, published for the Social Science Research Council.

KERR, C., and SIEGEL, A. (1954). "The interindustry propensity to strike." In A. Kornhauser, R. Dubin, and A.M. Ross (eds.), Industrial conflict. New York: McGraw-Hill.

KOHN, M. (1969). Class and conformity. Homewood, Ill.: Dorsey.

KORNBLUM, W. (1974). Blue collar community. Chicago: University of Chicago Press.

LIEBERSON, S. (1963). Ethnic patterns in American cities. Glencoe: Free Press.

MacDONALD, J.S., and MacDONALD, L.O. (1964). "Chain migration, ethnic neighborhood formation, and social networks." Milbank Memorial Fund Quarterly, 42:82-97.

NORTH, D.C. (1966). Growth and welfare in the American past. Englewood Cliffs, N.J.: Prentice-Hall.

NOVAK, M. (1972). The rise of the unmeltable ethnics. New York: Macmillan.

PARK, R.E. (1950). Race and culture. Glencoe, Ill.: Free Press.

PRICE, C. (1969). "The study of assimilation." Pp. 181-232 in J.A. Jackson (ed.), Migration. Cambridge: Cambridge University Press.

SANDBERG, N.C. (1974). Ethnic identity and assimilation. New York: Praeger.

SCHACHTER, J. (1972). "Net immigration of gainful workers into the United States, 1870-1930." Demography, 9 (1):87-105.

STEINBERG, S. (1974). The academic melting-pot. New York: McGraw-Hill.

TAEUBER, K.E., and TAEUBER, A.F. (1969). Negroes in cities. New York: Atheneum.

THERNSTROM, S. (1975). The other Bostonians. Cambridge: Harvard University Press.

THOMAS, B. (1973). Migration and economic growth. Cambridge: Cambridge University Press.

TREIMAN, D. (1975). "Problems of concept and measurement in the comparative study of occupational mobility." Social Science Research, 4:183-230.

WALLERSTEIN, I. (1974). The modern world system. New York: Academic Press.

WARD, D. (1976). "Ethnic pluralism and the division of labor in U.S. cities: 1870-1880." Unpublished paper.

ZOLBERG, A. (1978). "International migration policies in a changing world system." Pp. 241-286 in W.H. McNeill and R.S. Adams (eds.), Human migration: Patterns and policies. Bloomington: Indiana University Press.

Chapter 6

FRUSTRATED APARTHEID: RACE, REPRESSION, AND CAPITALIST AGRICULTURE IN SOUTH TEXAS, 1920-1930

David Montejano

For those who view history through the lens of class conflict and class interests, understanding the role of race in capitalist development generally raises difficult questions. In some "advanced" societies, race has become a key principle for the organization of the entirety of social life. Racism and race exploitation, rather than disappearing with economic "maturation" and progress, appear instead as intimate companions. How does one explain the "making" of these contemporary racial orders? No ready answers should be expected. When one reviews the abundant literature on social change and economic development, it becomes apparent quickly that the subject of race, if considered at all, is seen only as some social anomaly. The persistence of racism and race exploitation, rather than being integrated into theories of capitalist development, remains instead an unusual aberrant social "phenomenon."

AUTHOR'S NOTE: I would like to thank Wendell Bell, Stanley Greenberg, John Kendrick, and Paul S. Taylor for their encouragement. For their criticism of an earlier draft, I would like to thank the following: Tomás Almaguer, Michael Burawoy, Jorge Chapa, Philip Gonzales, and Andrés Jiménez. Finally, I would like to express my gratitude to the staff of Bancroft Library and the Chicano Political-Economy Collective at the University of California at Berkeley. None of the above mentioned, of course, bear any responsibilities for the views expressed in this chapter.

One manner by which we can approach the problem of race in capitalist development is through a suggestion by Barrington Moore, Jr.(1966), concerning the character and significance of "labor-repressive" commercial agriculture.[1] In this type of economy, agricultural production is based on a workforce tied to the land through violence, coercion, and law in other words, where workers are not free to sell their labor. Since these conditions require strong "undemocratic" political measures and mechanisms, labor-repressive commercial agriculture points to a distinct type of capitalist development—what Moore called a "fascist" road to the modern world. With some substitutions, we believe that Moore's emphasis on labor-repressive development can explain much of the "racial" experience in advanced capitalist societies.[2] To a considerable extent, as we shall see, race exploitation, separation, and exclusion can be understood in terms of the reactionary economic requirements and fortunes of commercial agriculture.

In the following discussion, we shall consider one episode in the making of a contemporary racial order which illustrates the interplay of race, commercial agriculture, and labor repression. The historical base for this detail is South Texas during the development of commercial agriculture in the 1920s. Occasional references are made to Central Texas and West Texas, areas which also had significant Mexican populations. The description of rural life presented here, in fact, could be generalized without much difficulty to cover most of Mexican Texas and extended a decade in either direction.[3] In rural Mexican Texas at this time, we find a clear but largely unexamined instance of racially based labor repression; more specifically, a situation where Mexican agricultural laborers constituted a restricted proletariat. It may seem "paradoxical" that some condition of labor repression should exist until 1930 (and well beyond that point) in a subordinate region of a modern capitalist democracy. But this apparent incongruity only suggest the compatibility of distinct types of development within a nation-state. Not until the late 1920s, in fact, does evidence of tension between the labor-repressive regional economy and the "national" requirements for free wage labor begin to surface. This tension obviously complicates the Texas story, but it does not weaken the argument. For the development of labor-repressive agriculture in Texas in the twentieth century cannot be seen as some "anomalous" capitalist transformation; rather it must be seen as the type of development made possible by racial domination in the internal peripheries of "core" states.

Unfortunately, we cannot discuss the nineteenth century history of this region; yet the Mexican War, annexation of old Mexican settlements, governance by cliques of Anglo merchants and land lawyers, and displacement of the traditional Mexican landed elite all point to some of the critical features of this chapter. In regard to commercial agriculture, we should note that its introduction in the early 1900s was one literally sponsored by a post-War Anglo elite, composed predominantly of merchants, cattlemen, and land agents. The most enterprising businessmen, in fact, joined together, built a railroad into South Texas, formed real estate and irrigation companies, sliced their ranches into farm tracts, and boomed towns on their property. The result was one of the best planned and greatest land movements in the history of the West. Farmers from the crowded Midwest and North bought the land and settled in the towns planned by the retiring cattlemen (many of whom now became the town bankers); they chose the most profitable cash crop that could be cultivated and began to recruit Mexican day laborers. An agricultural "revolution" had begun.

This revolution basically unfolded between 1900 and 1910. Another surge of agricultural expansion occurred between 1920 and 1930, but by then the basis for the new society of commercial farming had been laid in South Texas. By 1930 much of the famous "cradle" of the Texas cattle industry had been turned into farm land. Agriculture thoroughly dominated four South Texas counties and was challenging ranching in another nine; the ranch life remained uncontested only in six counties. The population in the farm counties, like that of the ranch areas, would be mainly Mexican, but the society of the farm areas is so dissimilar from that of the ranch districts that we must draw a sharp line between the two. In this chapter, we will consider only the world of the "new-comer" farmers. As our discussion will make clear, this was a world where the demands and fortunes of commercial agriculture shaped basic features in Mexican-Anglo relations.

In terms of primary historical sources, the excellent interview material which Paul Taylor collected in South Texas in 1929 and 1930 forms the core of our documentary evidence. Through these interviews with farmers, businessmen, and officials, we can reconstruct the racial order of the time and see that labor repression was no accident or imagined experience. On the contrary, they reveal the conscious manner in which the "new-comer" commercial farmers attempted to organize production for a competitive world market.

THE WORLD OF
CAPITALIST AGRICULTURE, 1920-1930

In the context we have outlined, then, we can place the exploitation and oppression which the Mexican in Texas experienced in the first third of this century. In this chapter we will not be concerned with detailing the extent and intensity of this experience, which appears as a matter of fact to the most casual historian of Mexican Texas. Mexican consular reports, accounts in Mexican and U.S. newspapers, the interviews which Taylor had with white farmers, sheriffs, and other officials, all attest to the brutal and volatile character of Mexican-Anglo relations at this time (Hidalgo, 1940). Rather, the thrust of this article will be directed toward outlining the logic which shaped racial oppression during this period of rapid agricultural development. "Labor repression" captures in both a theoretical and empirical sense the force underlying the exploitation of the Mexican at this time. In the following discussion, labor repression refers basically to the use of compulsion for organizing the recruitment, work activity, and compensation of wage labor. Immobilization of sharecroppers and pickers through debt is perhaps the most obvious case of labor repression. Horsewhipping and other types of physical punishment to discipline workers also constitute obvious examples. The dismissal or removal of wage laborers for the purpose of avoiding payment or compensation is yet another type of labor repression. Under this latter type fall a number of specific historical examples: shotgun settlements, the cancellation of credit at the local store, the timely "leak" to the Border Patrol, and so on. Finally, the formulation of labor policies designed to restrict the movement of wage laborers qualifies as another distinct repressive form. The Emigrant Labor Agency Laws which aimed to "restrain" the out-of-state movement of Texas Mexicans comprise a clear example of such policies. In brief, by labor repression we are speaking of "labor controls." More precisely, in the context of Mexican Texas we are speaking of "racial" labor controls. These various types of controls, then, suggest the breadth of exploitation to which Mexicans were subjected.

In the following discussion, we shall describe the manner in which the racial exploitation of this period was basically a response to the development of commercial agriculture. This we shall do by first discussing the market situation of commercial farmers which moved them to devise labor controls and other repressive policies. Then we shall outline the logic which weaves the variegated instances and expressions of control into an integrated pattern. Before proceeding, however, we should describe the manner in which work on South Texas farms was organized. By outlining these labor arrangements, the racial and class divisions of this rural society will be given some concrete meaning.

THE ORGANIZATION OF WORK

The well-known problems with census data concerning the Mexican population of the Southwest preclude any unambiguous description of the rural order during this period. Nonetheless some characteristics can be suggested. In 1930 the Mexican population in Texas consisted of 683,681 residents, or nearly 12% of the total state population. Almost half of the 236,201 "gainfully employed" Mexicans—this statistic includes all those gainfully employed above the age of 10— were agricultural workers (Farm Placement Service Division, 1940:5, 70). The portrayal of work situations we present here, then, suggests the quality of life for approximately half of the Texas Mexican population during the 1920s. To put it another way, the features of the racial order we describe were experienced by virtually the entire Texas Mexican population residing in farm areas.

We get a clear perspective of the rural order if we look at the composition of the migratory labor force. In 1940 the Texas State Employment Service estimated on the basis of its experience and records that of the 200,000 to 300,000 "full time" migrant laborers in Texas, 85% were Mexican, 10% were white, and 5% were black. As we move closer to the South Texas region, the Mexican character of this migratory labor force becomes even more pronounced. Crystal City, the seat of Zavala County, had in 1930 a population of 6,600, five-sixths of which was Mexican. Approximately 96% of the Mexican families in this Winter Garden town were migratory (Menefee, 1941:3, 15). In neighboring Dimmit County where 75% of the 12,000 residents in 1930 were Mexican, virtually all the field work was done by Mexicans. Even the distribution of the Mexican population in this country was determined mainly by the location of irrigated crops, a not uncommon pattern in semiarid South Texas. Along the coastal plain, in Karnes County, 85% of the farm laborers surveyed by the U.S. Farm Security Administration in 1936 were Mexican; the remaining 15% were evenly divided between whites and Negroes (Vasey and Folsom, 1937).

To complete our sketch of the racial character of the rural order, we have to look at another important layer of the agriculture labor force which included nonpropertied cultivators. This consists of the tenant farm population which must be divided between those on "thirds and fourths" and those on "halves." Those on thirds and fourths, commonly known as "tenant farmers" or "share tenants," were essentially cultivators renting land and a house from a landlord. The tenant farmer provided the rest—the seed, equipment, a team of horses or mules, his own labor, and usually the labor of his wife and children as well. At the end of the harvest season, the tenant farmer would pay the landlord one-third of the grain and one-fourth of the cotton he and his family had cultivated during the year. Sometimes the landlord exacted a cash rent instead of payment in kind. In contrast to these "regular" tenant farmers were those cultivators on halves, commonly known as "sharecroppers;" they were basically laborers who were compensated by payments in kind in lieu of cash wages. Under a halves agreement, the sharecropper furnished only his labor (and that of his family), for which he could keep one-half of the cotton cultivated on the acreage assigned him by the landlord.

The tenant farm population, then, was not one homogeneous class. Significant variations in the contractual agreements with landlords, in the freedom to cultivate and market a crop, and in ownership of the "basic requirements of production," to use a phrase of the U.S. Department of Agriculture, separated the market situation of regular tenant farmers, those on thirds and fourths, from that of sharecroppers (Johnson, 1926:33-34; Shannon, 1945:88-95; Taylor Collection: 102-692). A basic distinction must be drawn between these two groups. In South Texas, in fact, there was very little difference between the actual earnings of Mexican sharecroppers and migrant laborers. Nonetheless, because croppers were under less supervision than wage hands, perhaps because it appeared that they had a different relationship to the land and the workplace, croppers were generally regarded as a higher class than wage laborers.

Again the various weaknesses of census data do not allow any easy racial breakdown of the tenant farm classes. A rather evident pattern of "segmentation" along racial lines, however, suggests the relative proportions of tenants who were white and Mexican. A close look at the historical record uncovers a common tendency for white landlords to contract Mexicans on halves and whites on thirds and fourths (or on a cash rent basis). For example, about half of Nueces County, according to one local farmer, was farmed by white tenants on thirds and fourths, who in turn had Mexican families do the work for them. A few Mexicans were on thirds and fourths, but very few—"not 5% of the country."[4] Even in Central Texas, where Mexican sharecroppers had displaced white tenant farmers between 1890 and 1900, we see that this pattern holds. In Caldwell County, for example, the county agent for the U.S. Farm Service estimated that of the 2,300 tenants, 200 were white, 450 were black, and the remaining 1,650 were Mexican. Ninety-five percent of the Mexican tenants were half in rents (Taylor Collection:78-669; 31-36).

As far as landownership is concerned, we have no reliable estimates of the number of landowners in any one county, much less a breakdown of their racial composition. With the exception of a few border counties, however, we can discount Mexican landowners as a significant class group in the farm areas of South Texas. In 1914, for instance, there was only *one* Mexican landowner in Nueces County, and he owned a meager 30 acres. By 1929 the number of Mexican landowners in the county had increased to 29, most of whom owned less than 100 acres of land. In Dimmit County, where we find a similar pattern, the observation of a prominent resident may stand in place of numbers:

We have a high type of white citizens here. We have no white trash. The Mexicans are all the labor class of people.[Taylor, 1930a: 437]

On the basis of this evident class organization along racial lines, we can return to the census statistics of the period and use them to illuminate the typical class structure and labor arrangements of rural South Texas. Selecting the two counties of Dimmit and Nueces, where the Taylor interview material documents the racial-class segmentation just described, we can categorize the number of farms according to type, average size, and the likely identity of the farmer. Table 1 illustrates the common pattern. The information in this table helps highlight several features concerning the organization of labor in rural South Texas. As is obvious, sharecroppers generally received considerably less land to cultivate than tenants on thirds and fourths. Usually landlords provided about 30 acres, only enough land for one team of horses or mules. When the sharecropper in question was a Mexican, however, landlords sometimes provided even less land. Landlords had an explicit idea of what was "too much" for the

Table 1. Farms in Two South Texas Counties According
to Tenure, Average Size, and Probable Race
of Farmer, 1925.

	DIMMIT COUNTY (main crop: onions)		NUECES COUNTY (main crop: cotton)	
	No. of	Ave. size	No. of	Ave. size
Owner-operated (Anglo):	150	(289)	450	(272)
Tenant-operated Cash and Share (Anglo):	81	(333)	715	(143)
Sharecroppers (Mexican):	63	(76)	743	(49)

SOURCE: U.S. Census of Agriculture, 1925, Part II, *The Southern States*, pp. 1117, 1131

Mexican (Taylor Collection:101-691). In South Texas, Mexicans
were rarely given more than 10 to 15 acres per plow hand. This
suggests once more that in the new South Texas cotton belt sharecropping was basically a means of securing cheap resident labor. The
landlord-farmer dependent on seasonal labor to plant, chop, and pick
his cash crop still needed someone around to do whatever miscellane-
ous chores had to be done. Contracting sharecroppers on small parcels
adjoining the landlord's farm was viewed as an excellent way of
ensuring the availability of cheap resident labor throughout the year.
Thus it is hardly surprising that landlord-farmers had calculated a
proper ratio for the number of sharecroppers one needed according to
the size of their farms. Nueces County cotton farmers, for instance,
figured that one Mexican sharecropper on 15 acres was "about right"
for every 160 acres on their farm (Taylor, 1971:98-125). This brings
us back to one central point: in the 1920s sharecropping was
essentially an adjunct to an expanding system of migratory wage labor.
    At this point, some idea of the size of the migratory workforce
needed to work the farms of a county might be given. Ample
information concerning cotton cultivation in this period allows us to
construct a suggestive hypothetical example (Johnson, 1926:33-47,
56-59, 73). Let us focus on Nueces County, one of the leading cotton
counties in the state, and assume for the sake of discussion that the 450
"owner-operated" farms had all their acreage planted in cotton.
Theoretically, over the 10-week picking season the 450 owner-
operated farms in Nueces County would require 90 crews, each with
25 workers, or approximately 2,250 laborers altogether. This figure,
however, greatly underestimates the actual number of Mexican

laborers who worked Nueces County, because as a rule most cotton growers wanted their cotton picked immediately. Particularly when the timing of market sales was important, we might have a situation where all 450 farm owners desired to have their cotton picked within the same week. Such a situation, a not uncommon one in a speculative year, would require a force of 22,500 laborers.[5] These hypothetical estimates, then, provide us an approximate idea of the great size of the seasonal labor force needed to work one Texas cotton county. The great range between our two estimates, moreover, points to one of the most perplexing motifs in Texas agricultural history: the fear of a labor shortage. This possibility, a scarcity of labor at the critical picking or harvest season, was a source of considerable anxiety for the commercial farmer. It was, as we shall see, sufficiently bothersome to move him to devise ways by which the seasonal Mexican worker could be immobilized.

This, then, completes a composite description of how cotton was cultivated and worked in one South Texas county. Slightly more than half the farm acreage in Nueces was in the hands of nonpropertied cultivators; these in turn were sharply divided between white tenants on thirds and fourths and Mexican tenants on halves. The remaining farm land was tended by white farm owners and worked by a large transient Mexican labor force at the appropriate picking season. Given these work arrangements, it is no surprise that South Texas farmers had a reputation as men who sat around town and let the "Mex" do the farming. In Nueces County, one well-educated resident described the local farmers there as a "leisure class." In Dimmit County, farmers were similarly characterized as "drug store farmers." (Taylor, 1971: 88-89, 1930a:319). The farmer, for his turn, believed the white tenant depended too much on Mexican croppers and laborers. Since white tenant farmers generally subcontracted part of their rented land to Mexican sharecroppers, they often had the time to join their landlords in town. Such dependency on Mexican labor, of course, was more often seen as a privilege, an advantage of living in South Texas, rather than a matter for derision.

This local scenario could be drawn repeatedly for the agricultural counties of Texas; it represents the "mold" for South Texas as well as for Central and West Texas. This again suggests the extent to which migrant work and sharecropping were essentially racial labor arrangements. Having described these arrangements in some detail, we can now discuss the interests of the commercial farmers which led them to devise a number of "suitable" labor controls.

THE DILEMMA OF COMMERCIAL FARMERS

The farmers of South Texas shared two basic concerns: one, they wanted cheap labor; two, they wanted it at the right time and in sufficient numbers. These concerns do not distinguish the South Texas farmer from his counterpart elsewhere: these interests essentially reflect a common class position. The folk image of the hardy farm family which worked its land primarily for its own subsistence was, like so many other features of a disappearing frontier, no longer a tenable view of the rural population. By the close of the nineteenth century, according to one economic historian, the American farmer had become a businessman "as tightly enmeshed in the web of a world market as a Boston banker or a New York merchant" (Degler, 1967:78). Farmers now devoted their time and energy to the cultivation of a commodity for profit. What makes the story of the manner in which they seized on the "racial" character of the work force to improve their market situation. In competition with foreign crop imports (e.g., Egyptian onions and cotton) as well as with domestic production, South Texas commercial farmers sought to minimize their overhead by cutting costs in the one area most amenable to their control—wages. To eliminate the possibility of competitive bidding for labor, local farm organizations would meet before the season opened and determine the prevailing rates to which all growers of a particular crop or in a certain locality were expected to follow (Scruggs, 1957; Taylor, 1930a:352, 1971:119). "Wage-fixing," however, could not be an effective way by which to minimize production costs unless the movement of wage laborers to workplaces with higher wage scales could be constrained. For in an unfettered labor market, the commercial farmer or urban industrialist who offered relatively attractive wages, whether the workplace was within the same county, in a neighboring county, or in a distant state, would tend to upset any local wage-fixing. To maintain a "cheap" wage scale in South Texas, then, the mobility of the agricultural worker had to be restricted. Let us describe in more detail the advantages and difficulties farmers saw in maintaining a cheap migratory labor force.

There were no scruples among Anglo settlers in South Texas that a major asset of the region consisted of an adequate labor pool which was the "cheapest" to be found anywhere. Agribusinessmen, their Chambers of Commerce, and local county newspapers constantly emphasized this great advantage of the area. Appeals made to attract investment characteristically stressed the presence of cheap and ample labor. One land prospectus in the Winter Garden region, for example, pushed the "sell" in a succinct statement: "The cheapest farm labor in the United States is to be had in this section" (Scruggs, 1957:123). Some four hundred miles to the east, the Houston Chamber of Commerce wooed New England textile manufacturers by pointing out in their commercial bulletin that "unorganizable Mexican labor in inexhaustible numbers can be secured in Texas for new textile mills" (Taylor, 1971:105-106). Newspapers like the *Galveston News* and the *Corpus Christi Caller* likewise invited prospective agribusinessmen and industrialists to invest in South Texas, citing the presence of ample cheap labor. So cheap was Mexican labor, in fact, that the introduction of mechanization on commercial farms was effectively retarded by the higher costs and less profitable returns from machines (Taylor, 1971:109-113, 1930a:325-335). The degree to which these wages were depressed surfaces clearly when the Mexican wage scale in Texas is compared with those in neighboring states. According to information compiled in a 1926-1927 study of Mexicans in the United States, the average wage of Mexican laborers working cotton in the Southern and Southwestern states was lowest in Texas (Gamio, 1971). A Mexican laborer working Texas cotton received a daily wage of $1.75. In Arizona the Mexican laborer received $2.75 a day for the same work, in California, $3.25; in Arkansas, Louisiana, and Mississippi, $4.00. Mexican labor in Texas, in fact, was so cheap that most Anglos made a sharp distinction between "white wages" and "Mexican wages."

In the eyes of most farmers, these great differences between Mexican wages and white wages were basically adjustments to the minimum living standards of Mexicans and whites. The "cheaper" lifestyle of the Mexican, in fact, framed a common argument that farmers used in justifying their preference for Mexican labor over that of whites. One land development agent put it this way: "The white people won't do the work and they won't live as the Mexicans do on beans and tortillas and in one room shacks" (Taylor, 1930a:340). Likewise the same commercial prospecti which invited agribusiness and industrial investors to South Texas discouraged the settlement of any white who did not have capital or some skill or profession to offer. In the Winter Garden district, the Carrizo Springs Chamber of Commerce cautioned through its pamphlet, appropriately entitled "Your Opportunity May Be Waiting in Carrizo Springs, Texas," that "American laborers" should stay away because of the unequal competition with the living standards of Mexican labor. In Nueces County one farmer explained the matter to Taylor (1971:300-308) in this way:

> The Mexicans are the only class of labor we can handle. The others won't do this work; the white pickers want screens and ice-water. To white pickers I say, "If you will accept the houses we have for the Mexicans, you can work." They said they were broke and they had to.

Exceptions to the racial-class boundaries in South Texas, as we see, might occur, and a farmer might contract whites as sharecroppers or pickers, but they were exceptions. Generally whites were denied work as pickers or sharecroppers. White men who could not finance a crop, that is, go on thirds and fourths, were considered unfit as far as most farmers were concerned. A prominent Nueces County landowner echoed the sentiment of white farmers in the area: "I prefer any Mexican to a sorry white man." These preferences were based not only on considerations of wages and lifestyle, but also fundamentally involved the question of tractability and powerlessness. There was a sharp distinction drawn between what was considered a proper setting and proper treatment for a white worker and what was considered proper for a Mexican. A landlord-farmer could determine the character of the work relationship much more readily with Mexicans than with whites. One cotton farmer summed it up compactly: "Whites cannot be as easily domineered, led, or directed as the Mexicans" (Taylor Collection:188-777).

As we stated earlier, South Texas farmers shared two basic concerns. On the one hand, they wanted cheap wage labor. This, as we saw, they had. As the second basic interest, we noted that farmers wanted temporary or seasonal wage labor, labor available for the critical picking and harvesting seasons. Sharecropping, once an adequate way of anchoring cheap labor to the land, was no longer economically sound. Texas cotton farmers, as the Rural Land Owners' Association declared, simply could not "support 12 months in the year the large amount of labor required for a few weeks only." Likewise vegetable growers could "make more money by working the Mexicans than by leasing to them" (Taylor, 1971:200, 1930a:366). This desire for cheap but temporary labor, however, entailed an internal tension. Temporary wage labor meant that laborers had to be mobile. Mobility for the laborer, in turn, meant that Mexicans could work for the highest bidder for their labor. Such a competitive labor market, however, would undermine the low wage scale of the area. As it was, large commercial farmers in many South Texas counties were often concerned about "labor theft." Such accusations were regularly leveled at the small farmer and grower who, wishing his crop picked quickly, was willing to offer slightly higher wages than the "fixed" local norm. The problem of labor theft, however, was not one limited to the intracounty movement of Mexicans as well. Why not travel to a neighboring county where they were offering 10¢ a hundred pounds more? Or why not emigrate to Arkansas where they paid $4 a day in picking wages as opposed to $1.75 in Texas? This, then, framed the basic dilemma confronting the commercial farmers of South Texas. Wishing to preserve their cheap labor resource, they had to restrict the movement of Mexican laborers in some way.

Nowhere do we have a clearer view of this overriding concern to restrict labor mobility than in the attitude of farmers toward road building programs and ownership of cars by Mexican laborers (Taylor Collection:78-699, 101-691, 196-735; Taylor, 1971:309-311). Cars and roads, the much heralded symbols and carriers of the new world, had penetrated the old cattle country of frontier Texas, but their introduction resulted in no "automatic" freedom of movement for the landless Mexican. Large landowners in particular were expressedly against the good roads movement and the ownership of cars by Mexicans. Given their concern in securing cheap and stable Mexican labor, their position is hardly surprising. One large cotton farmer said he had Mexicans on halves "but never more" because they would spend their earnings on old cars. "The Mexicans stay better on halves." But car ownership had apparently "spoiled" the transient Mexican as well. The auto had ruined the Mexicans, according to one farmer, because now they would say "All right, if you don't give me what I want I will go where I can get it." One prominent Nueces County cotton grower informed Taylor that it was best to get the Mexican in trucks. "If they have their own cars, they travel every week to see where the cotton is. If they have no way to move about, it is better." Another cotton grower expressed the sentiments of his counterparts in the area: "The majority of farmers prefer Mexicans without transportation. They are going to stay with you then until they are through." In fact, this dislike among landlords and farmers of Mexican car ownership frequently expressed itself in attempts to attach cars in order to satisfy debts at the end of the season. The comments of one Corpus Christi judge in reference to peonage laws suggest what must have been a common practice among Nueces County farmers:

> You can't attach a Mexican's auto; it has been decided that an auto is a "wagon and team," and so protected by the laws for attachment. You might get them under the laws against swindling. I think they (the Mexicans) ought to believe it that they can be put in jail for leaving when in debt.

The difficulty with Mexican labor, then, centered on its mobility. How did the Texas farmer resolve this problem? Debt, as we have mentioned several times, constituted one common basis for the immobilization of cheap labor. This type of control, however, was ill-suited for a migratory labor system. Other measures had to be developed.

THE WEB OF REPRESSION

When we survey the various labor practices and policies which commercial farmers devised and experimented with in attempting to restrain the movement of Mexican labor, we find no general single response. Rather we are confronted with some individual attempts with an ad hoc character, and some collective efforts with more formal features. Horsewhipping, chains, armed guards, near-starvation diets, to name a few of the props involved, portray the more brutal side of these labor controls. Vagrancy laws, local "pass" systems, and labor "taxes" point to a more institutionalized dimension; and we could continue to point to other aspects of this repressive experience. The labor controls put into effect in this period of agricultural development are striking for the astounding variety in their detail. Some farmers even put gamblers among their Mexican pickers to keep them broke (Taylor Collection:102-642). The variety—even ingenuity—of these practices suggests a complex, puzzling patchwork of exploitation. Clearly these diverse responses to the problem of Mexican mobility all point in the same direction—toward control of movement. Nonetheless, on the surface such an inchoate web appears to weaken our central idea of labor repression. In what sense can we say that these variegated forms of exploitation and control composed an integrated pattern of labor repression?

The variety in labor controls can be attributed to three sources. In the first place, labor controls were tailored to the labor arrangement; different sets of controls, in other words, were associated with sharecropping and migratory labor. Secondly, the number of controls represents the experimentation of new-comer farmers with various methods for immobilizing Mexican labor. In many ways, such experimentation involved a search for a political solution that would assure them a cheap labor reservoir. It is not surprising, then, as farmers sought effective control over migratory labor, that they turned at each step to political agencies with increasingly broader jurisdiction and power. The various labor controls can be placed on an ascending scale according to their sponsorship; individual farmer of agricultural company, local agribusiness organizations, county government, and finally state government. Preliminary evidence indicates that this scale also represents chronologically the involvement of these political actors. Finally, the labor controls were related to the condition of the labor market—which control might be imposed depended on whether a labor "shortage" or "surplus" existed.

In the following discussion, we shall describe the most common controls associated with sharecropping first; then we shall proceed to describe those associated with migratory labor. The ascending scale of political sponsorship which farmers obtained in their efforts to create an effective repressive apparatus will become evident. In a final section, we will discuss how the condition of the labor market and other market factors shaped the form of repression.

Debts and Shotguns: Regulating the Sharecropper

In reviewing the cases of coercion associated with Mexican share-croppers, we find two distinct trends. On the one hand, large landowners attempted to immobilize the cropper through debt (Taylor Collection:125-294). The frank words of a San Antonio official of the U.S. Employment Service should suffice to reiterate this point:

> Some of the farmers here advance from $250 to $500 a year to the Mexican families. They use the debt as a club to keep them on the place. They bluff the Mexicans through fear of the law and personal violence. This is more prevalent with the big landowners.

On the other hand, we find cases throughout the length of Mexican Texas where the landlord would terminate the contract of the sharecropper in order to appropriate the cropper's cotton (Taylor Collection:59-64, 32-37, 83-673; Taylor, 1930a:350). The Mexican Consul in El Paso, drawing on his experience with conditions in West Texas (as well as throughout the state), told Taylor that landlords often terminate the contracts of croppers on the pretext that they failed to follow some instruction. "They may be then ordered off the place by a deputy sheriff and probably the horses and chickens are attached to pay the debts." In Central Texas, a U.S. Farm Service official noted that some landlords cut the tenants' store allowance in June or July when the crop looks good. By cutting their allowance, the landlords were able to run the Mexicans off the place. The Mexican Consul in Corpus Christi described the difficulties of the local Mexican population in this Gulf Coast region in similar terms:

> Almost all of the difficulties we encounter are because the farmers tell the Mexicans working on halves to leave without their pay or share of the crop. Almost all of these difficulties are arranged. There isn't much difficulty over payment of the pickers.

Finally, the Mexican Vice-consul in McAllen reported similar experiences in deep South Texas in the late 1930s. In a letter addressed to an inquiring Mexican congressional deputy, the Vice-consul noted that in his region the landlord "rentistas" have studied innumerable ways of legally breaking their contract with their Mexican croppers and, with this in mind, look for some difficulty so they can remove him from his work—"por supuesto, cuando éste ya está terminado" (Hidalgo, 1940:45). These legal maneuvers were at least a bit more sophisticated than another common method of breaking sharecropping contracts— the so-called "shotgun settlement," a tactic whereby an armed farmer drove off his cropper or laborer in lieu of payment of wages.

At first sight, expulsion of a sharecropper may seem to be an ironic form of labor control. The irony consists only of semantics, however, for shotgun settlements and other methods used to terminate work contracts were fundamentally means of securing subsistence labor. During the tenure of the contract, the expelled laborer, either a "regular" wage hand or a sharecropper, had basically worked for subsistence wages, that is, for the monthly advances given to feed his family. If his horses, chickens, or automobile had been attached to pay for the farmer's advances, then the expelled laborer had, in fact, worked for much less than subsistence. He had actually *borrowed* in order to live and work. Expulsion, then, appears to be an inverted form of peonage. It was one, however, suited to the labor arrangement. Migrant laborers occasionally might be expelled at the discretion of the farmer, but generally this type of labor control was practiced with *resident* labor. To put it another way, the emphasis of labor controls associated with *seasonal* labor lay in "recruitment." Controls geared to resident labor, from debt peonage to shotgun settlements, revolved around the question of retention or expulsion—for lack of a better word, on the "exit" side of a labor contract.

A word might be said about the circumstances facing the farmer which made for the use of debts and shotguns. In large part, these "diverse" tendencies of peonage and expulsion reflect the particular market situation of the commercial farmer. Agribusinessmen with extensive holdings, for instance, were the "farmers" most concerned with having stable resident labor throughout the year. They were, in other words, the segment of commercial farmers most likely to immobilize sharecroppers (and migrant laborers) and the ones least likely to run them off. A Nueces County farmer figured it this way: "There isn't much in it for a farmer to run a Mexican off with a small acreage; besides the farmer wants the Mexican to stay, therefore he doesn't run him off" (Taylor Collection:96-686). Conversely, the small farmer or tenant farmer on thirds and fourths would be the one most susceptible to running their cropers and pickers off. In a much more marginal and vulnerable market situation than the agribusiness-man, the small farmer might be tempted, in a good crop year, to settle his contractual agreements with a shotgun. In a bad year, he might be forced to. In short, the labor controls associated with resident Mexican labor were in a sense "appropriate" for the labor arrangement. Let us now turn to another way of obtaining cheap labor, a system of migratory wage labor, and discuss the controls which accompanied its development.

Promises and Passes: Recruiting Seasonal Labor

Farmers dependent on seasonal Mexican labor were concerned with immobilizing them at the proper time. There were several ways of accomplishing this objective, but perhaps the most common method was through recruitment of contract laborers under false pretenses. Labor recruitment and contract labor, we should note, constituted the only manner in which the migratory labor system was organized in

Texas until the mid-1930s. Needless to say, with little state super-vision or regulation, such organization of the work force was suscep-tible to considerable manipulation on the part of commercial farmers and labor contractors (Farm Placement Service Division, 1940; Final Report, 1916:9200-9205). Emilio Flores, secretary of the Mexican Protective Association in San Antonio, explained to the fact-finding federal Commission on Industrial Relations (1915) how such manip-ulation was arranged. Employment agencies and labor contractors would go down to the border and recruit Mexicans by making attractive but false offers. The contracted laborers, however, would not discover the actual terms of the contract and conditions of their work situation until they arrived at their destination. The result? As Flores testified before the Commission:

> When they (the Mexican laborers) sometimes refuse to comply, because of the promises of the employment agency at the border or at San Antonio, they are guarded until they work out what they owe. I have known a number of Mexicans to be chained in Gonzales County and guarded by armed men with shotguns and made to work these moneys out. This was officially reported and is of record.

Flores then named a score of Central Texas and South Texas counties and towns where Mexican workers had been subjected to brutal force, including instances of whipping and murder. Such episodes of coercion were an integral element of the work experience of the Mexican contract laborer during this period of rapid development. One Mexi-can interviewed by the sociologist Manuel Gamio in 1930 recalled his personal experience with Texas farmers and authorities about the year 1912. The passing of the years had done little to erase the bitterness (Gamio, 1931:150-151):

> In San Antonio we were under contract to go and pick cotton in a camp in the Valley of the Rio Grande. A group of countrymen and my wife and I went to pick. When we arrived at the camp, the planter gave us an old hovel which had been used as a chicken house before, to live in, out in the open. I didn't want to live there and told him that if he didn't give us a little house which was a little better we would go. He told us to go, and my wife and I and my children were leaving when the sheriff fell upon us. He took me to the jail and there the planter told them that I wanted to leave without paying him for my passage. He charged me twice the cost of the transportation, and though I tried first not to pay him, and then to

pay him for what it cost, I couldn't do anything. The authorities would
only pay attention to him, and as they were in league with him they told
me that if I didn't pay they would take my wife and my little children to
work. Then I paid them.

This incident was no isolated or exceptional case. It was only a
reflection of a "pass" system which local farmers and authorities had
instituted in order to have the cotton picked.

Another common practice used to immobilize seasonal Mexican
labor occurred through the timely enforcements of vagrancy laws. It
seems to have been customary in Texas for vagrancy laws to be applied
at the beginning of each cotton picking season, especially if there was a
labor shortage or, to put it more accurately, if laborers refused to work
for the wages offered by local farmers (Final Report, 1916:9001-
9003). Vagrancy laws, in fact, provided the "legal basis for one of the
more elaborate local arrangements used to control Mexican labor in
South Texas—the "hiring and pass systems" of the lower Rio Grande
Valley. In 1927 court testimony at the "Raymondville Peonage
Cases" uncovered a fascinating "compact" between local cotton
farmers, the county justice of the peace, the county attorney, and the
county sheriff and his deputies in Willacy County (Taylor, 1971:149-
156, 325-329). During times when labor was needed, local farmers
would recruit contract laborers who discovered, upon arrival, that the
terms they had agreed to were misrepresentations. Any who then
refused to work were picked up by the local deputies, found guilty of
vagrancy, and fined double the amount owed the farmer for transportation or food. The convicted were then given the option of "working off"
the fines by picking cotton for the farmer who had recruited them. Any
laborers passing through the county during the picking season also
experienced the same fate: convicted of vagrancy, they were informed
that the fines should be worked off in the cotton fields. Naturally such
"convict labor" was routinely guarded by armed deputies while
working cotton. To complement this method of recruiting labor, a pass
system was instituted to prevent unauthorized pickers from leaving the
county. Laborers leaving the area had to have passes signed by one of
the local farmers involved in the compact.

In this deep South Texas district, generally only Mexicans ended up
being "hired" through the Willacy County system. In practice, it was
essentially a racial labor control mechanism. This repressive apparatus, however, apparently could operate in a color-blind fashion
whenever white "vagrants" wandered into Willacy County. In fact,

this "color blindness" appears to have been partly responsible for the downfall of the Willacy pact, which occurred shortly after two young white men had stumbled into the "hiring" net. These white pickers provided, for a local attorney who was "politically hostile" to the sheriff, the necessary ingredient for removing the sheriff from office: in these white vagrants, the attorney had unimpeachable victims and witnesses, traits which Mexican and black laborers lacked before white juries. The court proceedings resulted in convictions, and five officials, including the sheriff and the justice of the peace, were sentenced to terms ranging from one month to 18 months. The convictions were a shocking and unexpected blow to the Texas farmers. Many observers, Anglo and Mexican alike, commented that the trial and convictions had occurred because Raymondville officers had involved two "white boys."

At the present we have very incomplete information concerning the duration or extent of such hiring and pass systems in South Texas. After reviewing the situation in Nueces County in 1929, Taylor concluded that peonage did exist, sometimes as a result of "coercion," sometimes because of "submission," fear, and ignorance of the law. Peonage in this frontier, in fact, was seen "simply as a fact," a common labor practice, even as "an ethically approved institution." The popular white reaction to the Raymondville convictions, moreover, indicates that the support of Mexican peonage was quite widespread. For these convictions created a profound sensation throughout the South Texas cotton belt. In Nueces County some farmers had an "aggrieved feeling" that the law had left them helpless. Considerable sympathy was extended to those convicted: the sheriff, in fact, was given a celebration in his honor on his release from imprisonment. An official from the U.S. Department of Justice defended the convicted authorities (Taylor Collection:169-758)

> They ought to be able to make Mexicans work out their debt. The peonage cases were extreme. There was a labor shortage in 1926. They don't generally do that (that is, guard the pickers with guns).

The Justice official was making the popular but circular argument of many farmers and politicians of the day. Naturally fear of labor shortages moved commercial farmers to devise ways to immobilize labor; this condition, after all, provided the impetus for labor repression.

In sum, we see that repression of "transient" Mexican laborers focused on some aspect of labor recruitment, and that two common methods of recruitment centered on misrepresented contracts and vagrancy laws. "Entrapment" is undoubtedly a more accurate description of this type of repression. The frequent companion of such entrapment was physical force; for the effectiveness of this labor control lay in the quick and emphatic suppression of any initial resistance by the Mexican workers. Likewise the supervision of entrapped labor generally carried with it the treat of physical discipline. In fact, the "success" of entrapment as a labor control, perhaps to a greater degree than other types of control, lay in the constant and visible threat of force. This corresponds to one suggestive observation in the testimony of Emilio Flores regarding contract laborers. "Many cases of outrages," with these unfortunates have been "traced back to the manner in which said labor is secured" (Final Report, 1916:9201-9202). Again this points to an interesting relationship between labor arrangements and certain types of coercion and control. Mexican sharecroppers and other resident laborers, although often threatened with physical force, were generally spared such brutality because of the farmer's need for stable, year-long labor. At least for the duration of the contract, paternalism tended to characterize the farmer's relationship with his Mexican "regulars." In contrast, the temporary character of seasonal labor undermined any need for paternalism and emphasized the instrumental nature of the work relationship. Thus, where the oppressive features of this relationship became too transparent, as for entrapped migrant labor, force and discipline had to play the necessary lead role.

Licenses and Taxes: Protecting the Migrant Stream

The character of racial exploitation during the early twentieth century was thus largely a response to the "imperatives" of commercial agriculture. A straightforward economic interpretation, however, does not explain the quilt-like quality of labor repression in rural Texas. For whether or not labor controls might surface depended in large part on what was possible locally. Where consensus among local farmers and authorities could be negotiated, some control along the lines of the Willacy County system might be attempted. Internal "dissent," however, could threaten any plan, as we see in the frequent complaints about farmers who engaged in "labor theft" and exceeded "fixed" wage levels. Given the varying political conditions in South Texas—a subject we cannot discuss here—the techniques and strategies established to control Mexican labor were expectedly different from county to county. There was no uniform response to the "problem" of Mexican mobility.

The county, in any case, constituted a singularly inadequate base for regulating the movement of Mexican migratory labor within the state. The cotton circuit alone stretched from the southern tip of the state to the northwestern edge of the Panhandle, a round-trip of nearly 2,000 miles (McWilliams, 1941:231-232). Thus, even where the farmers of a county were in agreement concerning wages and the form of labor recruitment, the lack of a regulatory agency which could coordinate the movement of Mexican labor within the state jeopardized the efforts. North Texas and Central Texas farmers, for instance, depended heavily on the Mexican labor of South Texas and regularly commissioned labor contractors to recruit for them in that area. In this manner, competing farmers from various counties could upset any local arrangement to immobilize Mexican labor.

Here, then, we have the elements of the ichoate web of labor controls in rural Texas: a varied county response to the Mexican labor problem and the absence of an intercounty organization which could coordinate the movement of Mexican labor. Thus, labor repression in Texas consisted of a set of ineffective and inefficient labor controls. Nowhere is this more evident than in the contradictory positions farmers were driven into. On the one hand, they "hampered" the movement of Mexican labor; on the other, they competed with each other for this labor. These dual features were major characteristics of South Texas agriculture (Taylor, 1930a:331). What must be emphasized are the conflicting directions of these two tendencies. In fact, the element of competition between farmers was undoubtedly responsible for the "freedom" which Mexican wage laborers did have at this time. This competition, actually the underlying source of dissension within the ranks of the white commercial farmers, points to the *internal* circumstances which made for a fragmented labor repressive web. We must ask, however, why farmers were unable to organize behind a common program that would circumvent the need to compete for Mexican labor. Why were farmers, recognizing the general ineffectiveness of their labor controls, unable to go beyond their "labor thieving" ways? Undoubtedly this failure to formulate a common labor policy has much to do with the peculiar difficulties that beset organizations of commercial farmers. Farm communities as a rule have been characterized as divided by individualism, competition, and suspicion (Olson, 1965; Paige, 1975). Texas farmers, confronted with the possible loss of their cheap Mexican labor pool in the late 1920s, rallied and proposed a solution to the problem of Mexican labor mobility. A set of bills, designed to restrain Mexicans from leaving the state, was introduced and passed by the state legislature (Taylor, 1971:142, 281, 1930a: 331-333). In these Emigrant Labor Agency Laws we find the initial impulse to create a formal state-wide repressive labor policy. Again competition between employers for the same source of cheap labor would cause these efforts to fail; this time, however, the competitors would be agricultural and industrial concerns in the Midwest and North. Thus, to understand why labor repression in Texas remained a patchwork of individual and localized efforts, we must look at the *external* political and economic interests which blocked the development of a repressive labor policy on the state level.

As long as additional cheap Mexican labor could be recruited from across the border, Texas farmers were apparently not overly disturbed by the overall ineptness of their labor controls. Toward the late 1920s, however, a number of events moved farmers to search for a legal and more effective basis for regulating the movement of Mexican labor. Perhaps the most significant event was the "discovery" of Mexicans by Midwestern and Northern industry in the late 1910s and early 1920s. In a 1929 interview, the passenger agent for the Missouri, Kansas, and Texas Railway in San Antonio described the intense recruitment activity of those days (Taylor Collection:206-377). In 1917 or 1918, a competing railroad had shipped several thousand Mexicans from San Antonio:

> The Pennsylvania shipped two or three years in succession and shipped about one thousand the second year. Some of their Mexicans used the bath tubs for coal bins (in order to keep warm).

The agent recalled other shipments: the Pittsburg Plate Glass Company shipped about 600 Mexicans from San Antonio in 1923 and about 1,800 the following year; Inland Steel was shipping Mexicans out of North and South Texas, and United States Steel was shipping Mexicans mainly out of North Texas; in 1925 alone the Missouri, Kansas, and Texas Railway shipped about 4,200 Mexicans out of San Antonio; and so on. Naturally, at the receiving end of these labor "shipments," the increase in number of Mexican workers was quite apparent (and in some cases provoked resistance by white and European workers). On 16 railroads in the Chicago-Gary region, for instance, the number of Mexicans employed in "maintenance of way" work was insignificant in the 1910s. This number, however, increased rapidly in 1920 and 1922. By 1923 Mexicans comprised 22% of the 10,000 workers in "maintenance of way"; by 1928 they comprised 43% of this work force (3,963 of 9,228 employees). In 15 industrial plants in the Chicago-Gary area—five meat packing plants, seven metal and steel plants, a cement plant, a railroad-car repair plant, and a rug factory—the increase of Mexican workers followed a similar pattern. Their number during the 1910s was insignificant; 1920 and 1922 registered increases; a steady growth followed until by 1928 Mexicans constituted nearly 11% of the work force in these industrial plants, or 7,050 employees of the total of 65,682 (Taylor, 1930b:206-207).

The circumstances which stimulated the interest of these distant companies in the Mexican population of the Southwest and of Mexico were, quite simply, the restrictionist quotas placed on European immigration in the early 1920s. At least for one business, the Michigan sugar beet industry, the shift to Mexicans as its source of cheap labor was nearly complete. The result was a thorough ethnic transformation of the Michigan sugar beet industry, the shift to Mexicans as its source of cheap labor was nearly complete. The result was a thorough ethnic transformation of the Michigan agricultural work force from "Slavs" to Mexicans. Plainly sensitive to the mounting criticism from Northern labor as well as from Texas farmers, the San Antonio-based labor agent for a Michigan sugar company blamed the immigration laws for these adverse effects. Before the restrictionist laws, Michigan farmers had shipped German and Russian immigrants out of Cleveland and Chicago for sugar beet work. "The biggest crime of the quota law," noted the agent, "was to keep that class of people out" (Taylor Collection:203-376). This was, of course, the familiar lament of Midwestern and Northern agribusinessmen and industrialists toward restrictionist immigration legislation. By the end of the 1920s, Texas farmers would join in such complaints and protests. For by this time, the continuing efforts of American restrictionists, including organized labor in the North, had led to a partial closing of the Mexican border as well. In the eyes of the Texas farmer, the people necessary for the development of the country, the Mexican laborers, were being kept out. As one Dimmit County farmer put it: "We have got to have a class of people who will do this kind of labor" (Taylor, 1930a:333).

In the 1920s, then, the Texas farmer saw his labor supply jeopardized in two ways. On the one hand, the enforcement of immigration laws endangered his "inexhaustible" source of cheap labor in nearby Mexico. On the other, the activities of these distant "outside" employers threatened to siphon off his domestic source of cheap labor—the Texas Mexican—as well. Increasingly the Texas farmer found himself competing with agricultural and industrial concerns with considerable capital. As if this were not enough, in 1927 the Raymondville convictions served to discourage any "local initiative" in responding to this challenge. The situation for the commercial farmer was critical, because his advantage in the competitive agricultural market was based in large part on the cheap restricted Mexican labor he had. Under these pressing circumstances, the Texas farmer reacted. In 1929, with the support of the South Texas Chamber of Commerce, the Winter Garden Chamber of Commerce, and the West Texas Chamber of Commerce, the state representative from Carrizo Springs (Dimmit County) introduced legislation explicitly designed to "protect" the cheap Mexican labor reservoir in Texas (Taylor Collection:51-641; Taylor, 1971:281, 301; 1930a:331). Through occupation taxes, variable county tax surcharges, and the posting of a return transportation bond in each county were laborers were recruited, the Emigrant Labor Agency Laws directly aimed to restrict the recruitment of Texas Mexican labor by outside industrial and agricultural interests. The Texas State Employment Division expressed the intent in plain language: "The occupation taxes were established to discourage invasions from outside on the State's labor and mobile workers" (Farm Placement Service Division, 1940:30; Menefee, 1941:31). The author of the Labor Agency Laws explained to Taylor how they were basically a response to the restriction of Mexican immigration:

> It is the same situation as where you have had a stream of water running through your ranch. If someone turns its source off you want to put up a dam to hold what you have got.

The state representative continued his explanation, saying that this state law could open the way for federal immigration law to be amended to permit seasonal labor along the border. In the representative's words: "If other parts of the country could feel free (from) having Mexican seasonal labor dumped on them, they would not object to a seasonal supply here" (Taylor Collection: 51-64). This "theory of restraint," in fact, was often proposed as a compromise to demands from organized labor for restrictive immigration legislation. As one Dimmit County resident argued, immigration authorities could stop Mexicans "from going out of the four border states; they could stop them there as well as they can on the river here" (Taylor, 1930a:332). In this vein, the Labor Agency Laws were also seen as protecting white workers in the North from competition with Mexican labor. Thus, the Texas A. F. of L., apparently moved by a spirit of "solidarity" with their Northern brethren, joined with the Chambers of Commerce in supporting the labor bills. Organized labor in Texas, however, was no disinterested party—some unions wanted Mexican immigrants put back in Mexico and Texas Mexicans kept in agriculture (Taylor collection 51-641; Wilson, 1933:114-117). The political situation for the Mexican in Texas then appeared quite ominous. With 85% of the state's migratory labor force composed of Mexicans, the thrust of these labor laws was unequivocally clear: they were in essence a set of racial labor controls.

The particular outside employers Texas farmers and politicans had in mind when they drafted the Emigrant Labor Agency Laws were the Northern sugar beet companies. Together these various companies formed one of the most formidable competitors for seasonal labor, annually recruiting approximately 10,000 Texas Mexicans to work the beet fields of Michigan and northern Ohio (McWilliams, 1941). It comes as little surprise, then, that Texas farmers frequently explained the need for the labor laws in terms of the recruiting activity of these beet companies (Taylor, 1971:281). One group of Nueces County farmers put it succinctly:

> We got a law passed to keep the Mexicans in Texas and out of the beets. The border states need a temporary passport for Mexicans; put a boundary on Texas.

Another group of Nueces Country farmers interpreted the labor laws similarly, adding that the legislation constituted *only a first step:*

> We wish to prevent the transportation of Mexicans where they don't belong. Through employment agencies he gets to where he has no business, where he gets in competition with union labor. Congress does

not care so much if we keep them here, so our first step was to make it as hard as possible for the agents of the beet sugar companies to get labor. . . . We propose a deadline, beyond which the Mexicans could not go North.

Such a proposal apparently never proceeded beyond the point of being resolutions endorsed by local farm organizations, because the best companies, recognizing the intent of the Labor Agency Laws, immediately responded to these initial measures. The first state bill, which levied an occupation tax of $7,500 on out-of-state labor recruiters, was enjoined by a federal court on the petition of a Michigan sugar beet company (Taylor, 1930a:331; Taylor Collection:51-641). The response of the state legislature was equally determined and swift. "There was the danger of its being declared unconstitutional because of the prohibitive fee," explained the legislator from Carrizo Springs, "so we repealed it and then passed the second law." The second law required only an annual occupation tax of $1,000 and variable county surcharges from $100 to $300, depending on the condition of the local labor market. Supervision of the Emigrant Labor Agency Laws was placed, appropriately, in the hands of the State Commissioner of Labor Statistics. In addition to this emergency legislation, a third bill was passed in order to satisfy the "imperative public necessity." This law, which the representative from Carrizo described as "a policy power measure," required the labor agent to post a $5,000 bond in order to "protect" the return of the recruited laborers. This return transportation bond was to be posted *in each county* where the agent recruited. A provision in the law, however, allowed for a dispensation if the recruited laborers waived their "rights" before the county judge. The bond provision was subsequently ruled unconstitutional by a federal court, again on legal action pursued by Michigan sugar beet companies.

Considering the repeated defeats of such legislation in the federal courts, it is difficult to assess how successful these labor laws may have been in restricting the movement of Mexican labor. As it was, in their diluted form, these Labor Agency Laws constituted no more than a harrassment on the recruiting activities of out-of-state interests. Likewise we can only speculate about what repressive measures may have followed had these legal precedents been successful (or had not been challenged). South Texas farmers, after all, only saw them as a first step. Certainly the Labor Agency Laws pointed to an effective strategy, because the migratory labor system at the time was primarily organized through the labor contract method. Approximately 60% of the cotton picking in Texas, for instance, was handled through labor contractors (McWilliams, 1941:232-233). Thus legal restrictions—licensing and taxation being the primary vehicles—on the activity labor contractors appeared to be the logical and most promising manner by which to regulate the movement of Mexican migratory labor.

In their design, then, the Emigrant Labor Agency Laws constituted a blueprint, a preliminary model, for an effective labor repressive apparatus. Even county officials, generally quite suspicious of state encroachment on their local autonomy, were provided critical supervisory roles through the administration of county tax surcharges and the posting or waiving of transportation bonds. Future legislation could readily have extended the principles of the Emigrant Labor Agency Laws to include *all* labor contractors and, in this fashion, regulated the movement of Mexican labor within the state as well. Nor is this just idle speculation. In 1929 in Dimmit County, the home district of the legislative sponsor of the labor laws, growers from the town of Asherton were able to use similar state laws to successfully restrain the movement of Mexican labor *within the county*. Upset at neighboring Catarina growers whose wage offers had lured away Mexican laborers, the Asherton growers filed a set of injunctions accusing the Mexican labor contractors (who were handling the recruitment for Catarina) with not having the necessary labor agency licenses. The temporary injunctions were subsequently overruled, but in the meantime they had intimidated the Mexican contractors and thus accomplished their purpose (Taylor, 1930a:330).

We see, then, the extent to which repression of Mexican labor was attempted in Texas, and the manner in which it was frustrated. In the Emigrant Labor Agency Laws we have a set of formal racial labor controls in embryonic form. There was, obviously, no altruism involved in the court challenges with the sugar beet companies directed against these laws. Even the weakening of the Labor Agency Laws, however, did not clear the web of controls through which the Mexican in Texas had to move to find work which paid more than subsistence wages. The federal court decisions had dealt serious blows to the establishment of a de jure labor repressive apparatus. This does not mean that labor repression evaporated, only that its legal institutionalization was checked. Consequently labor repression in Texas never progressed beyond an immature condition: it remained based, for the most part, on individual predilection, local custom, and administrative fiat. A good example of the latter can be seen in the common practice of Texas highway patrolmen to use any pretext— motor vehicle violations, even the diluted labor agency laws—to interrupt the journey of Mexicans traveling out-of-state. In 1941, years after the federal court challenges to the Texas labor laws, McWilliams described the movement of Mexicans north as one "shrouded in conspiracy and intrigue." On the road Mexicans constantly had to be on watch for agents of the Texas Bureau of Motor Carriers as well as for patrolmen in other states. Thus Mexican truck drivers, loaded with their cargo of Mexican laborers, usually drove at night, through back roads, following a zig-zag course to the beet fields of Michigan. Even when the Mexican workers "are not trying to evade the law, they are under the constraint of concealing, if possible, the nature of the enterprise in which they are engaged." The traffic of sugar beet workers from Texas to Michigan, in McWilliams' incisive characterization, was a virtual "underground railroad" (1941:264).

The right of a Mexican to sell his labor, then, was quite tenuous during this period of capitalist agricultural development. Nor should we have expected less; because the extension of political and economic rights to the Mexican in Texas would have signified, for the commercial farmer, the loss of the region's most valuable asset, its cheap labor. The history of Mexican labor from the early 1900s to the end of World War II demonstrates that commercial farmers and state authorities, in the absence of formal and effective controls, were willing to experiment with other means which could minimize the competition they faced from outside industry and agriculture with considerable capital resources.

SHORTAGES AND SURPLUSES: THE LOGIC OF REPRESSION

Having described how the complex array of labor controls reflected different labor arrangements and different levels of political jurisdiction, we can now turn to one last factor which helps us comprehend the market dynamic underlying labor repression. Here we have to look directly at the condition of the labor market, that is, at the manner in which a labor "shortage" or "surplus" influenced the imposition of certain labor controls.

The relationship between labor market condition and control is a straightforward common-sensical one. During times of abundant labor the farmer need not be concerned about the consequences of running his Mexicans off. Replacements could be readily obtained. Conversely, in periods of shortages or expected shortages, farmers tend to "hold" their Mexican labor. The web of labor repression we have described follows a simple logic: the various controls not only correspond to the two principal types of agricultural labor, sharecroppers and migratory wage workers, they also reflect the condition of the local labor market as assessed by the commercial farmer. This "assessment," it should be emphasized, was not actually a measure of the supply of laborers so much as an indication of the market situation of the farmer. For shortages and surpluses were summary references to the labor costs the grower was willing to incur, the urgency with which he wanted the crop marketed, and the willingness of Mexicans to work under those conditions. Usually urgent advertisements and reports of shortages were circulated to ensure farmers that they would have a sufficiently abundant labor force to keep local Mexicans from pressuring for higher wages (Taylor, 1930a). The statements of South Texas farmers make it clear, moreover, that by shortages they meant shortages of cheap, tractable labor. In other words, in regard to repression, the imposition of controls more directly reflected the market circumstances confronting the farmer than any problem with the labor supply. Table 2 represents the connections between labor controls, labor arrangements, and market situation of commercial farmers. In short, whenever the farmer could not obtain a sufficiently

Table 2. A Logic of Repression

		Labor Arrangement	
		SHARECROPPING	MIGRATORY LABOR
Market situation of farmer	**LABOR SHORTAGE**	(a) dept peonage	(a) vagrancy laws (b) local "pass" systems (c) recruitment through misrepresentation (d) labor agency laws
	LABOR SURPLUS	(a) shotgun settlements (b) breach of contract (appropriating the cropper's share)	(a) breach of contract (nonpayment)

cheap or tractable labor force through the "normal" play of the market, labor controls provided the logical alternative. Thus migratory labor controls—vagrancy laws, misrepresented contracts, and so on—expectedly followed a seasonal pattern and were invoked whenever farmers and growers could not get local laborers to work for the fixed wage scale. Likewise shotgun settlements, as we discussed earlier, were apparently indications of the vulnerable market position of the small commercial farmer. In this context, then, let us examine more closely the market circumstances which created shortages and moved farmers to repress Mexican wage labor. The Willacy County pass system in 1926 will serve as an illustrative example.

Shortages: Competing in a World Market

A survey of the labor needs cited by South Texas farmers readily suggests that shortages were relative matters. As mentioned before, much depended on how quickly the farmer wished his crop picked and marketed. This decision, in turn, depended on extra-local conditions, such as the market trend in crop prices, crop production regionally and nationally, competition with foreign producers, and so on. Onion growers around Carrizo Springs and Laredo, for instance, were sensitive to competition with Egyptian onions; they were vigilant in following "the daily fluctuations in the market price of Bermuda onions in New York"; and consequently they were quite aware of the importance of moving their crop to market at the right time (Taylor, 1930a:314-315, 332; McWilliams, 1941:241). For the Winter Garden area then, these world-wide market linkages and contingencies generated an interest in having a large disposable labor force which could be rushed into the fields one day and withdrawn or transferred to other fields the next.

Like onion growers, cotton farmers had discovered that they could reduce the cotton harvest from a matter of weeks to a matter of days by using a large migratory labor force. In the hypothetical case presented earlier, we saw how a force of 2,250 laborers would be sufficient to work Nueces County cotton farmers over a span of 10 weeks, the duration of the picking season. However, if market conditions (e.g., a sharp rise or decline in cotton prices) prompted these farmers to have their cotton picked within the same week, a migratory army of 22,500 laborers would be needed. It is within the context of these extralocal market circumstances, then, that a commercial farmer could claim a shortage of labor. If these market factors created a severe shortage, that is, if the farmers of a county wished their crop picked immediately and cheaply, then the farmer might be pressed to restrict the movement of Mexican wage laborers. This apparently was the setting for the Willacy pass system of 1926; "extralocal" market factors generated an acute labor shortage and subsequent efforts to entrap migratory Mexican labor. The condition of the Texas cotton market at this time offers a likely scenario for the South Texas county.

Texas cotton farmers found 1926 to be a particularly bad year for them; cotton prices declined sharply from previous years, apparently as a result of overproduction (USDA, 1951:28). In 1925, for instance, the average yield per acre was 115 pounds; in 1926, the yield increased to 152 pounds. Thus, although the number of acres in cultivation remained practically unchanged in these two years, 5,623,000 bales were produced in 1926 compared to 4,163,000 bales produced the year before, an amazing increase in production of 35%. The 1926 cotton crop, in fact, represented then the highest output ever produced in Texas, a level that would not be surpassed until 1949. At the same time that cotton production was at record levels, however, cotton prices in 1926 declined to their lowest point in a decade. From 20.33¢ in 1925, Texas cotton prices plummeted to a low of 12.73¢ in 1926. These market conditions suggest the concrete features behind labor shortages and labor controls. The great 1926 crop required additional labor. Depressed price levels, moreover, meant that farmers would be extemely pressed to reduce production costs in the area most subject to their control, the cost of labor. Finally, given the bleak market outlook for Texas cotton, farmers most likely were anxious to market their cotton before prices dropped even lower. The demand for this cheap labor, in other words, was an immediate and urgent one. How could they secure such a cheap and temporary work force quickly? Entrapment of migratory Mexican laborers was one sure way of accomplishing this end, as the Willacy "hiring and pass systems" illustrate. This type of "peonage," at least before the 1927 federal convictions of the Willacy authorities, was undoubtedly a common practice in South Texas. The point which should be emphasized is that this practice was a *market-conditioned* response.

The 1929 Winter Garden injuctions against Mexican contractors also demonstrate the relationship between labor controls and market circumstances which Texas farmers considered extreme or pressing. Again, this was a situation where growers had misread the market and overcommitted their farms to a poorly priced crop. The speculative and competitive character of Texas commercial agriculture played a critical role in the shaping of rural labor relations. At least for the repressive side of this experience—we shall describe white benevolence and protection for the Mexican on another occasion—it seems clear that the manner in which the Mexican laborer was treated by the white farmer was in large measure related to the fluctuations of capitalist agriculture itself. Whether to increase profits or minimize losses, white farmers in Texas sought to accomplish this by fixing local wages and restricting the movement of their local Mexican labor force.

Shortages: The Flight of Mexican Labor

On the other hand, a basic dimension of this farm problem lay in the emigration of the rural Texas Mexican population to Texas cities and to places outside the state. The importance of such emigration, as we saw, was explicitly recognized by farmers concerned about the loss of their cheap Mexican labor. It was this concern that compelled them to attempt a more effective organization of the labor market in a repressive manner. The other side of the labor shortage issue, in other words, lies in the fact that Mexicans were exercising their fragile "legal" right to sell their labor. We have already indicated the extent to which Texas Mexicans were willing to travel in their search for better working and living conditions. During the 1920s, the agricultural and industrial Midwest witnessed the introduction of Mexicans as a significant addition to their working population. In the 1930s, over 66,000 Texas Mexicans were leaving the state annually to find work (McWilliams, 1941:257). The fact that Mexicans searched for higher paying work and were sensitive to workplace conditions is an obvious but critical point—one largely obscured by a romantic literature which has portrayed the Mexican as passive. Let us emphasize the obvious: Mexicans were conscious of the world they lived and worked in. In their constant search for work in Texas, Mexicans were sensitive to rumors about bad treatment and poor working conditions at particular farms; for them, it was a matter of protection. White farmers, in other words, acquired favorable and unfavorable reputations which circulated among the local and migratory Mexican population. One disliked grower in Dimmit County, for example, had to bring Mexicans from San Antonio, over a hundred miles away, because local Mexicans would not work for him. Even then another landlord had to "front" for him in the hiring and supervising of these imported laborers (Taylor, 1930a:351). Likewise Mexican workers who found themselves in intolerable situations often took the only recourse open to them—escape. In the rural world we can reconstruct from the extensive interview material, in fact, debt peonage and escape surface as commonplace events in the life of Mexican sharecroppers and pickers. The massive emigrations to other states present no less dramatic evidence of the Mexican response to their world in Texas. There were, of course, other responses—abortive strikes, attempts at political organization, instances of violence. But escape, flight to the cities, emigration to other states—in the 1920s and 1930s, these comprise the dominant reaction, perhaps the form of resistance, to oppression. The meaning of this response is expressed eloquently in one piece of memorabilia of Mexican life during this period—in a popular Texas Mexican ballad, "El Corrido de Texas," recorded in San Antonio in 1929. In this corrido, the hero—a Texas Mexican laborer recruited to work for an Indiana company—feels dejected because he has to leave the woman he loves. Why must he leave? In the refrain he tells us repeatedly—the lyrics are straightforward and powerful at this point—

> Goodbye State of Texas
> with all your fields,
> I leave your land
> so I won't have to pick cotton.[6]

In a sense, the theme of this corrido points to the basic argument of this essay. The fact that Mexicans had some freedom to leave Texas cotton fields is not a matter for presumption; it is rather a question that needs to be examined and explained. An excellent point of departure rests, as in the case of the corrido's hero, in understanding the part played by the Nothern capitalist.

SUMMARY

In large part, the brutal experience of the Mexicans in Texas in the twentieth century can be understood in terms of a labor-repressive capitalist agriculture. Racism, coercion, exploitation were common everyday events, integral features of the rural order. This racial experience, however, was not guided by some blind force whose blows struck at random. On the contrary, underlying the complex array of detail from horsewhipping to a license check by a Texas patrolman is a comprehensible logic of repression.

Essentially this repression took form in the various measures and strategies commercial farmers and authorities used to maintain a cheap Mexican labor force. Vagrancy laws, local pass systems, manipulation of labor contracts, labor agency laws, suggest the character of controls used to restrict the movement of Mexican wage laborers. These restrictions comprise the core of the practices and policies we have described as "labor repressive." Since they accompany the rise of a migratory labor system, these various controls focus, not surprisingly, on the recruitment and placement of wage laborers. In one sense, the different types of migratory labor controls illustrate the experimentation and various political steps which farmers took as they attempted to create an apparatus which could guarantee them a supply of cheap seasonal labor. These migratory controls, however, never become crystallized in a coherent and effective "system" because of external political challenges undertaken by Michigan agribusiness. Thus, in 1930 labor repression in Texas remained an inchoate web— responsive to the interests of local commercial agriculture, limited by the interests of Northern agribusiness.

Further historical research into this neglected chapter of Mexican Texas should be able to piece together a more definitive picture. One aspect of this story, however, is quite clear. Labor repression in Texas failed to become a formal, coherent system because of external limitations. "Imperial Texas," as D. W. Meinig (1969) described the pretensions of the former Republic, was not a sovereign state which could chart an independent course of economic development. Despite many heated defenses of "States" rights," Texas could hold its labor resources only as long as they did not become valuable elsewhere in the country. This hold became somewhat tenuous with the restriction of European immigration in the early 1920s, because Midwestern and Northern agricultural and industrial interests then began a search for a domestic source of cheap labor, which they found in the black and Mexican communities of the southern states. The regional controls restricting this desired labor were challenged *at this point*. "Free" labor market policies were invoked and any de jure repressive plans weakened by federal court decisions. Thus, the extent to which labor repression developed in Texas is basically a political question. What merits closer examination in future historical work is an outline of the various political interests and forces which could support or challenge such practices and policies. Equally important is understanding how distinct sectional societies, with distinct class relations, can develop, persist and change within a nation-state. In this manner, by asking why repression did not become formally instituted, we will be able to identify the historical specificity of distinct patterns within capitalist development.

What type of development was blocked in Mexican Texas can be suggested by what was in fact created. For the newcomer farm settlers had a clear vision of the foundation on which their society rested. The beliefs and attitudes of the white settlers, from town bankers to tenant farmers, express definite ideas of separate development for the "races." The features of such a vision have repeatedly been made plain in descriptions of rural Mexican Texas from the 1920s to contemporary times: separate neighborhoods, churches, schools, stores, cemeteries, and so on (Meinig, 1969:98-101; Taylor, 1930a: 288-431; Rubel, 1966). One reason such dual development never proceeded beyond a fragmented and localized basis lies unquestionably in the failure to establish effective labor controls. It lies, in other words, in the failure of white commercial farmers (and white industrial workers) to keep Mexicans in the fields. In this sense, twentieth-century Mexican Texas seems best portrayed as a case of "frustrated" apartheid.

NOTES

1. I would like to thank Stanley Greenberg for his suggestion that I consider Moore's analysis.

2. In an important critique, Theda Skocpol, (1973) has pointed out that the critical questions which need investigation are "how are these mechanisms organized?" and "who controls the mechanisms?" Skocpol is correct; but the answers to her questions, as we will see, do not weaken the strength of Moore's argument.

3. For our purposes, we can basically describe "Mexican Texas" as a 200-mile-wide band paralleling the Mexican border; it thus includes portions of West Texas, Central Texas, and all of South Texas. A second point: in the text, "Mexican" refers to both "Texas Mexicans" and Mexicans born in Mexico. "Texas Mexican" is generally used only when it is important to stress the matter of citizenship or group identity. The latter issue, of course, has a long and complex history, but here that will not trouble us. Our discussion focuses primarily on the attitudes and interests of the white settlers who

generally collapsed such internal distinctions among the Mexican population in Texas. In the 1920s, in particular, Mexicans were simply Mexicans.

4. Taylor (1971) himself estimated that there were probably not 100 Mexican tenant farmers or sharecroppers with large acreages in Nueces County, and that their number may be considerably less.

5. This figure corresponds to Paul Taylor's (1971:99) estimate of the seasonal labor force in Nueces County for the 1929 harvest.

6. See the long-playing album entitled *Chulas Fronteras*, Arhoolie Records, Berkeley, California. The translation is Arhoolie's.

REFERENCES

DEGLER, C.N. (1967). The age of the economic revolution, 1876-1900. Chicago: Scott, Foresman.

Farm Placement Service Division (1940). Origins and problems of Texas migratory farm labor. Texas State Employment Service, September.

Final Report of the Commission on Industrial Relations (1916). Vol. X. Washington, D.C.: U.S. Government Printing Office.

GAMIO, M. (1931). The Mexican immigrant, His life story. Chicago: University of Chicago Press.

———— (1971). Mexican immigration to the United States. New York: Dover, originally published by the University of Chicago Press, 1930.

HIDALGO, E. (1940). La proteccion de Mexicanos en los Estados Unidos. Mexico: Secretaria de Relaciones Exteriores.

HOFFMAN, A. (1976). "A note on the field research interviews of Paul S. Taylor." Pacific Historian, 123-131.

JOHNSON, W.A. (1926). Cotton and its production. London: Macmillan.

McWILLIAMS, C. (1941). Ill fares the land. New York: Barnes and Noble.

MEINIG, D.W. (1969). Imperial Texas. Austin: University of Texas Press.

MENEFEE, S.C. (1941). Mexican migratory workers of South Texas. Washington, D.C.: Federal Works Agency, Work Projects Administration, Division of Research, U.S. Government Printing Office.

MOORE, B. (1966). Social origins of dictatorship and democracy. Boston: Beacon Press.

OLSON, M. (1965). The logic of collective action. Cambridge: Harvard University Press.

PAIGE, J.M. (1975). Agrarian revolution: Social movements and export agriculture in the underdeveloped world. New York: Free Press.

PERALES, A.S. (1937). En defensa de mi raza, Vols. I and II. San Antonio: Artes Fraficas.

RUBEL, A. (1966). Across the tracks: Mexican Americans in a Texas city. Austin: University of Texas Press.

SCRUGGS, O.M. (1957). A history of Mexican agricultural labor in the United States, 1942-1954. Unpublished Ph.D. dissertation, Harvard University.

SHANNON, F.A. (1945). The farmer's last frontier: Agriculture, 1860-1897. New York: Farrar and Rinehart.

SKOCPOL, T. (1973). "A critical review of Barrington Moore's *Social Origins of Dictatorship and Democracy*." Politics and Society, 4 (1):1-34.

TAYLOR, P.S. (1930a). "Mexican labor in the United States: Dimmit County Winter Garden District, South Texas." University of California Publications in Economics, 6 (5):293-464.

_____ (1930b). "Research note." Journal of the American Statistical Association, XXV, 170 (June):206-207.

_____ (1971). An American Mexican frontier: Nueces County, Texas. New York: Russell and Russell, originally published by the University of North Carolina Press, 1934.

_____The Paul S. Taylor collection. Berkeley: Bancroft Library, University of California, Berkeley.

U.S. Department of Agriculture (1951). United States cotton statistics, 1910-1940 by states. Washington, D.C.: Bureau of Agricultural Economics.

VASEY, T., and FOLSOM, J. (1937). "Survey of agricultural labor conditions in Karnes County, Texas." In Survey of Agricultural Labor Conditions. Washington, D.C.: U.S. Farm Security Administration.

WILSON, W. (1933). Forced labor in the United States. New York: International Publishers.

PART 4

INCORPORATION AND RESISTANCE
IN THE PERIPHERY

Chapter 7

THE PERIPHERALIZATION OF CHINA: NOTES ON THE OPIUM CONNECTION

Dilip K. Basu

China's incorporation into the world capitalist economy is usually supposed to have begun with the Opium War and the Nanking Settlement (1840-1842). In bourgeois historiography, the war marks the "opening" of China, initiating the destruction of a Sino-centric, culturally chauvinistic Chinese world order and the gradual creation of a Chinese national consciousness. In Marxist and nationalist historiography, the war begins the process that converted the Chinese Empire, later the Republic into a "semi-colony." In both views, therefore, the war is conceived as the most important turning point. While this emphasis has not been wholly wrong-headed, the war is perhaps better viewed as culminating the first phase of a peripheralization process that had been long in the making. To see this, we must turn to the decades preceding the Opium War, to discuss first the "pidginization" of the Hong merchants of Canton, and then the role of the foreign participants in the opium traffic.

PIDGINIZATION

The Ch'ing government (1644-1911) has been roundly condemned by contemporary Western traders and later by scholars for its visceral hostility to trade and commerce, an interpretation which is now seriously questioned. A major reason for holding such a view was the organization and function of the Canton commercial system (1760-1842) through which the Ch'ing attempted to administer and control its foreign commerce. From 1760, Canton was the only Chinese port open to foreign traders. Government patrol boats were required to check the entry and exit points from Canton to the sea, and the emperor had his own man, a member of the Imperial Household, the Hoppo (the maritime customs commissioner) placed on location to supervise the trading operation. Under his authority, government-appointed Hong or "security merchants" (*pao-shang*) were given a monopoly of dealing with foreign traders on a day-to-day basis as well as being charged with the responsibility for foreigners' conduct. The authorities attempted to exclude competition among the Chinese merchants by insisting on fixed prices. The foreigners were housed in secluded factories on the Pearl River front in Canton with their free movement severely restricted (Chang, 1964:3-9). Most Western scholars have viewed this system as a classic example of Ch'ing anticommercial policy based on the Confucian ethic and the traditional tributary system. Few if any have attempted to look at it from a broader, comparative standpoint.

This was obviously a case of "administered trade" that was a commonplace phenomenon in much of the precapitalist world. For comparative purposes, the two complementary approaches that are relevant are the concept of "Port of Trade" of Karl Polanyi, and Wallerstein's world-system approach to precapitalist trade as trade between "external arenas."

"Port of Trade" is Polanyi's name for a settlement that acted as a control point between a market and a nonmarket economy when commercial intercourse between them had become inevitable. Trade of this kind was normally treaty-based and administered by officially appointed authorities; competition was excluded and prices set over long terms. Polanyi makes a distinction between "embedded" (non-market) and "disembedded" (market) economies. Trade and market were only marginally important in a nonmarket economy. When they occurred, there were fixed prices and official supervision. In these situations political authority—what Wallerstein would later call world-empires—was usually located inland. It shunned the coasts and the vagaries of external trade. If coastal or foreign trade still developed, there was an attempt to neutralize the effects with enforced control (Polanyi, 1957:114-188). Even a cursory view of the Ch'ing commercial policy and the "Canton Commercial System" described above will suggest enough similarities between Polanyi's theoretical projection (some of his students empirically worked it out in case studies of Eastern Mediterranean and African ports) and the situation that existed on the South China coast. But was Canton really a "port of trade" during the 1760-1842 period?

In attempting to answer this question, I find Wallerstein's work more germane. Wallerstein focuses on the origins of what he calls the world-capitalist system with its core, semi-periphery, and peripheral areas. Colonial or semicolonial port cities fall in the latter category where the ensuing trade with the "core" results in their "peripheralization." "External arenas," on the other hand, belonged to world-systems—Polanyi's embedded economy—outside the capitalist world-economy. Trade between these two, when they occurred, were in "preciosities," or luxury items. But once these luxury items started to become vital to the world-economy, like slavery had become, the external arenas fall under the threat of peripheralization (Wallerstein, 1974). The rise of the tea trade from China and its great importance in the late eighteenth century in the commerce of the world-economy can be viewed as a transition from a preciosity to a vital item of trade. Was Ch'ing commerce and the Canton system then inevitably, if subtly, being peripheralized? The answer to this question will help us decide to what extent Canton, during the pre-1842 period, succeeded in maintaining its "Port of Trade" like characteristics.

To attempt an answer to this question we can turn to a model suggested in my empirical materials. Looking at the advent and impact of Western trade, especially in its later, "vital" form, I find Asian merchant classes in the port-cities facing two entrepreneurial choices. First, one could work within and/or for the superimposed Western commercial institutions such as the Agency Houses, Managing Agencies, commercial banks, and joint stock companies. Many who worked *for* such institutions were no more than factotums, but then there were a few brilliant entrepreneurs who, while working *within* these institutions, attempted to relate and engraft them onto the existing Asian institutions. The result could be something viable that was both Asian and non-Asian, syncretic if you will. Such developments appear to have taken place in port cities which were already colonized or semicolonized. Dwarkanath Tagore's remarkable entrepreneurial innovation in the 1830s and 1840s in Calcutta would come close to this condition. One may hasten to add, this was probably more an exception than a prevailing trend. The second choice was a frank acceptance of the status quo, of the existing constraints imposed by both Asian and non-Asian institutions and making the best of a bad bargain, as it were.

If the first is syncretic, the latter is eclectic. If joint stock companies and commercial banks were the preferred form in the first, "loose" partnerships and business relationships based on trust among Asian and Western traders was the practice in the second. The common element that both shared, which was the dominant impact of Western trade on the Hong merchants and their institutions, is "pidginization." It is an insular term in the sense that it represents a local phenomenon and derives its name from the local business dialect, Pidgin, but the process it describes is structural and of value in analyzing the second situation from a comparative standpoint.

I am not, however, the first person to use it. Louis Dermigny, in his magisterial tomes on Canton trade, has used it, though in a much more general way. Anthropologists and linguists recently have been looking at pidginization from cultural and linguistic standpoints (Dermigny, 1964 (I):340). Dell Hymes, the noted anthropologist, has edited a volume which shows that pidginization has fascinating social and cultural ramifications and may, in fact, represent a new science of communication (1971:13-42).

My purpose in employing the term in Canton's context is more modest. Pidgin was the medium through which the Europeans, Americans, Chinese, and other Asians communicated with each other. Chinese, English, Portuguese, Hindustani, and Malay words were freely intermixed, though the basic Chinese syntax and structure remained unchanged. I am suggesting that in day-to-day commercial intercourse, Chinese and non-Chinese traders in Canton related to each other essentially at the level of the language they used to communicate with each other. This communication level extended to their mutual business relationships; it profoundly affected their credit operations and, to some extent, their social life and perception of each other.

Unlike Pidgin, a language in which Chinese syntax and structure pretty much remained intact, the process of pidginization, I argue, resulted in structural erosion due to the exposure of the "external arena" to the world-economy. The traditional Chinese merchant institutions, like the Kung-so and Hui-Kuan, were no longer (did they ever?) serving the mutual aid interests and deliberations of the merchant guilds, but were instruments of the entrepreneurial few who, in turn, were dependent on and conditioned by the interests of foreign trade and Western traders.

Let me just summarize what I have presented elsewhere along these lines (Basu, 1978). First, we face the Hong merchants in the early eighteenth century as an Imperially anointed group. They were appointed specifically to deal with Western trade when Canton was reopened for intercourse with the outside world in 1685. A Western trade "Hong" was created. We know from available sources that this Hong essentially attempted to deal with Western traders in a traditional guild-like fashion. In 1720 they formalized their guild operations, but the Europeans did not like it because the guild always dictated prices. In their search for competitive prices, European traders in Canton went outside the Hong monopoly system and attempted to deal with "outside shopmen,"—the nonmonopoly Chinese merchants who were willing to oblige. The result was that the "administered" trade of Canton did not really work.

A second attempt was made during 1760-1772 to administer the trade again from above, with dictated prices and tight-fisted guild control of the Hong, but the result was again disastrous. Many Hongists who had entered the trade without adequate credit or collateral were bankrupted completely and even the official "monopoly" in its formal sense could survive only after a large infusion of foreign credit contracted by the chief Hongist, Puankhequa.

With this began the structural erosion of the entry of the world capitalist element into the picture. The huge "Hong Debts" that were created in 1772, soon after tea had become a "vital" trade, were owed by the majority of the Hongists to Europeans. They continued to snowball in the 1770s and 1800s and were not liquidated until after the Nanking Settlement of 1842. I would argue that the debts introduced a control mechanism which gave Western traders considerable leverage, reducing the Hongists to a position of dependence.

H.B. Morse (1910), one of the early writers on the Canton trade, characterized the Hong merchants' predicament as one between "the devil and the deep sea." There is no doubt that the merchants had trouble from both ends, but in this analysis the "deep sea" elements were certainly more difficult. One of the best sources on the Hong debts is a Consoo account book that I found in the Chinese documentary piles at the Public Record Office in London; this book spells out in vivid detail the bonds imposed on most Hongists by their commercial debts. The mechanism established for the settlement of the notorious Hingtae debt of 1836 illustrates the nature of the bonds. The foreign creditors of Hingtae challenged the Tao-Kuang emperor "to respect and enforce the rules he has himself laid down." Three senior Hongists and three foreigners would constitute a committee to examine the claims and agree on a final settlement. Sitting in the Hong merchants' guild-hall, the six trustees worked out the detail of the nine-year schedule of payment on a debt of $2,261,439 that the Hingtae family owed the foreign creditors. The Western bookkeeping method was introduced to the Consoo books. Instead of recording the debts in the traditional cash-book style which often left room for "jumping" the account by keeping a secret cash-book, the new practice spelled out in corresponding English and Chinese columns the names of creditors, the amount of claims, interests, and the payment schedule.[1]

The officially appointed Hong merchants were never a large body— the number varied from eight to 16 at any given time. Only three or four among them were solvent and commanded the fabled wealth that is attributed to them. They were called the "senior merchants" in the English records. Though the recognition of Hong leadership goes back to the Chinese mercantile tradition, the "seniority factor," I argue, was critically important to the pidginization process. If, in the past, seniors were responsible to the Chinese authorities for the solvency and proper mercantile behavior of the juniors, they now were guarantors on the juniors' behalf to Western traders who otherwise would probably not have advanced the loans in the first place.

There was a good reason why senior merchants would be willing to do that. The Hong merchants, according to Chinese law, were not allowed to invest in internal enterprises. (Some did own real estate, and trade-related property like tea gardens.) Those with the idle capital, therefore, turned to external possibilities. Houqua, the wealthiest among the Hongist and, in the estimation of some Westerners, the wealthiest merchant in the world, looked for opportunities for investment in contemporary international trade. He established close personal business relationships or what can be called "fraternal partnerships" with American traders, John P. Cushing and John M. Forbes, among others. In 1836, he provided the seed money for the establishment of John M. Forbes and Company in Boston to the tune of half a million dollars. In the Forbes Company's account books, the Houqua money was entered in as the American Investment Fund and American Stock Investment.

John Forbes, of course, was a pioneer railroad builder in the mid-nineteenth century (Johnson and Supple, 1967:24-30). He funneled Houqua's capital to the Iowa Land Association, the Burlington Railroad, and the Michigan Central Railroad, among many others. The business relationship was continued until 1880 with Houqua's descendants. Houqua's case was not an isolated one. His predecessors in the eighteenth century had similar relationships with the Swedes; one can find evidences of such relationships among other Hongists who were Houqua's contemporaries. I cite him as a case study only because the documentation is strongest.[2]

As an analytical construct, pidginization pinpoints a particular aspect of peripheralization—the growing dependence of the Hong merchants, whether through debts or through individual investments abroad. When a commodity exported from external arena to core moves from preciosity to necessity, from luxury to staple, peripheralization is likely to follow. Before China could be "opened" or "semicolonized," it was inevitable that the elaborately devised, Ch'ing-administered Canton commercial system should break down.

THE OPIUM PENTANGLE

In the expansion of global trade after 1750, a pentangular set of relations emerged in the Asian arena. No doubt uneven and unequal, these relations joined together Britain, the British Indian colonial state, the United States, and Ch'ing China. Because of the importance of the Spanish silver dollar in trade transactions, Hispanic Phillipines also played a crucial role.

If one applies the world-system approach to the Opium War, the historiographical debate between the Europocentric view that opium was "incidental" and that China's cultural arrogance deserved to be punished, and the Asianist view which holds the opposite line reach a point of uncomfortable resolution. The requirements of the multilateral trade had turned opium into a vitally important commodity that could not be substituted for by rice or molasses. On the other hand, the expansion of the capitalist world-economy (not the old-fashioned "expansion of Europe") inevitably brought the Chinese world empire and the external arena of the Canton system into clash with the core state, Britian. As China, the largest extant world empire, became exposed to the process of peripheralization, the war that was waged in its wake could not have been an isolated "episode." Here Wallerstein's line of inquiry helps articulate the mechanisms of imperialist action that closely followed or often accompanied the incorporation of the periphery by the core. Taking his cue, I would argue that the international entanglements and ramifications of the Opium War were significant enough to give it a deserved rank of the first major modern colonialist/imperialist war in Asia. It was prosecuted with the direct as well as back-up economic/commercial and police support of semi-peripheral areas: the first was provided notably by the United States, and the second by the British Indian colonial state. As in most colonialist wars, the rhetoric was couched in a deceptively convincing ideological position which often has been mistaken for its root cause.

One must start with a long-range view to understand the specific historical conjunctures that in effect transformed the old Asian trade, an inveterate mix of commerce and politics, into the flame and gunfire of war in China. This has the disadvantage of telescoping developments over at least an 80-year period (1757-1842), but it is necessary. The Battle of Plassey (1757), often referred to as a war won in a "fit of absent-mindedness," marked a watershed. It virtually ended the old cash-and-carry basis of East India Company's bilateral trade and began a process which involved raising the cash in Asia itself. A mercantilist war, it nevertheless helped lay the foundations of a colonialist state. The growing power of the latter as the years wore on explains why the theory of comparative costs, increasingly popular among the policy-planners at the metropole, failed to attract adherents in Asia. The Company records show that its servants, instead of pursuing the precepts of comparative costs, were following what can be best termed as an "absolute advantage" trade strategy. Since this neatly coincided with the Company's avowed policy of revising the traditional inward flow of silver and treasure to Asia, there was little grumbling even among the theorists. Commercial combines with Asian merchants along the coasts or with other European trading powers were entered into only insofar as these reinforced the desired absolute advantage.

So single-minded was the Company in balancing its budget over the India trade during the early period that it refused to be enticed by the prospect of an East Asian trade. But Plassey gave considerable relief.

Tea, regarded as a "pernicious article of luxury" with a 200% sales
duty on it in Britain, had started to become a beverage with wide
markets in Europe and America. In England it would keep the new
factory workers at work at their posts. As a staple item, tea now
received the Company's top priority. As Parkinson (1937:2-4) has put
it, "the only commercial interest the Company had had since then was
in the China trade. All else was grist to the tea trade mill."

As an aide, notice the irony latent in the attitude of the Company and
the growing number of Free Traders. The quickness with which tea had
become a popular beverage in Europe was comparable to a similar
growth in the opium-smoking in China. Both enabled the Company to
earn windfall profits based on inelastic supplies, and both encouraged
smuggling. As W.A. Cole (1957-1958:395-397) has argued, the high
tariff walls in eighteenth-century Europe provided stimulus to massive
smuggling operations through fraudulent entries at the customs,
relending of goods entered for re-export, as well as direct import
smuggling. But while the British government and the East India
Company were alarmed at the extent of this tea smuggling and its effect
on their revenues, they turned the other way when the opium traffic
posed a similar problem to the Chinese government in the 1830s. The
Free Traders' position was also equally contradictory: in England
they pointed at the evil of smuggling as justification for Free Trade; in
Asia they organized and ran the opium-smuggling networks.

If the rise of a staple trade in tea and the ability to support it with
Bengal revenue solved the anxieties of the Company's authorities in
England, it posed, as is well-known, a vexing problem to the mangers
of the colonial state in East India. The Bengal Council was continuously
pressured for providing bullion support for the China trade. If it
resented this Cinderella-like treatment, it was told point-blank: "You
must take every opportunity to buy up the same (bullion) for the use of
your China trade."[3] The solution was to be found in opium, but not
"accidentally" at the opportune moment. The records show that the
Company as well as the Free Traders had been considering it for a long
time. As early as the 1770s opium was a fact of trade; it was being
carried to the Malaccan Straits by private traders. Colonel Kyd of the
Calcutta Botanical Gardens had gotten hold of one Poorhan Giri, a
peripatetic Hindu merchant (*gossain*) with wide travel experience in
Tibet and China. Giri possessed "a diary of his several journeys . . .
that affords plenty of material for perfecting our knowledge" of the
poppy plant—how it could be further improved to suit the Chinese

tastes.[4] Kyd also gathered intelligence from the Company's servants in Malacca and Canton and succeeded in transplanting the Patna poppy to Bengal's nonpoppy-producing areas. Later, a private trader had written Warren Hastings a series of five letters, suggesting that the China trade, "rather a commerce of necessity than choice," be converted into a channel of remittance and sale of Bengal goods, including opium. Should the Court of Directors object to indulging in a contraband trade, he suggested the informal connection with the private traders and the Agency Houses (Five Letters, 113-116). The recommendations proved prophetic for soon both the Bengal government and the Agency Houses began their implementation. If the Court worried about annoying the Chinese government, especially after the 1796 Ch'ing edict which declared opium unequivocally illegal, it could blame the Free Traders and corrupt, rapacious Chinese officials. Prevarication of this sort helped smooth liberal public opinion at home, making both the Company and the British government look clean. Private traders bought the opium at the Company's auction sales in Calcutta, and carried the contraband in Company-licensed private country boats. From 1816 onward a clause was inserted in the license declaring it void if the boat carried any opium which did not bear the Company's premium trademark. But the sailing orders of the Company's ships bound for China strictly prohibited opium on board, "lest the Company be implicated." As Jardine later said, most Company ships carried opium on "privilege" account; the Canton supercargoes maintained an interest in these accounts as well (Greenberg, 1951:109).

Such collaboration between the Company and the Free Traders extended even further when third parties—members of the expansive world trade system over whom the British exercised no political control—were involved. Since the Spanish silver dollar was the favored currency in Canton, involvement of third parties in multilateral relations was inevitable. The two parties that came to play significant roles and about whom we have not known much so far are the Hispanic Philippines and the United States. I would therefore like to provide some detail.

A continual need for silver had persuaded the Company as well as the Free Traders to seek direct trade with Manila. Manila had maintained for over 150 years an exclusive monopoly that barred all Europeans other than the Portuguese in its lucrative silver trade to Acapulco on the Mexican coast. In 1785 the Royal Spanish Philippine

Company was established. It supplied through its Lima and Cadiz connection a new source of silver to Manila and Canton. The Bengal government in Calcutta attempted in 1790 to set up a direct commercial relationship with the Spanish Company but it fell through. In 1810 Spanish American revolts finally snapped the Royal Spanish ties with Eastern Trade. A direct trade developed between Calcutta and Latin America, the erstwhile Spanish mercantile system now being made open to all foreign shipping. The Agency Houses quickly grabbed this opportunity, establishing close ties with Manila from both the Calcutta and Canton ends. From 1818 onward Spanish merchants followed the British way and started to operate as private agents and traders. Manuel Laruletta, the ex-chief of the Spanish Company in Canton, along with Xavier Yrissari, José Uriarte, andJosé Mendietta established Laruletta and Co. in Calcutta in that year. At the same time, Laruletta's arch foe, Lorenzo Calvo, set up a Spanish Agency in Canton (Cheong, 1970:227-247).

From the beginning, Calvo and Laruletta's business, though sharply competitive, enjoyed the advantage of an access to the source of the silver dollar. This quickly brought them the avid attention of the British private traders and both found themselves enmeshed before long in the opium business. In 1821-1822, Calvo successfully speculated in both Maiwa and Bengal opium; Laruletta also entered the market in conjunction with McIntosh and Co. in Calcutta. Through this Calcutta Agency House, he came to know Matheson, and a long relationship between the three firms, Laruletta and Co., McIntosh and Co., and Matheson and Co., began. Laruletta was admitted to McIntosh and Co. as a partner and Xavier Yrissari went out to Canton with a view to establishing an agency there.[5]

Yrissari was destined to play a crucial role in opium smuggling. He hit upon the idea of setting up a permanent opium depot off Macao Roads, away from the reach of the Chinese river police. The idea impressed Matheson, because a permanent depot in effect would provide teeth to the smuggling operation: they could control supplies and maintain prices. Yrissari began his operations in earnest, styling himself as Yrissari and Co., a branch of the McIntoshes in Calcutta.[6] Yrissari's activities inspired Calvo to join in the competition. He admitted Magniac to his extensive opium speculation. Together they provided the atmosphere of edgy competitiveness characteristic of the opium trade under the control of what W.E. Cheong has called "Anglo-Spanish Agency Houses" (1963:257-318). The permanent floating depot centered on Yrissari's first opium-carrying boat, the *Merope*. He thought it would be safer to fly the Spanish ensign upon it. The Spaniards enjoyed special privileges at Macao with the Portuguese and were the only Europeans who had, thanks to the long tradition of Sino-Philipino trade, access to the Fukien coast. The floating depot was still insufficient as smuggling moved to a new high in the 1820s. Contraband depots were considered at Macao, Manila, and Singapore. Since these possibilities seemed remote, Matheson and Yrissari, by now no tyros in the art of smuggling, focused on Amoy because it had the advantage of being open to Spanish trade. The Amoy merchants showed considerable interest in a revived Fukien-Manila trade and Yrissari throught the trade could be a cover for carrying opium. The prospect was indeed tantalizing. There was a flurry of activity among the opium smugglers who turned eastward, attempting to circumvent Amoy's lax and relatively inexperienced, at least insofar as opium was concerned, coastal checkpoints. The Dents, the Magniacs, and the Portuguese all followed suit in sending out their surreptitious expeditions (Cheong, 1963:282-294). Before Yrissari could further actualize this plans, he passed away in 1826 on his way to Calcutta. He nevertheless had already done his part. Soon Jardine Matheson and Co. had emerged as the conglomerate after incoporating both Yrissari and Co. and Magniac and Co. within its fold. In the 1830s, it contended with less powerful competitors—Dent and Co. and the American firm, Russell and Co.

After the decolonization from Britain, Americans started to participate in world trade on their own account. The U.S. economy can be regarded as semi-peripheral during the early nineteenth century. Semi-peripheral areas, in Wallerstein's model, trade in both directions, often maintaining peripheral relations to the core while engaging in core-like activities in relation to the periphery. I suggest that the United States played the latter role in Canton where they quickly became identified as "the second sort of Englishmen." American traders accepted British hegemony without much demur, moving into those "service" areas which the East India Company and the major Agency Houses had left to the private traders. A common mode of American operation in Asia was to enter into informal partnerships with Banian, Hong, and Parsi merchants who occupied a lower rung of the trade hierarchy. However, if this enabled the Americans to be competitive with the British, which they often were, the basic relationship between the British and American traders remained as one of collaborativeness.

The magnitude of American involvement in the carrying and smuggling of opium has eluded most scholars. The fact that American vessels were barred from the India-China carrying trade through treaty agreement has led to the assumption that American involvement was minimal. The fact that of the 20,283 opium chests captured by Commissioner Lin only 1,437 belonged to the American traders has reinforced this assumption.[7] The American role in the Turkish opium traffic has been recognized by Stelle (1941) and more recently by Downs (1968); but the Indian connection has remained undocumented.

The Jay Treaty of 1794, which had stipulated that the Americans could only indulge in a direct trade with India without the right of stopping enroute in Europe, was never effectively enforced. American traders were sailing directly from India to Europe by merely touching at an American port on their way to Europe. They furnished the British West Indies and the British North American colonies with Indian and Chinese goods and engaged in inter-Asian and coastal trade. If the London authorities were not pleased with such violations, British officials in India were friendly. At the European end participation in the agency and commission business, in collaboration with the Baring Brothers of London, was also common. The standard pratice was to buy bills of exchange in London on the basis of American products shipped to England and use the bills to balance off their Canton trade. A similar process worked at the Canton end in the reverse order. The bills often appreciated in value through investment in coasting and inter-Asian trade while in transit.

That opium formed a significant part of these transactions there is little doubt. As an irate British Free Trader remarked, "Both in the Act which originated the dispute, and the insults and outrages consequent thereon, our transatlantic brethren have had their full share."[8] Its exact amount and extent will be difficult to quantify or pinpoint. From the American China trade archives, we can, however, draw a general picture of how the American opium trade interest worked. The early American import of Turkish opium had often posed a threat to the British. The fear was not that it might replace Indian opium in the Chinese market but its value in adulteration. In 1820 the Court of Directors, after careful deliberation with the Bengal Board of Trade, laid down its policy vis-a-vis the American trade in Turkish opium: Americans would have the minor markets for Turkey in non-Chinese Asia and England where, incidentally, the demand for opium for medicinal purposes was substantial.[9]

The records, however, show that Turkish opium never really disappeared from the Canton market as the Indian was increasing. During the crucial 1820s and 1830s, it was in their service role in the smuggling networks along the China coasts that the Americans made the most impact. In 1821, the "Terranova incident" has pushed the opium-laden American ship *Emily* to the other anchorages away from Whampoa. After suffering some initial difficulty, the American traders turned this into a decisive advantage. Unlike the East India Company and the Agency Houses, Americans owned both the cargo and the boat. They could keep the opium on board as long as they waited until they got the desired price. The new development led them to use one of their ships stationed off Lintin as a floating depot, a method adopted by Yrissari and Matheson later (Stelle, 1941:5-74). The technological superiority of the American clippers enabled them to anchor off the coasts, away from the reach of the Chinese patrol boats. By the 1820s, Lintin Island had become a counter-thrust to the Canton system: anything that was not possible in Canton could be accomplished with impunity at Lintin. Captain Robert B. Forbes was the mastermind behind the Lintin operation. He handled all three categories of Indian opium—Patna, Maiwa that came via Bombay, and Malway that came via Damoun. The Company's trademarks as well as those of the non-Company illicit opium were clearly identified along with quantity, the names of the importing ships, and the method of sale which, barring two, was smuggling. A total of 1,575 chests of Indian opium passed through his hands during the April-August period of 1831.[10]

The family papers of a Banian merchant family that I have consulted show that the American traders had succeeded in establishing direct contact with the Calcutta opium market. Russell and Co. was represented in Calcutta by J. Church, J.B. Higginson, P. Dixwell, and Philip Ammidon. Benjamin Wilcocks and John Latimer, Philadelphia merchants, personally went to Calcutta to establish contact. The Rajkissen Mitter family papers show that Ashutosh De, the noted Banian merchant and the son of the great Banian Ramdulal De, who had made considerable fortunes through his contacts with American traders earlier in the century, had opium dealings with at least 20 Boston merchants and numerous others from New York, Philadelphia, and Salem.[11] Among the Parsi merchants, the Forbes family had close ties with Jamsetji Jeejoebhoy of Bombay and Rustomji Cowasjee of Calcutta.[12] Both maintained agents in Canton.

The role of the China trade fortunes, notably those of John P. Cushing and John M. Forbes, in the nineteenth-century American economy, especially in railway development, is now fairly well-known. What is not sufficiently emphasized, however, is the probable impact of the huge influx of specie from the China trade on the American economy during the 1830s. Temin (1973:293-314) has recently suggested that the inflation resulting in the Bank War during the 1830s was caused by the high flow of specie. The American specie stock in 1836 was about $40 million higher than it was in 1831. The decline of silver exports to China was large enough to make the annual amount of silver rise from zero in the late 1820s to its 1836 high. He attributes this to the opium trade's phenomenal increase in the 1830s and the rise "in the demand for Bills on London among the Chinese purchasers of opium. The Second American Bank facilitated this change by introducing the long-dated bills of exchange for the Eastern trade." Obviously, if it was possible for a core country like Britain to absorb the surplus silver, it was not easy for a semi-peripheral country.

It now remains to identify briefly the role of the British Indian colonial state. While much of India was undergoing the process of peripheralization, the colonial state using the port cities of Calcutta, Madras, and Bombay as beachheads had succeeded in establishing reciprocal linkages with its capitalist core. These linkages not only facilitated economic and commercial relations, but helped conduct the military and political affairs as well. It is in this limited sense that the British Indian colonial state can be construed as semi-peripheral, performing the major functions in the core's thrust toward China. First, it provided revenues, after Plassey, for financing the staple trade in tea; later it produced opium under monopoly control, merchandized the drug through smuggling networks, and ploughed a considerable amount of revenues back to its coffers. The second function relates to the role of the British Indian Army in prosecuting the war—a function which emerged as the paradigm for many a colonialist battle during the high imperialist period of the late nineteenth century, as more and more of the globe was incorporated into the capitalist world-economy.

NOTES

1. Public Record Office, London (P.R.O.): FO 233/24.
2. John M. Forbes and Co., Boston: A.S.I. Account Books, I, J, K, L, JA, JB, JD, JE of the 1858-1879 period.

3. The National Archives of India (NAI), Fort Williams-India House Correspondence, Letter from Court, May 17, 1769.

4. NAI; Home Public, January 14, 1779, No. 22.

5. Jardines S. Matheson Papers, Cambridge University (JM), India Letter Book, Vol. IV (1819-1921), pp. 10-11. Much of this story is based on my research among the Jardine papers, although the pioneering work is that of Cheong (1970).

6. JM; Private Letter Book, Vol. I (1820-1821), pp. 31-61.

7. Boston Athenaeum (BA); "Journal of Occurrences at Canton During the Cessation of Trade at Canton, 1839," W.C. Hunter, March 26, 1839.

8. China Monopoly Examined, London, 1939, pp. 43-44.

9. P.R.D.: FO/677/1B, "Resolution of the Government of Bengal on Opium, 1820."

10. Baker Library (BL), Harvard: Forbes Papers, Vol. H7, R & Co.; Indian Opium Account.

11. Rajkissen Mitter Family Papers, Calcutta. I have produced much of this evidence in my unpublished paper, "Calcutta-Canton Trade: The American Connection 1784-1840."

12. Baker Library, Forbes Papers, July 10, 1833.

REFERENCES

BASU, DILIP K. (1978). Colonial port cities in Asia. Santa Cruz: Center for South Pacific Studies.

CHANG, HSIN-PAO (1964). Commissioner Lin and the opium war. Cambridge: Harvard University Press.

CHEONG, W.E. (1963). "Some aspects of British trade and finance in Canton, 1784-1834." Unpublished Ph.D. dissertation, University of London.

COLE, W.A. (1957-1958). "Trends in eighteenth century smuggling." Economic History Review, Second Series, Vol. X.

DERMIGNY, L. (1964). La Chine et l'occident: Le Commerce à Canton au XVIIIe siècle, 1719-1833. 4 vols. Paris: S.E.V.P.E.N.

DOWNS, J.M. (1968). "American merchants and the China opium trade, 1800-1840." Business History Review, 42(4):418-442.

Five Letters from a Free Merchant to Warren Hastings, Eq. (1783). London.

GREENBERG, M. (1951). British trade and the opening of China. Cambridge: Cambridge University Press.

HYMES, D. (ed.) (1971). Pidginization and creolization of language. Cambridge: Cambridge University Press.

JOHNSON, A.M., and SUPPLE, B.E. (1967). Boston capitalists and western railroads. Cambridge: Harvard University Press.

MORSE, H.B. (1910). International relations of the Chinese empire. 3 vols. London: Longmans.

PARKINSON, C.M. (1937). Trade in the eastern seas, 1793-1813. Cambridge: Cambridge University Press.

POLANYI, K, (1957). Trade and market in early empire. Glencoe, Ill.: Free Press.

STELLE, C.C. (1941). "American trade in opium to China, 1821-1839." Pacific Historical Review, 10(1):425-444.

TEMIN, P. (1973). New economic history. London: Penguin.

WALLERSTEIN, I. (1974). "The rise and future demise of the world capitalist system: Concepts for comparative analysis." Comparative Studies in Society and History, XVI, 4, September.

Chapter 8

ISLAM AND RESISTANCE IN NORTHERN NIGERIA

Paul Lubeck

   Nigeria has emerged as the preeminent power in the African region of the world-system. By any standard used to evaluate the trajectory of capitalist development at the periphery, Nigeria possesses the potential for making the transition to a semi-peripheral position in the world-system. Population (75-80 million), petroleum-based wealth, a centralizing state apparatus, and a comparatively advanced indigenous capitalist class are critical assets for Nigeria's transition; especially when compared to its rival states in Africa—Zaire, Kenya, Ivory Coast, or Ghana. As Nigeria prepares for a return to civilian rule with an American-styled constitution, questions of uneven distribution of the benefits of the petroleum boom are certain to be raised. Of course, most students of the world-system who are familiar with Nigeria's regions are reminded of the Nigerian Civil War and the ethnic or "tribal" animosities that are alleged to provide an explanation. While it is not my intention to review the causes of the civil war, I do intend to explain the origins of regional nationalism in one region—the north— in structural terms rather than solely in terms of cultural values or ethnicity. Further, I shall argue that the development of Islamic nationalism as a regional nationalism is best explained by examining the historical relationship of that region to the capitalist world-

AUTHOR'S NOTE: I would like to acknowledge receipt of a grant from the National Endowment for the Humanities and the Academic Senate Research Committee of the University of California, Santa Cruz.

economy with attention paid to modes of incorporation and resistance, as well as subsequent collaboration between indigenous rulers and colonial administrators.

Such an approach avoids the error of reducing regional or ethno-national conflict within a state to the continuing influence of primor-dial values or similar mystiques. In fact, the structural origins of ethnic conflict in Nigeria are located in an earlier period—the eighteenth and nineteenth centuries—when the northern and southern regions were developing radically different societies and profoundly divergent relations to the expanding capitalist world-economy. To understand regional nationalisms, such as Islamic nationalism in states like contemporary Iran or Nigeria, culture must be viewed in a dialectical relationship with structures such as class, the state, or the world-system. Finally, in order to assess the significance of anticapitalist tendencies within nationalist movements at the periphery or semi-periphery, one must examine the historical relationship of those regions to the expanding capitalist world-economy. In this essay I shall develop this argument by examining the consequences of incorporation and resistance in the northern region of Nigeria during the first decades of the twentieth century.

THE PROBLEM

Interpreted as concepts for the analysis of an expanding capitalist world-economy, *incorporation* and *resistance* refer to the reciprocal relationship between two modes of production: one capitalist and the other precapitalist.[1] Once incorporated, the history of any society cannot be explained by the logic of either mode taken by itself; rather only the action of each upon the other, or the "articulation"[2] of both, can explain the historical development of that society. The case in point concerns a conquest situation in which, after a period of informal empire on the West African coast, British capitalism penetrated the interior and incorporated the Muslim states of northern Nigeria, but only after encountering armed resistance, a millenarian movement, and a peasant rebellion.

Beyond documenting yet another example of capitalist incorpora-tion of a precapitalist society, what are the important questions flowing from this case study? If we begin by accepting the fact that the Sokoto

Caliphate, together with the city of Kano as its economic center, represents the largest, most complexly organized and economically advanced precapitalist state in Africa, then the questions of how it developed in relationship to the capitalist world-economy is significant.

In the context of northern Nigeria, Islam is an important feature of both resistance and incorporation. Given the integrative power of Islam as a state-building ideology in precapitalist societies, the problem of interpreting "articulation" emerges when one attempts to explain how Islam could function first as the ideological source of resistance and then, after a period of social disorder, as the basis for class collaboration between Muslim aristocrats and colonial adminis-trators. Finally, regarding the commoner classes, what are the consequences of incorporation and resistance for subsequent political movements? In answering these questions I shall examine the origins of the dominant Muslim state—the Sokoto Caliphate—and its rela-tionship to the capitalist world-economy during the nineteenth century and then devote the remainder of the essay to interpreting resistance and incorporation, especially the form that articulation took during the early colonial period. Finally, I shall advance some propositions regarding the consequences of incorporation and resistance for politi-cal movements and the development of regional ethno-nationalism.

ISLAM AND EXTERNAL DEVELOPMENT

Although Islam was accepted by certain ruling classes of northern Nigeria at least from the year 1000, it was not until the formation of the Sokoto Caliphate by a "Jihadi" movement (1804) that a large-scale Muslim state system emerged. Like capitalism, Islam was alien to the indigenous societies of West Africa. Unlike capitalism, however, Islamic Jihadi movements were led by indigenous Muslim clerics. Further, though the Jihadi states were integrated into a Muslim system and world perspective at the cultural level, the Sokoto Caliphate became neither an economic dependency nor a political-administrative appendage of the declining Muslim empire of North Africa. This combination of cultural attachment to, and political autonomy from the Muslim world allowed Sokoto as the political center and Kano as the economic center to take advantage of the technological, organiza-tional, and ideological advances flowing from contact with the Muslim world (e.g., the "Hajj" to Mecca and the trans-Saharan trade), while enabling them to avoid becoming tributary to a more powerful Muslim state or North African Empire (Last, 1967; Smith, 1960).

The Caliphate's relationship to the burgeoning capitalist world-economy was also advantageous to state building and economic growth and development. For example, when the Atlantic slave trade was abolished by the British in 1806, economic depression and political disorder occurred in the southern regions of Nigeria because the trade in slaves had integrated those regions into a single division of labor and created a dependency on the part of Africans for European goods: firearms, gunpowder, textiles, spirits, and other manufacturers. Subsequently, Christian missionaries, British traders, and formal annexation of Lagos (1851) followed economic dependency.

Without reviewing the complex history of southern Nigeria during the late eighteenth and nineteenth centuries it is certain that, while the northern states remained *external* to the capitalist world-system, much of the southern region was undergoing peripheralization through the slave and palm oil trade.

Accordingly, new forms of political authority based on commerce rather than traditional criteria emerged in many states; Victorian Christian missionaries, offering education and modern medicine, challenged indigenous and Muslim cultural systems; local crafts declined; and European communities were established on the coast as early at 1851 at Lagos. For all these reasons I argue that regional differences within Nigeria derive from the mode, timing, and degree of incorporation into the capitalist world-system as much as from the peculiarities of each ethnic group or the alleged clash of cultural values.

In contrast to the peripheralization of the southern regions, however, the abolition of the slave trade created an incentive for the settlement of slaves as servile producers within the Sokoto Caliphate. It follows from Jihadi ideology that the boundaries of Islam must be extended. This, of course, entailed enslaving non-Muslims under the control of the ruling class—the "Sarakuna," who benefited from the raids by settling slaves on productive estates, selling them to commoners, or incorporating them as bureaucrats, soldiers, or craft workers. The incorporation of millions of non-Muslims into the Caliphate not only allowed a more complex division of labor and the development of export-oriented industries such as indigo dyed textiles and leatherware, but it also succeeded in socializing captives into an

Islamic perspective. In sum, remaining external to the capitalist world-economy allowed Muslim political and ideological expansion and, equally important, it enabled a complex predindustrial economy to develop, characterized by literacy, long distance trade, handicraft production, and a comparatively advanced peasant agricultural system (Lovejoy, 1973; Shea, 1975; Chamberlin, 1975; Last, 1967).

If we search for the enduring and most significant consequence for Nigerian history of the north's remaining unincorporated during the nineteenth century, it must be the formation of an integrated Muslim ruling class. Unlike Yoruba city-states to the south, this ruling class developed a class identity and a set of interests that extended beyond the city-state or lineage that an individual member immediately ruled. As an integrated ruling class the Sarakuna recognized the primacy of the Sultan at Sokoto, arranged marriage alliances between themselves and other West African Muslim rulers, and formed a distinct status honor group, marked by dress, the use of Arabic, and the emulation of Muslim aristocratic lifestyles.

The state apparatus created by the Sarakuna was organized into a series of fiefs which were distributed by the emir on the basis of loyalty to free and slave office-holders. The system lacked fealty in the European sense and, following Weber (1968:259), is best described as prebendal feudalism: the fief holders were urban residents and collected tax revenues in cash and in kind (Lubeck, 1977). What is important to emphasize is that the state apparatus, even as a slave, was an advantage over a free person performing the same task. State officials were the major consumers and controllers of social surplus that was extracted from the producers. Thus, in many ways the state apparatus formed a corporate group.

After Sokoto, Kano was the most powerful emirate. But unlike Sokoto, whose power was politically and religiously based and whose revenue depended on tribute from subordinate emirates, Kano's power flowed from dense market-oriented agriculture, an extensive technically innovating and export-oriented textile and leather industry, and its role as entrepot for local and long distance trade. Recent research (Shea, 1975) indicates that the emirate encouraged the immigration of skilled craftspeople, assessed tax rates on market crops to stimulate production and, in contrast to other emirates, exempted export-oriented industries such as indigo dying from craft taxes. The essential point here is that although the state dominated the merchant class and never allowed rich traders to threaten Sarakuna hegemony, it also facilitated economic development through enlightened fiscal measures.

Finally, it should be emphasized that Islamic learning flourished during the nineteenth century both because of the need for literate bureaucrats in order for Muslim rule to function according to the *Shari'a* (Muslim Law), and because of a genuine intellectual revival of Muslim learning (Last, 1967; Paden, 1973).

Prior to conquest, the Sokoto Caliphate possessed autonomy and integration at the political, economic, and ideological level. Without informal empire, which tends to corrupt the integrity of indigenous institutions, the Caliphate leadership was not unaware of but was largely unprepared for the rapidity with which capitalist forces moved from the coast and into the interior (Adeleye, 1971).

PERCEPTION AND RESISTANCE

When initial contacts by the British suggested that European penetration was imminent, the response of Sokoto was to obstruct and to discourage British requests for concessionary privileges. From the first travellers' accounts, however, it is certain that the ruling class perceived European expansion from a Muslim perspective. Clapperton in his visit to Sokoto (1830) "recorded that he was regarded as a spy in Sokoto and that it was the common talk of the town that the Europeans intended to take Hausaland as they had taken India" (Adeleye, 1971:120). Furthermore, British requests for concessions violated Muslim law and if granted could be grounds for removal of a Sultan because of the emir's responsibility to resist infidels. The perspective of the ruling class is described best in the letters written by emirs to Caliphate officials regarding the incursion of the British. The first is from the emir of Kano and is addressed to the Vizier of the Caliphate (Blackwell, 1927:73):

> I have found no more useful plan for all Muslims and for us and for you than as I wrote in my letter which my messenger brought to you, that we leave this country all of us—this is my clear conviction—as these dogs have surrounded us and threaten to overcome us.

In the following letter the Muslim obligation of withdrawal from control of the infidel (*hijra*) is referred to in correspondence to the Sultan of Sokoto from a prince who was subsequently Sultan of Sokoto (1915-1924).

we have no more news beyond what we have sent to you and are awaiting the arrival of the spy we sent. If we hear any news of them [Christians] we will send it to you. Further I earnestly beseech you in God's name let no one hear a suggestion of our departure from your mouth in this land as this would mean the ruin for our affairs. Our subjects and people, who are within the boundaries of our land, would certainly throw off their allegiance to us on hearing such news. . . . If circumstances indicating departure arise, let us depart. [Blackwell, 1927:74]

Before moving to the final letter, we should note the reference to unrest among their "subjects." The last letter received by the Sultan came from Yola which was one of the first conquests of the British (Blackwell, 1927:68):

After greetings to inform you of the trouble which has befallen us. The Christians have brought war on us . . . the rule of the Christians has reached our town Yola. . . . You will learn of the position between us and the Christians. I will not be double faced toward you and the Christians. My allegiance is to you by Allah and the Prophet and after you to the Imam Madhi. I shall not follow the unbelievers even if my towns are captured. The prophet declared that he who joins his abode with the unbeliever or dwells with him, is among him.

The letters indicate that, because the invaders were Christians, resistance was obligatory, and that if defeat were certain, then withdrawal to a Muslim state was required of all Muslims. It is also clear that their perspective derived from a Muslim worldview. Subsequently, the Sultan with thousands of his followers attempted to escape from the British but were defeated; the Sultan was slain, together with over 600 followers at the second battle of Burmi (1903).

More interesting in relationship to resistance at the popular level is the last letter's reference to allegiance to the Mahdi. Mahdist movements are well-documented manifestations of popular resistance to imperialism. They occurred in Algeria, the Russian Caucasus, Ghana, and most famously, in the Anglo-Egyptian Sudan. According to Islamic tradition, when the end of time is near a profound crisis will ensue, marked by social disorder, political strife, and moral degeneration. Under these conditions a divinely inspired caliph (Mahdi) of the Prophet Mohammed will appear to conduct a Jihad against backsliding Muslims and unbelievers. Furthermore, a Mahdi will not be bound necessarily by established dogma, and the period between the end of the world and the appearance of the Mahdi will be, for those who heed the Mahdi's call, a period of peace, justice, and prosperity. Other traditions associate the Mahdi with the second coming of Christ (Isa).

Mahdist movements were common during the first years of British rule. Lugard noted in 1906: "I do not think a year has passed since 1900 without one or more Mahdist movements" (Al-Hajj, 1971:136). British fears of a major rebellion continued through World War I, when Pan-Islamic propaganda in support of the Ottomans brought a revolt in French Niger (Tomlinson and Lethem, 1927). Note that the successor to a Mahdist movement within the ruling house of Sokoto was considered so politically dangerous by the colonial authorities that he was kept under house arrest until 1959.

MAHDISM AND THE POPULAR CLASSES

That Mahdist expectations were involved in the Sultans' futile attempt to reach Mecca is certain. But from the perspective of structural change the most important aspects of Mahdism are found in its mass appeal, and in its opposition to both British and Sarakuna rule. Revolts against British-appointed emirs and their representatives occurred in rural Kano and at Hadejia. In rural Kano many peasants in the western districts refused to pay taxes, demanded the abolition of slavery, and requested village autonomy from the British. Meanwhile, many slaves of the ruling class deserted their masters. Though the British abolished the trade in slaves and the enslavement of free individuals, their need for Sarakuna collaboration would not permit them to abolish slavery itself. Lugard, the originator of "indirect rule," saw the necessity of maintaining the traditional ruling class and feared that if sudden emancipation occurred "a state of anarchy and chaos would have resulted, and the whole social system of the Mohammedan States would . . . have been dislocated (1970:223). Such an act, Lugard feared "would dislocate the whole social framework in Moslem States, and result in pauperizing and destroying the ruling classes, which it was the object of Government to preserve and strengthen" (1970:221). Accordingly, Lugard argued that slaves be recognized as real property among the "Mohammedan population" and that (1970:224):

it was important that the latter [farm slaves] should not leave their accustomed employment as agriculturalists, and flock into the cities as "free" vagrants without means of subsistence. Residents were therefore instructed to discourage wholesale assertion of freedom, and where similar circumstances still exist the same course will be pursued.

Hence from the perspective of the commoners, both slave and free, British incorporation of the Caliphate into the world capitalist economy promised little in the way of easing their burden. Taxes were to be collected and slaves were to remain enslaved at least in the short run. It is in this context, where a combination of social disorder, political crisis, and attempts by the producer classes to free themselves of ruling class exactions, that the last Mahdist revolt should be evaluated.

The Satiru rebellion (1906) was one of the last violent acts of resistance to incorporation. Satiru was a village north of Sokoto where in 1904, and again in 1906, the village head declared himself Mahdi and appealed to all Muslims for support against the British. A major crisis ensued when a British force sent to put down the rebellion was unexpectedly defeated by peasants armed with bows, arrows, hoes and axes, resulting in the death of the British Resident of Sokoto, two British officers, and 25 mounted infantry. Moreover, the Mahdists at Satiru captured a maxim gun and the rifles of the fallen soldiers (Adeleye, 1971:323-327).

Despite support from anti-British emirs, reaching as far as Zinder in French Niger, the Satiru rebellion was put down, but only with active support by the Sarakuna (Muslim ruling class) "with cavalry although they had not been asked to do so" (Smith, 1960:205). M.G. Smith recognized that Satiru represented an attack on both the British and the ruling class, and provided the first instance of class collaboration between the two dominant classes: the Sarakuna and the colonial administrators.[3]

Thus the revolt at Satiru changed relations between the British and the ruling Fulani from superordination based upon force to a near parity based upon common interests. [Smith, 1960:205]

Before leaving Mahdism, the role of Islamic ideology as a resource for the expression of social protest and rebellion against both national and class forms of exploitation requires emphasis. During the political party period of the first Nigerian Republic, the opposition party—

N.E.P.U.—attempted to mobilize sentiments of anti-imperialism
Muslim nationalism, and class struggle against the ruling party of the
Sarakuna and wealthy merchants (Dudley, 1968; Sklar, 1963).
Again, in the 1970s as I have documented elsewhere (Lubeck, 1975),
the Adebo strikes illustrated the same combination of Islamic nationalism and class consciousness among industrial workers. Moreover,
data collected by participant observational techniques and in structured
interviews verify the relationship between high Muslim institutional
participation and support for strikes and working class organizations
(Lubeck, 1979). Hence, one clear empirical example illustrating how
articulation between the capitalist and precapitalist modes continues
to influence political expression is the way in which Muslim nationalist
ideology both reinforces and constrains the class struggles of the
commoner classes in three distinct cases: the Mahdist revolt of Satiru,
the N.E.P.U protests, and the working class struggles surrounding the
Adebo pay award.

ISLAM AND THE COMPRADORE RULING CLASS

Fears of a widespread Muslim rebellion directed against the British
continued to influence colonial policy. Only when the railway reached
Kano in 1912 did the colonial officers feel militarily secure. Once the
railway reached Kano, thus integrating Kano's agricultural production
in the world economy, the Caliphate can be seen as fully incorporated.
Therefore, it is in the decade prior to the railway, 1902-1912, that the
terms of incorporation, i.e., indirect rule, were negotiated between
British-sponsored emirs and colonial officials.

Earlier accounts provide the evidence that the disorder following
conquest created a situation in which the Sarakuna and the colonial
officers truly needed each other's cooperation to maintain a ruling
position. An important agreement focused on the place of the Islamic
religion, with which the British agreed not to interfere; this included
not allowing Christian missionaries to proselytize in Muslim areas.
British reforms included: rationalizing the fief system into districts but
often employing the same personnel (i.e., the emirs' clients and
slaves); introducing free wage labor, usually through state expendi-
ture; reforming the currency system; and fixing salaries and responsibilities of the emirs and emirate bureaucracy. How successful the

British were in reforming the "abuses" remains controversial. M.G. Smith's account of Zaria in the late 1940s indicates that the reforms took place only in the presence of the British officers. He suggests that the nineteenth-century system moved from the cities, where the residents officiated, into the rural districts; further, colonial officers were accompanied by an emir's representative when they were on tour in rural areas. Slavery and slave raiding, however, stopped; but it is clear that some former slaves living on former slave estates as well as their descendants continued to contribute unfree labor for the office holders who claimed the land (Smith, 1960).

In reviewing the vast colonial literature on indirect rule and the role of Islam, it is clear that both the British conquest and their policy actually increased the depth and importance of Islam in two ways: through Islamic nationalist reaction to their dominance, and through their indirect rule policies that supported Islamic institutions and especially the institutionalized prerogatives of the Muslim ruling class. For example, Muslim states to the east, such as Bornu, which rejected the Jihad during the nineteenth century were integrated into the same protectorate. This facilitated contact between two previously estranged Muslim ruling classes. Similarly, Muslim district heads were forced upon non-Muslims in the non-Muslim border areas of the Caliphate because under colonial rule these middle belt areas became part of the protectorate of northern Nigeria. Later, Christians from these areas were systematically discriminated against by colonial administrators for entry into the most advanced secondary school in the protectorate. For example, it was only in 1936 that the first Christian was admitted to Katsina Training School, which became the training center for the post-war political elite (Hubbard, 1973).

While it is clear that the British needed the ruling class to rule, the leverage possessed by the emirs and the Sarakuna is less obvious. By agreeing not to interfere with Islamic religious principles, the British allowed the ruling class to define virtually all prerogatives of their class as Islamic in nature. Similarly, at the mass level, the commoners were told to avoid Western education because it would corrupt their religion, while at the same time the ruling class sent their sons to be educated; though not without initial resistance. Islam, then, became the ideological screen through which the conquered manipulated the conquerors. Given the power of the emir as *imam* of the community and the unity of the political and the religious in Islam, especially in the face of Christian conquerors, any administrative reform regarding taxation, extortion, or other abuses had to be negotiated and usually under the threat of a Mahdist uprising, especially during the first decades of colonial rule. To be realistic, however, the British could do little else, for declining support at home for imperial ventures and expenditures limited their ability to reform or to rule more directly.[4] A declining core state is usually strapped even to maintain its empire, let alone reorganize it.

Once it became certain that the class alliance between the British and the Sarakuna was necessary, the British had to develop a policy for training the new generation of enlightened rulers. The model was clearly taken from the English gentry. Education was designed to create leaders, not for economic or occupational advancement. Military and gentlemanly values were stressed and reinforced by the introduction of elite sports such as rounds and polo. Hubbard (1973) found that over half the education officers (1910-1940) attended public schools and that 67% received either Oxford or Cambridge degrees. Note also that for political reasons, the implementation of reforms in education taking place in Britain was opposed by the education officers. This suggests that a declining class, or a group that identified with this declining gentry, organized and directed the educational system for northern Nigeria in an attempt to create in northern Nigeria what was lost in Britain. In retrospect, the fulfillment of the romance of the gentry was costly for the educational development of the region. Besides depriving commoners of educational opportunity, colonial educational policy contributed to regional uneven development, and thus regional tensions within contemporary Nigeria.

THE POLITICAL ECONOMY
OF INCORPORATION

Propagandists favoring the conquest of the Caliphate argued that, aside from reasons of imperial rivalry, the region was capable of producing cheap and reliable cotton supplies for British industry. Nevertheless, despite the support of the textile lobby, cotton failed to develop as the major export crop. Instead, groundnuts (peanuts) became the principal commodity export. Imports of cheap manufactured goods affected consumption patterns only slowly, but rail and motor roads altered nineteenth-century patterns of urbanization.

When the railroad reached Kano, groundnut sales from the peasants were organized by local merchants who sold to European companies or Levantine merchants (Hogendorn, 1966).

The British policy of indirect rule reinforced the emir's powers by eliminating traditional checks on centralized authority. Further, during the colonial period the emirs had the technical capacity of the British military and communications system to enforce their domination over the commoners. It is of interest, though apparently not planned, that groundnuts as an export crop did not upset the precolonial social relations of production in any major way. Crops such as groundnuts had been taxed in the precolonial state; and similarly both the crop and the individual producers were taxed by the emir's administrative apparatus, now called the "Native Authority."

Groundnuts are an annual leguminous crop that were grown, taxed, and even exported in the preincorporation period. Unlike many colonial export crops, such as cocoa or coffee, that depend almost entirely on world market demand in order to realize value, groundnuts are consumed locally and hence have *use* value as well as *exchange* value for the producer. Whereas cocoa production in western Nigeria required seven years of investment of labor and opportunity costs before realizing a profit, groundnuts are grown annually. Hence, a decline in the world market price allowed the producer to switch to a local food crop annually; or even to market the crop locally. In sum, groundnuts, while linking the region to the world market, created a minimum of dependency on its fluctuations.

Hence, colonial policy intentionally reinforced the social status quo, and groundnut exports further reinforced the stability of the system. As food crops were grown together with the leguminous groundnut crops, the region continued to remain self-sufficient in food. True, slavery was eliminated, but peasant cash crop farming existed prior to incorporation and continued as the dominant system after slavery was abolished. Moreoever, the major slave holders were the Sarakuna, and they were compensated by the British through the slavery ordinance and by becoming salaried officials of the British colonial administration. Incorporation of the Caliphate did not radically alter the relations of production between peasant producers and tax collecting emirate officials. The same centralized bureaucracy, with many of the same personalities, existed to exact surplus from the peasantry before and after incorporation.

INCORPORATION AND ARTICULATION

The question one must pose is: how did the two structures or modes of production relate to each other during the pre-war period? It is clear that there developed a class alliance between the British and the Sarakuna and that the nineteenth-century period of external development was crucial to the development of the Sarakuna as a self-confident and culturally integrated ruling class. Of course, in this case we have another example of how incorporation into the capitalist world-economy does not necessarily abolish precapitalist social relations of production—not even slavery—but may increase the intensity of precapitalist exploitation.

Further, it is clear that the exploitation of the peasantry remained constant or may have even increased as the administrative apparatus was much more technically effective with the intervention of the British. Certainly, abolition of slavery did not improve, and possibly lowered, the status of the free peasantry, because after emancipation the enslaved joined the ranks of the free peasantry.

The two modes of production related to each other in contradictory ways. It is clear that gradually capitalist social relations developed in the cities among the wage labor and salaried classes and within the foreign firms. Nevertheless, because the native authority and the colonial state were the major employers, social change was limited. For the rural sector contact with the capitalist mode of production was limited to migratory visits to the city either as Koranic students or as wage workers. Gradually, the Muslim state apparatus rationalized its procedures, but the system of Muslim law remained dominated by the emirate authorities and thus reinforced the precapitalist system. The major change in class structure was closely related to the groundnut export trade. Here local merchants and entrepreneurs profited from their "agent" role in linking the peasantry to foreign companies such as Unilever. Merchants were also important in trading food, livestock, leather, and kola nuts within Nigeria. In sum, the relationship between the two modes of production, at least prior to the rise of post-war nationalism, was one where the precapitalist system remained nearly intact at the political and ideological levels, if not reinforced by its relationship to the capitalist mode of production. Part of the reason for this relationship is found in the ferocity of the Islamic resistance movement as well as the romantic paternalism expressed by the colonial officers who represented capitalist state interests. Tensions released from the joining of two modes of production were reconciled within the state apparatus, which was composed of the two administrative classes: Muslim officeholders and British colonial administrators. To rationalize the tensions arising from the interaction of two contradictory modes of production, the state's function, scope, and intervention into economic affairs increased accordingly. Forces antagonistic to this overly developed state, such as international capitalism or indigenous interests demanding Mulsim reforms, were unsuccessful in their efforts either to promote economic modernization or to reform the emirate system.

During the post-war period the strength of the precapitalist structures and their resistance either to opposition parties, such as N.E.P.U., or to the demands of southern Nigerian nationalists explains the success of the North in dominating the first Republic. It is only with the collapse of the First Republic and the resulting civil war that modern capitalist social relations begin to appear in the northern region. But one should expect that precapitalist structures and ideologies will continue to shape and mediate the impact of capitalism and the class structure that will emerge.

NOTES

1. I have intentionally avoided labeling northern Nigeria as a specific mode of production as is fashionable at present. It was not feudal in the European sense; nor was it Asiatic in the traditional Marxian sense; rather it was a system created in the Muslim conquest tradition whereby conquering warriors *cum* aristocrats established a state which extracted surplus from peasant communities more or less according to Islamic law. For a discussion of the classical Muslim system of which northern Nigeria appears to be a variant, see Anderson (1974:462-520).

2. I am using the concept of articulation to refer to the coexistence of two modes of production in a single society or social formation in which the antagonistic and contradictory demands of the one, for the realization of any value or end, are mediated by the demands of the other. In practice this process creates institutions that behave in contradictory ways, usually producing some synthesis of the practices of both. In northern Nigeria the colonial state, staffed by Muslim aristocrats and colonial administrators, most clearly reflected the tension and articulation of both modes of production within one institution. For a discussion of articulation in the context of a world-systems approach, see Roxborough (1976) and Foster-Carter (1978).

3. Gowers, writing as Lieutenant Governor of the Northern Provinces in 1923, compared British colonial policy in the Sudan and northern Nigeria and stressed the advantages of ruling through the emirs rather than the Muslim clergy. "The policy of

indirect administration persued in Nigeria creates a body of chiefs whose interests are closely bound up with Government, where a purely religious leader will always tend to put himself in opposition to the infidel" (Tomlinson and Lethem, 1927:9). Elsewhere Tomlinson and Lethem note the importance of Mahdism as an ideology of resistance (1927:80): "Mahdism as the religious side of their spirit of resentment to European domination has had a wider appeal than it might otherwise have had."

4. As is well known, colonial administrators were but a thin layer superimposed upon an emirate political system. For example, in Kano during peacetime the European staff, numbering 11, was expected to administer a population of two and one half million. During World War II the number of European staff declined to five "during three months in 1944" (White, 1966:179).

REFERENCES

ADELEYE, R. (1971). Power and diplomacy in Nothern Nigeria, 1804-1906. London: Longman.

AL-HAJJ, M. (1971). "Hayatee B. Sa'id: A revolutionary Mahdist in the Western Sudan." Pp. 128-141 in Yusuf Fadl Hasan (ed.), Sudan in Africa. Khartoum: Khartoum University Press.

ANDERSON, P. (1974). Lineages of the absolute state. London: New Left Books.

BLACKWELL, H. (1927). The Occupation of Housaland, 1900-1904. Lagos: Government Printer.

CHAMBERLIN, J. (1975). "The development of Islamic education in Kano City, Nigeria, with emphasis on legal education in the nineteenth and twentieth centuries." Unpublished Ph.D. thesis, Columbia University.

DUDLEY, B. (1968). Parties and politics in Northern Nigeria. London: Frank Cass.

FOSTER-CARTER, A. (1978). "The modes of production controversy." New Left Review, 107 (Jan.-Feb.):47-78.

HOGENDORN, J. (1966). "The origins of the groundnut trade of northern Nigeria." Unpublished Ph.D. thesis, University of London.

HUBBARD, J. (1973). "Education under colonial rule: A history of Katsina College, 1921-1942." Unpublished Ph.D. thesis, University of Wisconsin-Madison.

LAST, M. (1967). The Sokoto Caliphate. London: Longman.

LOVEJOY, P. (1973). "The Hausa Kola trade, 1700-1900." Unpublished Ph.D. thesis, University of Wisconsin-Madison.

LUBECK, P. (1975). "Unions, workers and consciousness in Kano, Nigeria." In R. Cohen and R. Sandbrook (eds.), The development of an African working class. London: Longman.

_____(1977). "External development and the world system: Kano in the nineteenth century." Unpublished paper, Comparative History Seminar, University of California, Santa Cruz.

_____(1979). "The value of multiple methods in researching third world strikes." Development and Change, April (in press).

LUGARD, L. (1970). Political memoranda (third edition by A. Kirk-Greene). London: Frank Cass.

PADEN, J. (1973). Religion and political culture in Kano. Berkeley: University of California Press.

ROXBOROUGH, I. (1976). "Dependency theory in the sociology of development: Some theoretical problems." West African Journal of Sociology and Political Science, 1(2):116-133.

SHEA, P. (1975). "The development of an export-oriented dyed cloth industry in Kano emirate in the nineteenth century." Unpublished Ph.D. thesis, University of Wisconsin-Madison.

SKLAR, R. (1963). Nigerian political parties. Princeton: Princeton University Press.

SMITH, M. (1960). Government in Zausau. London: Oxford University Press.

TOMLINSON, G., and LETHEM, G. (1927). History of Islamic propaganda in Nigeria. London: Waterlow.

WEBER, M. (1968). Economy and society. New York. Bedminster Press.

WHITE, S. (1966). Dan bana. Net York: Heineman.

Chapter 9

LABOR IN THE EMERGENT PERIPHERY: FROM SLAVERY TO MIGRANT LABOR AMONG THE BAULE PEOPLES, 1880-1925

Timothy C. Weiskel

INTRODUCTION: THE PROBLEM

Throughout the nineteenth century the Baule peoples of the hinterland region of the Ivory Coast remained outside the area directly engaged in producing agricultural goods for European commodity markets. While many of the coastal regions in West Africa had adapted their productive systems to meet the rising demand in industrial European economies for palm oil, palm kernels, and groundnuts, the Baule continued to produce commodities of a higher value-to-weight ratio for exchange in an expanding inter-regional trade in luxury goods in the area beyond the direct reach of European commercial agents.[1] The Baule were by no means isolated from European trade. On the contrary, enormous volumes of European goods entered the Baule economy by way of trading connections with their southern neighbors; but in exchange for these goods the Baule continued to offer their coastal partners the trading objects of the

AUTHOR'S NOTE: This chapter is an abbreviated version of a paper originally presented to the Agrarian History Conference, Columbia University (April 1977) and subsequently revised for the Political Economy of the World-System conference at Santa Cruz in March 1978. I am grateful to participants in these two conferences for their constructive criticisms.

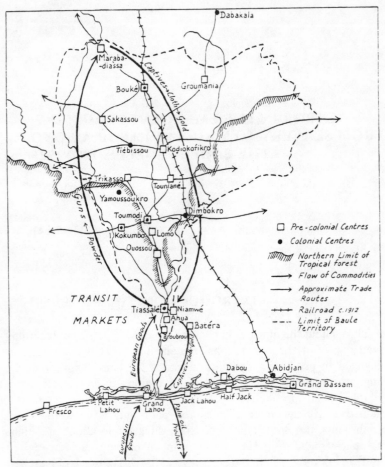

Baule Late Nineteenth Century Trade Patterns

"rich" or "royal trade"—ivory, gold, hand-woven cloth, and slaves.[2] (See map of trade patterns.)

In effect, the increased purchasing power afforded to the coastal peoples as a result of their integration within the periphery of European capitalism had the consequence of intensifying their demand for the luxury items that the Baule were accustomed to produce, and the Baule economy experienced a corresponding boom as it sought to produce these items in response to the new levels of external demand. Ironically, it was in large part the pervasive success of the "economic revolution" taking place among the coastal groups that enabled the Baule to maintain, and indeed expand, their relatively archaic economic system. In the event, the Baule economy remained external to the world capitalist system well into the period of formal colonial rule. Moreover, far from being moribund, the Baule economy flourished in its final years until it was abruptly destroyed and forceably restructured within the strictures of an emerging colonial economy. The historical problem at hand is to account for the transition which occurred as the Baule moved from their position as trading partners in an external arena to that of peasant producers on the periphery of a world-system of commodity production and beyond this to examine the ways in which this transition gave rise to and was itself brought about by new patterns of labor recruitment and control.

DOMESTIC SLAVERY AMONG THE PRECOLONIAL BAULE

Among the precolonial Baule the basic unit of production for the items that entered the external luxury trade remained the *awlô bô*, or household. This consisted in its basic form of a man, his wife or wives, and their children. Beyond the production of foodstuffs for domestic consumption, members of a household engaged to the extent that available manpower permitted in the mining of gold and the manufacture of woven cloth to provide themselves with articles for trade with their southern neighbors.[3]

Trade characteristically took the form of periodic expeditions to peripheral markets located along the ethnic boundaries of Baule country. There household heads sought to obtain desired goods on the best possible barter terms in exchange for the products of their own household's labor. As such the Baule household head was what A.G. Hopkins has aptly described as a "target marketeer," an agent primarily concerned with obtaining goods for their use-value at the best possible barter rate of exchange. Thus, among the precolonial Baule an independent class of indigenous merchants deriving its existence primarily from profit margins in multiple exchanges of commodities had not yet emerged. Trade continued to be the prerogative of household heads and, by extension, village chiefs, and it remained embedded in a complex set of socio-economic institutions. Most significantly, those in charge of trade were those who originated production.[4]

In these circumstances it was possible for Baule socio-political leaders to exercise a certain amount of control over the barter price to be paid for their goods. If the barter terms fell too far below their expectations of a fair price for their invested labor, they could simply withhold the luxury items until their expectations were met. Over time they could, if necessary, reallocate the labor at their disposal, adjusting their production to the types of commodities that guaranteed greater return. In this respect, although the Baule economy had become highly responsive to the external demands placed upon it in the precolonial period, Baule socio-political leaders still retained ultimate control over the essential economic decisions concerning the allocation of land, labor, and resources for market production.

Throughout the precolonial period the major constraint on the expansion of production was not land but labor. Population density was relatively low and settlement patterns were dispersed; land was generally available to any Baule who was in a social position to establish a household. As in other regions where man-to-land ratios were relatively low and the means of production were readily available, a market in "free" labor did not emerge among the precolonial Baule since the wage necessary to attract such labor would have been well beyond the surplus value it could be expected to generate. Consequently, to increase production, the Baule, like other West African peoples, had recourse to various forms of nonvoluntary servitude, or slavery.

In almost all instances slaves were captives taken in warfare.[5] Initially these captives may have been taken by the Baule themselves as they moved into the area of the central Ivory Coast from the region near the Ashanti kingdom, reputedly in the eighteenth century. Captives taken in local warfare of this sort, however, were difficult to control because both the incentive and the possibility for escape were relatively high as long as the slave remained close to his area of origin. By contrast, captives obtained from wars at a distance and transported through trading networks were potentially far more attractive as slaves, because problems of their control were reduced by the fact that their social alienation was reinforced by a geographical alienation. As the Baule expanded their participation in patterns of long distance trade over the course of the nineteenth century, it is probable that the proportion of slaves obtained by them in direct warfare decreased in relation to those obtained by trade with more distant groups generally to the north. Sometimes these slaves were captured in warfare hundreds of miles away from Baule country as far to the interior as the Niger bend. In 1891 when the French explorers reached the southern Baule town of Tiassalé, they encountered one captive who had been sold into slavery by Ahmadou as a result of one of his campaigns in the central Sudan.

In addition to buying their slaves from more remote regions, the Baule employed a number of other techniques to assure their control over slave populations. In the absence of a centralized political system with a monopoly over the means of coercion, emphasis was generally placed on mechanisms that would assist the process of assimilating slaves within exiting socio-economic structures as rapidly as possible. By far the most effective means of achieving this was to integrate incoming slaves within the domestic units of production as fictive kin of the respective household head. Thus, male slaves were referred to as "sons" and female slaves as "daughters" of the household head. Furthermore, adult slaves were frequently integrated in marriage relations with free-born dependents for two reasons. In the first place, he could expect to obtain residual rights over the labor of any potential offspring of such marriages by virtue of his role as the provider of a spouse for the slave. In addition, the chance for the slave to enter into a conjugal relationship and establish a domestic family of his own was in itself a means of anchoring the slave within a local nexus of kin obligations and prerogatives. This in turn effectively reduced his or her incentive to escape. Children of such unions were considered to be free among the Baule, and would not be subject to the kinds of control or arbitrary resale that could be inflicted on a newly arrived slave. To the extent that they had been socialized as Baule children, speaking the Baule language, and to the extent that they were capable of pointing to Baule lineage ancestors through their free-born parent, such children had succeeded in reemerging as social beings. They no longer shared the "desocialized" state with their slave parents, and were in this sense no longer slaves.

These assimilative mechanisms were for the most part highly effective as the means of controlling slaves and channeling their labor so as to increase the overall output of the *awlô bô*, but other more coercive means of control could be used as well. Slaves who resisted assimilation or attempted to escape could find themselves being resold by the Baule toward the coast. In addition, some slaves were customarily executed on the occasion of the burial of important Baule chiefs, and the choice of these slaves was not entirely arbitrary. Those slaves that continuously distinguished themselves by their loyalty and productivity were not likely to be singled out to "accompany" the deceased chief in this manner, but those who had proved to be a constant problem were more vulnerable in this regard. In short, the Baule pattern of domestic slavery was characterized by varying practices ranging from full-scale assimilation and marriage with free-born spouses on the one hand to rather arbitrary resale or brutal execution on the other. To a large extent the fate of a particular slave depended on his willingness to function within the recognized structure of Baule household production.[6]

In addition, however, there were external circumstances that impinged upon and conditioned the Baule slavery phenomena, and as these parameters changed over time so did the character of Baule master/slave relations. Specifically, the question of numbers was crucial in determining both the nature and extent of the assimilative process and the degree of coercion employed. Slaves were after all the product of warfare among groups to the north of Baule, and these wars were impossible to predict. While the occasional purchase of a single slave to augment the household's production posed no major problem to the mechanisms of assimilative control, the arrival of large numbers of slaves in a short period of time created an entirely different situation. Groups of recently arrived slaves were likely to be more difficult to control than individuals who had been absorbed one by one. In these circumstances, the more brutal practices designed to coerce slave submission would be employed more frequently, and the latent tension between master and slave could become markedly more pronounced. It is precisely the changes in these external conditions which deserve renewed attention in examining the transformations which Baule labor relations experienced as their territory became absorbed within the realm of the colonial economy.

EUROPEAN INTRUSION AND THE
TRANSFORMATION OF BAULE LABOR RELATIONS

French imperial conquest in the Soudan and later from the coast northwards toward the interior had a profound impact on the pattern of Baule master/slave relations. Campaigns of the French colonels against Ahmadou in the 1880s stimulated an active commerce in slaves. In exchange for captives flowing southwards African warriors in the interior demanded arms and ammunitions to wage their wars of resistance. As the demand for arms and ammunitions increased and the captives from the internal wars became more plentiful, the price of slaves on the northern borders of the Baule dropped to very advantageous levels for the Baule. The net effect was a massive influx of new slaves into Baule territory, particularly as Samory moved into the Ivory Coast hinterland during the early 1890s. Slaves were within the purchasing range of virtually every household head. No precise data exist on the quantity of slaves absorbed among the Baule in the 1880s and 1890s, but it is likely that the quantities reached a total figure in the tens (if not hundreds) of thousands. In the later years of Samory's resistance, particularly after Colonel Monteil destroyed food supplies for Samory's troops in the Djamala and Djimini region of the Ivory Coast during March 1895, Samory exchanged captives with the Baule in return for basic foodstuffs. It was possible to buy slaves for a few chickens or a pile of yams, and the Baule responded by purchasing slaves on an unprecedented scale.[7]

The massive influx of slaves posed new problems of social control, particularly since many of the slaves were mature adults. Slaves in this situation may have resigned themselves to their captive position while their own villages and territories were being ravaged by rival French and Samorian troops, but were this condition to pass the possibility of returning to their homelands was a prospect that could not have failed to occur to them. Under these circumstances the Baule had at best only a precarious control over their newly acquired slaves. In response, they appeared to employ the full range of strategies available to them to foster or coerce loyalty. The patterns of slavery became correspondingly diverse as the "carrot and stick" were variously applied in differing local circumstances. Some slaves appeared to enjoy a remarkable degree of freedom; at the same time, however, it seems that the incidence of slave executions at chiefly burials and the scale of slave resale increased markedly as well.[8]

The pattern of French intrusion into Baule country from 1893 further aggravated the problem of slave control. Initially the French were not interested in controlling Baule country per se, but as part of their effort to defeat Samory they launched a military expedition with instructions to cross Baule country and defend Kong from Samory's eastward advance. The Kong expedition under Colonel Monteil proved to be a military disaster. Monteil found himself bogged down in Baule country with logistic and supply difficulties resulting from a well-coordinated Baule revolt. Before he had the chance to engage his forces with Samory's *sofas*, the Minister of Colonies ordered his retreat.[9]

The motives for the first Baule revolt derived directly from the problem of master-slave relations among the Baule. Because the Bandama river was not navigable beyond Tiassalé, the expedition depended for its progress on conscripting porters to carry supplies and ammunition northward overland through Baule country to the Kong region. Porterage work was traditionally the work of slaves, and if the direction of travel had been anywhere else but northward, the Baule may well have been amenable to French demands for porters. As events developed, however, it became evident to the Baule that if their slaves were to act as porters for the French expedition, they would probably never see them again. Carrying the supplies for the French meant that the slaves would be traveling under French protection back to the regions from which they had originally been captured. Secondly, once they had arrived in the north, there was no rational necessity for them ever to return to Baule country. The supplies they were carrying were to be consumed, and their services would not be required for the troops to withdraw to the coast. Furthermore, if the French expedition were to be successful in defeating Samory, the Baule slaves—most of whom were only recently acquired as a result of Samory's earlier expansion into the northern Ivory Coast—would have every reason to remain in the north, reestablishing themselves once again in their homelands.

In effect the nature of French demands for porters from among the Baule exacerbated the latent conflict between the newly acquired slaves and their Baule masters. The slaves had everything to gain if the French defeated Samory; the Baule had everything to lose. Not only would a large number of slaves they had recently acquired disappear, but it would also be impossible to replace them with new ones, for their lucrative trade with Samory would have been brought to a halt.

The situation was thrown into dramatic relief when several Baule slaves escaped from their masters and sought refuge with the French troops, entreating the French to provide them protection.[10] They asserted, no doubt quite accurately, that if the French returned them to their Baule masters, they would face certain execution. The French Lieutenants, fresh from experience in the French Soudan, followed the military custom in their earlier campaigns against Soudanese resistance movements. Escaped slaves were "liberated" in the name of humanity and resettled under French protection in what became known as the "villages de liberté" in close proximity to each of the military posts.

The French policy of liberating escaped slaves was, to say the least, ill-considered under the circumstances. The Baule reacted swiftly and massively. In a series of coordinated ambushes on the French supply columns the Baule succeeded in grinding the French advance toward Kong to a total standstill.[11] Rather than provide the necessary finances and troop support that would have been required to conquer the Baule at the time, the Minister of Colonies, Chautemps, opted for withdrawal in February 1895. The first encounter between the French and the Baule had erupted in a swift struggle over the effective control of Baule labor. The Baule made it quite clear that they were prepared to fight to retain control over their newly acquired slaves, and the French initiative ended in humiliating defeat and retreat.

This initial encounter, however, did not resolve the fundamental differences between the French and the Baule for long. Indeed, over the next 15 years the French and the Baule clashed repeatedly over the same issue: who would have ultimate control over the disposition of Baule labor. As the conflict developed it broadened to include the labor of the Baule freemen themselves as well as that of their slaves.

Briefly, the conflict unfolded along the following lines. As the French sought to assert their administrative authority in the central Ivory Coast there were two further waves of Baule revolt. The first lasted from 1898 to 1903, and was inspired by the Baule effort to maintain control over their slaves after the capture of Samory in September 1898. With Samory defeated the French attempted to facilitate the return of Baule slaves to their areas of origin in the north, and predictably the Baule resisted this move vigorously.[12]

A period of relative peace followed from roughly 1903 to 1908 during which the Baule began to be integrated into a pattern of production for the capitalist world-economy. Specifically, the early colonial rubber boom brought the Baule from the first time into direct exchange relations with Europeans. The demand for rubber increased markedly during the 1890s and early 1900s, and by collecting the latex from wild rubber trees and vines the Baule took their first steps toward providing bulk agricultural produce for European industry.[13] They had, as it were, stepped tentatively over the threshold separating the European world-economy from the external economies surrounding it. It became apparent in the years that followed that for the Baule there would be no retreat.

As long as the Baule and their slaves were willing to extract enough rubber to support an expanding petty commerce and meet their symbolic tax obligations, the French were content for the time being to leave the control of slaves to the Baule themselves. In 1901 one French administrative theorist badly justified using African domestic slavery as a cornerstone of the colonial economic structure. To have done otherwise, he argued, would have been to go too fast; African slaves were somehow not yet ready for emancipation (Florimond, 1901:77):[14]

> Le noir n'aime pas le travail et est totalement étranger aux sentiments de l'épargne; il ignore que l'oisiveté le maintient dans un état d'inferiorité économique absolue. Il faut donc utiliser les institutions qui le regissent, l'esclavage en espèce, pour améliorer sa condition, et ensuite le conduire doucement à l'apprentissage de la liberté. Méprisant le travail, le noir ignore que, pour nous, le travail ennoblit le caractère et l'homme: il faut donc passer par un état intermédiare, avant de lui donner la liberté telle que nous la comprenons.

Governor Clozel made it clear that he did not intend to proceed toward a full-scale liberation of Baule captives.[15]

After the famous slavery scandal in Senegal during 1904 involving the son of Félix Chautemps, the former Minister of Colonies, pressure was brought to bear on Clozel from above to "liberate" all domestic slaves in the colony. On the face of it Clozel did this in the official decree of 1905, but it was clear from the instructions given to administrators among the Baule that the measures were designed more for metropolitan consumption than for local reform. Local officials were advised:

> Il serait donc impolitique et imprudent de proclamer à grand bruit la nouvelle du décret.

Vous n'avez pas à vous occuper du passé; j'entends que vous n'avez pas
à ordonner aux maîtres le renvoi des captifs de case pas plus que vous
n'avez à conseiller à ces derniers de saisir une liberté dont ils seraient
d'ailleurs embarrassés.[16]

Thus, as long as production could be maintained, the status quo was
endorsed and the French turned a blind eye to prevailing patterns of
domestic slavery.

When production flagged, however, as it did for a combination of
reasons after 1906,[17] the colonial administration became convinced
that full-scale intervention was justified to reorganize labor relations
among the Baule for more efficient production within the colonial
economy. This direct French intervention precipitated the final phase
of Baule resistance from 1908 to 1911, provoking a major military
campaign by six companies of Senegalese troops under French
supervision.[18]

The resulting battles between the Baule and the French forces were
devastating, culminating in a thorough-going search and destroy
policy against the homes, possessions, and crops of the rebels. In the
aftermath of defeat Baule armaments were confiscated and destroyed,
heavy war fines were imposed, taxes were increased, and rebel
"leaders" were exiled. As a result of the military engagements and
the famine and epidemics that swept the area in their wake, the Baule
population appears to have been diminished by hundreds of thousands
of people.[19]

The Baule suffered considerable material losses, and in the process
they also lost all remnants of political sovereignty. But that was not all.
With the authority born of victory the French proceeded to transform
Baule relations of production to coerce both freemen and slaves alike
to produce new commodities cheaply for the world market in agricultural staples. In effect the Baule emerged from a valiant but ultimately
futile resistance struggle to find that henceforth they constituted a
peripheral area in the capitalist world-economy.

The newly imposed pattern of external economic ties paralleled an
equally marked shift in internal labor organization. The tributary
mode of production characterized by the institution of domestic
slavery among the precolonial Baule could only sustain itself as long as
the Baule remained external to the capitalist world-economy; but now
that they had been forcefully incorporated into that system, new
relations of production began to emerge as a result of explicit French
policy.[20]

The new emphasis of French policy from 1908 on is best understood when contrasted with the immediately preceding policy. During the lull between the second and third phases of Baule resistance from 1903 to 1907, Lieutenant-Governor Clozel counted primarily on market forces alone to attract the Baule to expand their production for world markets. He extended the transportation and communications infrastructure of the colony and hoped that with reasoned persuasion the Baule would of their own accord want to produce goods for sale in order to purchase the European imports they desired. Clozel (1906:8) wrote eloquently about his *laisser-faire* paternalism:

> les moeurs se modifient, les besoins se developpent, la production, s'accroît, avec la collaboration indespensable du temps, sous l'influence de causes multiples dont beaucoup échappent à notre action directe. Favoriser les courants naturels, les endiguer en quelques points sans les trop contrarier, c'est à quoi me parait devoir se borner le rôle des gouvernants.

This was all very well as long as the world prices for market commodities continued to be attractive to the Baule. But the progressive decline of rubber prices from 1907 on created a new situation in which Clozel's policies appeared obsolete. Market incentives were no longer sufficient in themselves to stimulate continued production, and Clozel's successor, Lieutenant-Governor Angoulvant, began to use "strong arm" methods to maintain and expand production.[21]

Angoulvant increased taxation and imposed forced labor to achieve his desired ends. Economic theorists at the time expressed the functional connection between the two policies quite succinctly:

> L'idée qui parait le meilleure pour permettre la réalisation de l'emploi de la main-d'oeuvre indigène, c'est d'établir des taxes relativement elevées sur les noirs; ceux-ci auraient le choix de les acquitter en nature, en fournissant aux exploitations européennes un travail prolongé, et, à defaut de paiement, ils encourraient une condamnation au travail forcé. [Lestideau, 1907:81]

Initially the forced labor that resulted from a default in tax payments was employed for immediate administrative concerns, including the construction of administrative buildings, and the provision and maintenance of public works and roads. The summary judicial procedures known as the "indigénat" were the mechanism through which the administration obtained this labor. Under these legal provisions the local administrator had the power to accuse, try, and sentence any Baule subject for alleged infractions of tax laws or other regulations of which he was often ignorant. In subsequent years when the administration's labor needs diminished the same related mechanisms of high taxation and forced labor were deployed to provide European commercial and industrial ventures with needed labor. Indirectly, the effect of these policies was to increase incentives for the Baule to develop cash crops, because the working conditions on administrative work projects or on European *chantiers* were something the Baule wished to avoid.

Angoulvant was not content, however, with the indirect effects of this policy. He sought in addition to develop an extensive program of coerced cash crop labor.[22] Administrators required villages to establish plantations of new types of crops including cotton, rice, rubber, cocoa, and coffee. These were variously located either close to the administrative post or on suitable lands near the villages themselves. In either case police officers or Senegalese soldiers acted as work foremen and obliged the Baule to cultivate these "champs collectifs" or "champs du commandant" to the satisfaction of the local administrator. In some cases the proceeds from the sale of crops were distributed by the administrator to the Baule who had performed the labor. As such the farms formed quasi-cooperatives that the French hoped would sufficiently demonstrate the advantages of collective labor for cash crop production.

In this respect at least the farms failed. As the economic stringencies of the First World War hit the colony, the Baule returns for their labor diminished and the pressure exerted on them increased in order to produce rice, cotton, and kapok for the war effort in Europe. The result was that although the Baule derived some limited cash returns from these government supervised plantation efforts, they nonetheless developed an abiding distaste for the entire system of government controlled production.[23]

In addition to the meager returns on their labor, the governmental plantations were repugnant to the Baule for other reasons related to their assessment of their relative social status. The system of coerced cash crop labor that the French imposed until the end of World War I had the effect of compressing the relative status distinctions between Baule freemen and their slaves. Both groups were expected to perform according to the dictates of the French administrator, and to a large extent they did. Nevertheless, manual or field labor for Europeans continued to be associated in the minds of Baule freemen with the status of slavery, and in so far as possible they sought increasingly to avoid direct labor service in the various forms of forced labor conditions. Those who still possessed slaves tried to pass the larger part of the French labor demands on to them. Many others simply emigrated, either to the regions in the south of the colony, or eastward as far as the Ashanti region in the Gold Coast. This made the burden for those who remained all the heavier, and their resentment toward the administration's plantation efforts increased.

In the post-World War I economic boom Baule freemen responded to market incentives by reasserting their autonomy from this system of coerced cash crop production. Generally, the collaborating chiefs, with varying degrees of enthusiasm, became the first Baule to experiment with cocoa and other forms of cash crop production.[24] A second group of early market farmers emerged from the non-Baule groups that had settled in Baule territory as a consequence of French intrusion. Specifically, the Dioula merchants, the residual residents of the "villages de liberté" surrounding the French posts, the Senegalese soldiers, and Fanti merchants all began to experiment with cocoa. In part this was because the commercial value of cash crop production may have been more evident to them than it was to Baule generally. In addition, however, these intermediary groups were likely to be attentive to French suggestions, because their survival and prosperity was dependent on continued French favor.[25] While it might be an exaggeration to say that the collaborating chiefs and these intermediary groups were forced to plant cash crops, neither would it be accurate to say that they exercised a large degree of choice in the matter.

A third group of planters began to undertake cocoa production among the Baule on a significant scale after World War I. This group consisted of young Baule males who, in order to escape the exegencies of forced labor and military recruitment in Baule territory, emigrated southward or eastward as far as the Gold Coast. In these new locations they had been employed by Agni or Ashanti farmers as temporary laborers on well-established cocoa plantations. There they acquired the technical skills and experience needed to clear, plant, tend, and harvest the cocoa tree, and the evident commercial success of Gold Coast cocoa farmers provided them with clear evidence of the profitability of the venture. When war-time military recruitment ceased and the exertions of coerced labor on administrative plantations diminished, these men began to filter back into the Baule region and establish themselves as independent planters.

As yet little is known in detail about this process of initial migration and subsequent return, but it is clear that this pattern of movement provided multiple advantages for the development of commercial production in the colony as a whole. In the first instance it provided the supplementary manpower necessary to expand cash crop production throughout the southern and eastern areas of the colony. In addition, a portion of the cash earned by these men returned with them to Baule country to stimulate the development of petty commerce in the interior. Perhaps most significantly, however, many of these men returned as conscious agricultural innovators, ready and capable to establish cocoa farms in Baule villages.[26]

It is likely that this group was numerically as important as the collaborating chiefs and resident aliens combined, although as yet precise statistics on this are lacking. More significantly than their absolute numbers, however, was their catalytic effect on the social context of production. Their return to Baule country had the effect of confirming the validity of the as yet tentative experiments that the collaborating chiefs and resident aliens were conducting. As each of the three groups began to derive palpable profits from their crop sales it is likely that they pushed one another to greater levels of production to consolidate or advance their own socio-economic positions with reference to one another. In the process, even those who had remained persistently opposed to all of the administration's cash crop initiatives were drawn at this point toward cash crop production to maintain their relative standing with reference to the others. The real origin of the dramatic upsurge in cash crop production during the early 1920s lay not in the initiatives of the government agricultural services, but rather in the unfolding of this pattern of indigenous innovation and dynamic rivalry in the context of rising commodity prices. Although the administrators were not reticent to take credit for the expanded production, in most cases it took them by surprise.[27]

So successful were the African experiments with cash crops that the idea of large scale capitalist production began to appear attractive to individual European entrepreneurs. Angoulvant had tried to attract European investment in the Ivory Coast from the outset of his career as governor, but because of his clashes with the Baule and other groups in the interior, European investors had been reluctant to venture capital in plantation experiments. In addition to the standard import-export firms, European activities remained generally confined to investment in infrastructure (railways) with guarantees of governmental support and to forestry concessions in regions close to the coast. In the 1920s, however, Europeans observed the profits that African farmers were deriving from cocoa farming, and they began to start plantations as well (Hay, 1967:12; Fréchou, 1955:8).

The cumulative pattern of cash crop development along with the expansion of European forestry concessions led to an increase in the demand for labor. The forestry *chantiers* needed a constant supply, and they called on the administration to assist them in recruiting the necessary manpower. Initially the administration assisted in recruiting workers from the Baule region, but the difficulties of obtaining a reliable and cheap labor force from this area proved intractable. Increasingly, the French began to direct their attention farther afield to the regions north of the Baule.

The administration's preference for laborers from the north dated from their early years of contact with the Baule groups. As one observer phrased it in 1896.[28]

> les Dioula sont infiniment supérieurs aux Agnis [Baule] la civilisation musulmane les a faconnés, ils sont industrieux, très commerçants, durs à la fatigue, une qualité très rare chez les noirs, très travailleurs . . . de la population agni nous n'avons rien de semblable à espérer.

In the course of the pacification of the Baule groups the northerners continued to provide faithful service to the French, and in the face of the reticence of the Baule groups to provide labor willingly after the resistance period, the French understandably turned to the northern groups to meet the growing demand for labor in the post-World War I era.

In addition to labor for their own needs, the administration took an active role in providing labor for European concessions. While the labor recruiters themselves may well have been employees of private enterprises, they depended on the administration for assistance. The administration intervened actively to provide the labor. Local officers would contact collaborating chiefs in the north and make them responsible for providing certain quotas of eligible men to meet the recruiters. In 1921 Governor Autonetti summarized the administration's role succinctly:[29]

> Un des buts essentiels de notre politique en Côte d'Ivoire doit être de faire descendre des populations de race soudanaise qui nous fourniront la main d'oeuvre nécessaire pour exploiter les richesses de la basse côte.

With the extension of the railway beyond Bouaké after 1912 the task began to be undertaken on a massive scale.

Independent of governmental initiatives, there were powerful forces contributing to a pattern of labor migration from the north toward the south (Berg, 1965). Because of the limitations of the available means of transport in the interior, populations resident in the Soudanese belt extending from the Soudan through Upper Volta to Niger found themselves in a region where cash crop production for European markets was not an attractive economic proposition. Furthermore, the ecology of the area reduced the range of crops for possible export. Cocoa and coffee were limited to the forest regions in the south as were palm oil and rubber. Cotton, which could be grown in the Soudan, had to compete with Egyptian and American output and could hardly expect to be remunerative. As a result, if residents were to gain a cash income from agricultural labor, their prospects looked brighter in other regions nearer the ports of European trade. Already in the nineteenth century laborers from the Soudan migrated to earn income on the Senegalese groundnut plantations, and a similar pattern of seasonal migration from Upper Volta toward the cocoa-producing areas of the Gold Coast had become recognizable as early as 1910. Since the rhythms of agricultural work complemented one another between Upper Volta and the Ivory Coast, the system of temporary migrant labor seemed particularly well suited for both areas.

What the objective circumstances favored, the colonial administration rendered virtually inescapable by its polyvalent intrusion. In the Soudan and Upper Volta the French increased the local need for cash income by imposing tax obligations and introducing petty commerce in European goods obtainable predominantly with cash alone. Given the limitations on the Soudanese export possibilities, this cash could most easily be obtained by migrating to work in the southern regions at least for a short period during the year. From some areas migrants moved southward on their own accord, taking up possibilities for employment in the Ivory Coast in much the same way that others had done in the Gold Coast. In other regions the administration assisted labor recruiters to engage workers in specific contracts before they left the north. In either case a pattern of migrant labor that can be described as partially voluntary and partially coerced emerged as the dominant feature of the Ivory Coast economy in the 1920s.

The subsequent evolution of the migrant labor system and particularly the rival demands placed on it by African farmers on the one hand

and the European planters on the other lies outside the scope of our present study, but it is significant that issues surrounding labor recruitment continued to provide the central focus for political and social conflict throughout the colonial period. African planters consolidated their position as independent producers of cocoa and later coffee, and as they did so they came into direct conflict with a small but influencial European settler class. The administration was far from neutral in the affair.[30] Active administrative participation in the recruitment of labor for European concessions and plantations developed a sense of grievance on the part of the increasingly important African farmers, and it was largely the sense of injustice felt among this group that provided the motor force behind the nationalist movement. The *Parti Democratique de la Côte d'Ivoire* (P.D.C.I.) emerged from the cooperative movement known as the *Syndicat Agricole Africain* (S.A.A.) whose primary achievement had been to focus the discontent of the African farmers against the inequities of the labor recruitment system. In 1946 Félix Houphouet-Boigny, a prosperous Baule cocoa planter, emerged as the national hero for his success in forcing the French to abolish the labor regulations that systematically favored the small group of European settlers (Morganthau, 1964; Zolberg, 1964). The nationalist movement, like the earlier resistance struggle, was animated in large part by the persistent effort of the Baule to assert their control over available labor resources.

CONCLUSION: THE BAULE, MIGRANT LABOR, AND THE STRUCTURE OF COLONIAL PRODUCTION

Over the period from 1880 to 1925 relations of production among the Baule underwent several radical and abrupt transformations as the central Ivory Coast entered the periphery of the world-economy. In part these transformations were a result of conscious European policy. The transition from precolonial domestic slavery to coerced cash crop labor was a clear case in point. The Baule struggled hard to resist this transformation, but after their defeat they were forced to accept it. The subsequent transition to independent cash crop farming and migrant labor, however, was less the result of explicit policy implementation than it was the outcome of a series of more diffuse changes stimulated by both positive and negative responses to European initiatives.

On the face of it, it may have appeared that the Baule farmer and the migrant laborer each enjoyed an increasing degree of choice as new relations of production emerged, but in reality both parties had become integrated in a hierarchical structure of colonial production that was more rigidly defined than anything they had known in the precolonial period. By focusing on the phenomena of urbanization, education, the crises of chieftancies, and religious revival movements, much of the social science literature about the colonial period fails to recognize this fundamental point. Just as the emphasis on trends in trade statistics tends to obscure the fundamental transformation that occurred in the early colonial economies, so too the preoccupation with particular facets of social change creates illusions about the fluidity of the colonial situation. Many changes did occur, but in the process a new and more intractable social structure emerged—one whose shape and capacities for change were henceforth determined less by the input of its local participants than by the exigencies of the expanding world-economy of which they now formed a part.

A review of the transformation in Baule relations of production over the period from 1880 to 1925 clarifies this process of social rigidification. The northern captive who became a Baule slave in the precolonial period would be assimilated within the Baule household and over time could rise to a position of considerable respect. Furthermore, his descendants could be fully integrated among the Baule depending on their capabilities. As a matter of course it was expected that they could amass goods for trading ventures and function as fully fledged Baule freemen. After several generations they effectively recreated a network of kin ties that reestablished their existence as social beings. It was the loss of these social ties that originally relegated them to the position of slaves; once these ties developed anew in the Baule social context, they were in effect "liberated" from their status as "desocialized" beings or slaves.

This form of social integration and relative mobility was no longer possible for the northerners who arrived among the Baule as wage-earning migrant laborers during the colonial period. These men were perpetually "strangers" in the land, confined to separate *quartiers* within the village or separate settlements near the plantations. Moreover, the descendants of these men remained "strangers" in the land, confined to separate *quartiers* within the village or separate settlements near the plantations. Moveover, the descendants of these men remained "strangers" in the land even though many received permission to settle and work for extended periods of time. Increasingly, the migrant laborer was denied sexual access to Baule women, and patterns of ethnic endogamy began to become pronounced. The migrant either went back to the north to establish a family or brought a wife south to live with him for the duration of his stay. Hence, while the migrant laborer and his descendants could earn significant cash incomes, they were kept socially distinct and in some sense perpetually subordinate by the Baule planters on whose land they worked. Their enlarged incomes could not purchase acceptance or integration; and as taxes, school fees, and prices increased, the real value of income deteriorated.

On a broader scale, the Baule planter could no longer engage in trading ventures on his own as his forefathers had in the precolonial period. Trade had become the monopoly of resident aliens, either Dioula, Syrian, or European. The petty traders were in turn usually mere agents of larger import-export firms who by the 1920s dominated the colony's commerce. The Baule could bring his cocoa harvest to the local agents of the big firms, but he could no longer bargain as effectively as his forefathers had for an advantageous price for the fruits of his labor. Prices for cocoa were largely determined by market mechanisms in Europe about which he had very little information and over which he could exercise no control. His options were to take whatever price was offered or to let his crop rot. In such circumstances he could and often did witness a decline in his real income despite expanded production on his part. Often this was concealed from him by the fact that instead of direct cash payments for his crop, he was offered payment in new kinds of European goods, some of which—like metal pots, machetes, hoes—he could no longer afford to do without, because he depended on them for subsistence as well as cash crop production. While it is true that for the most part he had succeeded in re-establishing his autonomy from the early colonial system of coerced cash crop labor, the Baule peasant was nonetheless not really free to reject cash crop production altogether.

Within the colonial society as a whole productive activities had become socially prescribed, and each sector was dominated by a particular ethnic group. The identity of these groups was in turn reinforced and defined by the specialized economic function that they had come to perform in exchange for cash payment. The entire stratified structure was supervised by a small group of European aliens with a monopoly on the means of coercion, acting for the most part through collaborating "traditional" chiefs.

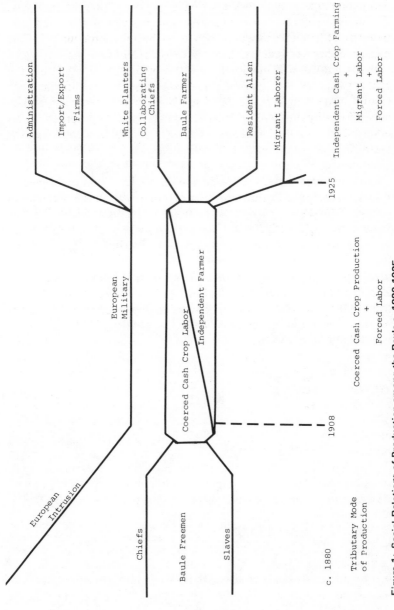

Figure 1: Social Relations of Production among the Baule c. 1880-1925

The transformation in relations of production that occurred among the Baule within the first 30 years of colonial rule created a substantially more hierarchical framework for social interaction than that which existed in the precolonial period (See Figure 1). Schematically the transformations can be thought of in terms of an initial destruction of the precolonial forms of labor organizations followed by a period of coerced cash crop labor during which the Baule themselves built up considerable motivation to reassert their autonomy as independent cash crop farmers. This they accomplished in the post-World War I era with the aid of migrant laborers from the north. Although the Baule succeeded in establishing themselves as independent producers with a greater degree of freedom than they had known during the period of coerced cash crop production, they were not masters of their own economic destiny in the way they had been in the precolonial period. Instead they had become incorporated in a permanently subordinate role in the new structure of the colonial political economy. By 1925 structural rigidity, not change, had become the hallmark of the system as the Ivory Coast fully emerged as part of the periphery in the capitalist world-economy. In its essential features this social framework of production was to endure throughout the period of formal European control and to persist in the postcolonial era until the present day.

NOTES

1. For historical studies of European relations with the coastal areas to the south of the Baule, see Atger (1962) and Schnapper (1961). Ethnographic accounts of peoples along the coast include Augé (1969), Mêmel-Foté (1969), and Niangoran-Bouah (1965).

2. For a good summary of the pattern of Baule precolonial trading relations, see Chauveau (1974). For a synopsis of Baule precolonial evolution, see Weiskel (1976, 1976-1977:Chap. I).

3. For a study of Baule gold mining activities at Kokumbo in the precolonial period see, Chauveau (1972). More research is needed on the organization of gold mining elsewhere among the precolonial Baule. The cloth industry is currently being reviewed by Mona Etienne.

4. The southern Baule trading mechanisms are discussed by S. Bamba (1975) and are analyzed as well in Weiskel (1976-1977:13-24, 47-56).

5. Evidence on the conditions of servitude and the conduct of the slave trading among the precolonial Baule is hard to come by. No direct eyewitness accounts exist, for it was not until after the annexation of the Ivory Coast as a colony that Europeans

began to penetrate Baule country. Nevertheless, three types of evidence are available: first, the indirect evidence culled from accounts of Europeans who heard of the Baule while visiting neighboring groups; second, the initial reports of early colonial administrators residing among the Baule; and finally, recent studies by social scientists and historians who have interviewed elderly slaves and slave descendants among the contemporary Baule in an attempt to reconstruct a faithful picture of precolonial conditions. The following account is based primarily on the second type of evidence available—that is, written observations of early colonial administrators. Published accounts of this type include Delafosse (1902), Nebout (1900-1901); Lasnet (1896), and Armand (1891). Unpublished material of this kind is abundant in the district and local reports from Baule country now preserved in the Archives Nationales de la Côte d'Ivoire (ANRCI).

6. As Delafosse (1901 ms:63-64) reported, "L'esclave est un client, un domestique sans gages, mais entretenu par son maître et faisant partie de sa famille, plutôt qu'un veritable esclave. Il n'y a même pas de mot dans la langue pour traduire notre mot 'esclave': un chef dit 'mes fils' en parlant de ses esclaves, ou 'mes jeunes gens' ou 'mes hommes', et ceux-ci appelent leur maître 'mon père'."

7. Price variations are hard to trace with any degree of precision. Isolated quotations of prices do exist, but changes between them are only sometimes indicative of trends. In 1891 a French explorer on the southern fringe of Baule country encountered a slave that costs the equivalent of 48 francs, probably at the point of purchase along the northern Baule border. He further stated that a good slave could sell for as much as four ounces of gold or the equivalent of 385 to 400 frances (Grisard, 1891:6-8). Captain Armand reported on the same expedition that the average price for a young male slave in southern Baule country was 150 to 200 francs and that of a woman around 240 francs (Armand, 1891:13). By 1896 the situation had changed because of the abundance of captives from Samory, and the regional variations in price were pronounced (ANRCI, X-31-32, Lasnet, "Mission du Baoulé," 12 août 1896).

8. There seems to have been a geographic variation in the severity of slave treatment. Generally the chieftancies in the northern areas of Baule country were reputed to deal more harshly with their slaves—at least, they had the reputation of killing more slaves on the occasion of chiefly funerals. This may have been simply because these chiefs thought of themselves as politically more powerful than their southern counterparts. On the other hand, it may have reflected a pronounced problem of slave control requiring exemplary executions. In any case, the supply of slaves was more abundant in the north, and although they may not have been obliged to sacrifice greater numbers of slaves at important funerals, they could perhaps "afford" to do so.

9. It is often asserted that Monteil withdrew because of his defeat at the hands of Samory. It is true that his troops were badly battered by Samory, but the order to disband the expedition was issued by the Minister of Colonies on February 18, 1895, before Monteil even contacted Samory's forces. Because of delayed communications, Monteil did not receive the order to withdraw until March 17, 1895, and by then he had been soundly routed by Samory (ANSOM, Afrique III, 19b, Chautemps to Monteil, Feb. 18, 1895).

10. ANSOM, Afrique III, 23c, Desperles to Caudrelier, Nov. 25, 1894, and Nebout to Caudrelier, Nov. 25, 1894.

11. ANSOM, Afrique III, 19a, Telegram, Monteil to M.C., Jan. 4, 1895.

12. Published accounts of the 1899-1903 wave of resistance include Cornet (1904), Privey (1904), and a series of anonymous articles summarizing field comman-

ders' reports appearing in the *Revue des Troupes Coloniales* and the *Almanac Annuaire du Marsouin* in 1903 and 1904. For an analysis of the unpublished archival record on this phase of Baule resistance, see Weiskel (1976-1977:154-216).

13. For an analysis of the rubber trade at the time, see Merlin (1913-1914). Dummett (1971), a recent study of the rubber trade in Ghana, is useful for comparison with the Ivory Coast experience.

14. More accurately—the embryonic colonial economies were not yet ready for the social disruption that was thought would follow upon immediate emancipation.

15. ANRCI, V-10-255, Gov. to Gov. Ge,. Jan. 8, 1904.

16. Clozel's instructions are cited in ANRCI, XIV-29-5, Commandant Charles to M. l'Administrateur de la circonscription de Toumodi, April 11, 1906.

17. Production sagged for two reasons: European prices dropped, and the rubber itself became increasingly difficult to collect. The tapping techniques in the early years of the rubber boom had been extremely destructive, and as the years passed the Baule and their slaves were obliged to search further and further in the forests for producing vines and trees. This required substantially more labor, and it appears that the Baule simply calculated that the return was no longer worth the required effort.

18. The major published account of Baule "pacification" during this period is Angoulvant's own work (1916). Additional articles in the *Revue des Troups Coloniales* provide detailed information. For an analytical study of the final phase of Baule resistance and Angoulvant's repressive policies, see Weiskel (1976-1977:262-317).

19. According to some population estimates Baule losses could well have exceeded one million people. This was not an exceptional feature of European colonialism at the time. As in earlier instances where precapitalist economies had been forcefully incorporated in the European world-economy (North America and Latin America in the sixteenth and seventeenth centuries), demographic catastrophe was common and widespread in early twentieth century Africa. In this connection, see Coquery-Vidrovitch (1976:37-38).

20. The notion of the "tributary mode of production" ("mode de production tributaire") is used in the sense outlined in Coquery-Vidrovitch (1976). Wallerstein (1974:86-91) has argued persuasively that different positions within the capitalist world-economy are characterized by particular relations of production. Thus, changes in the nature of external relations of a given social formation are necessarily accompanied by shifts in the internal relations of production themselves.

21. The phrase, "strong arm" ("la main forte") was coined by Angoulvant himself, and he used it with pride to describe his policies.

22. Angoulvant (1916); see also ANRCI, X-35-31, Angoulvant, Lettre Programme, October 26, 1908. By coerced cash crop labor we mean the condition succinctly described by Wallerstein (1974:91):

'Coerced cash-crop labor' is a system of agricultural labor control wherein the peasants are required by some legal process enforced by the state to labor at least part of the time on a large domain producing some product for sale on the world market.

23. A thorough study of coerced cash crop production and its use during the First World War has yet to be undertaken. Nevertheless, field interviews with elderly Baule concerning "l'effort de guerre" indicate the degree of hatred they developed for this intensive work, particularly in reference to cotton production (personal communication from Ph. Ravenhill).

24. For a discussion of methods of eliciting collaborators, see Weiskel (1976-1977:225-236). For a theoretical treatment of the phenomena of collaboration, see Robinson (1972).

25. Senegalese merchants like William N'Gom and Alassane Diouf and Sudanese auxiliaries like Bassoumou Traouré began to plant cocoa from 1912 on. ANRCI, XI-43-434, "Rapport économique et agricole," Toumodi, Dec. 31, 1913, and April 26, 1915.

26. The first reports of this came as early as 1917. ANRCI, XI-43-434, "Rapport Agricole," Dec. 31, 1917.

27. ANRCI, X-38-6, "Quelques notes sur la politique . . . ," Nov. 29, 1920.

28. ANRCI, X-31-23, Dr. Lasnet, "Mission du Baoulé, July 18, 1921.

29. ANRCI,X-38-6, Télégramme 172, Antonetti to Administrateur Bouaké, July 18, 1921.

30. Fréchou's study (1955) examines closely the interlocking relations between the European planters and the French administration.

REFERENCES

PRIMARY MATERIAL

Most of the evidence on Baule slavery exists in the form of comments in reports by early colonial administrators resident in Baule country from 1893 on. The reports are preserved in several public archival collections, including the Archives Nationales de la Republique de Cote d'Ivoire (ANRCI), the Archives Nationales de la Republique du Senegal (ANRS), Archives Nationales, Section d'Outre-Mer—Paris (ANSOM), the Archives Nationales—Paris (AN), and the Archives Nationales de la Republique du Mali (ANRM). The following archival guides are useful in locating the military and administrative reports relating to the Baule:

CHARPY, J. (1955). Repertoire des archives. Rufisque.

Conseil International des Archives (U.N.E.S.C.O.) (1971). Sources de l'histoire de l'Afrique au Sud du Sahara dans les archives et bibliotheques francaises: Volume I—Archives. Zug.

GAMBY N'DIAYE, A. (1967).Rapports politiques et periodiques, serie 2-G, 1895-1922. Dakar.

NIAKATE, M. (1974).Archives nationales du Mali: Repertoire, 1855-1954. Bamako.

WEISKEL, T. C. (1973). "Répertoire préliminaire des dossiers conservés aux Archives Nationales concernant l'histoire des peuples baoulés, 1893-1920." Abidjan.

PUBLISHED SOURCES AND SECONDARY STUDIES

A. BIBLIOGRAPHIES RELATING TO BAULE
HISTORY AND CULTURE

CHAUVEAU, J. P. (1972). "Bibliographie sur la société baoulé (histoire, anthropologie)." Pp. 223-251 in V. Guerry, La Vie Quotidienne dans un village baoulé. Abidjan.

_____ (1973). "Complements à la bibliographie sur la Société Baoulé (Histoire, anthroplogie)." Abidjan.

JANVIER, G. (1973). Bibliographie de la Côte d'Ivoire, II. Sciences de l'Homme. Abidjan.

B. PUBLISHED SOURCES AND SECONDARY WORKS

AMON D'ABY, F. J. (1951). La Côte d'Ivoire dans la cité Africaine. Paris.

ANGOULVANT,G. (1916). La pacification de la Côte d'Ivoire (1908-1915). Methodes et resultats. Paris

ARMAND, LIEUTENANT (1891). "La mission Armand." Afrique Française, 9:12-14.

ATGER, P. (1962).La France en Côte d'Ivoire de 1843 a 1893: Cinquante ans d'hésitations politiques et commerciales. Dakar.

AUGE, M. (1969). Le Rivage alladian: organisation et évolution des villages alladian. Paris.

BAMBA, M. S. (1975). "Tiassalé et le commerce précolonial sur le BasBandama." Paris, Mémoire de Maîtrise—Paris I.

BERG, E. J. (1965). "The economics of the migrant labor system." In H. Kuper (ed.), Urbanization and migration in West Africa. Berkeley.

CHAUVEAU, J.-P. (1972). "Note sur la place du Baoulé dans l'ensemble économique ouest-africain précolonial." Abidjan.

_____ (1974). "Note sur les échanges dans e Baoulé précolonial." Bondoukou.

CLOZEL, F.-J. (1906). Dix ans à la Côte d'Ivoire. Paris

COQUERY-VIDROVITCH, C. (1976). "La mise en dépendance de l'Afrique noire. Essai de périodisation, 1800-1970." Cahiers d'Etudes Africaines, 61-62, XVI (1-2):7-58.

CORNET, LIEUTENANT (1904). "Notes sur la Côte d'Ivoire." Revue des Troupes Coloniales, III:451ff.

DELAFOSSE, M. (1900). Essai du Manuel de Langue Agni. Paris.

_____ (1901ms). "Coutumes indigènes des Agni du Baoule." Ms. monographies de cercle conservees aux ANRC.

_____ (1902). "Coutumes indigenes des Agni du Baoule." Pp. 95-146 in F.-J. Clozel et R. Villamur (eds.), Les coutumes indigènes de la Cote d'Ivoire.

DUMMETT, R. (1971). "The rubber trade on the Gold Coast and Asante in the nineteenth century: African innovation and market responsiveness." Journal of African History, XII (1):79-101.

ETIENNE, P., and ETIENNE, M. (1963). "L'organisation sociale des Baoulé." Pp. 163-167, 191-194 in Etude Régionale de Bouaké. I. Le Peuplement. Abidjan.

_____ (1971). " 'A qui meiux mieux' ou le mariage chez les Baoulé." Cahiers ORSTOM, Sciences Humaines, VIII, (2):165-186.

FLORIMOND, A. (1901). L'Organisation économique de la Côte Occidentale Francaise: Liberté; réglementation. Paris.

FRECHOU, H. (1955). "Les Plantations européennes en Côte d'Ivoire." Bordeaux, thèse.

GRISARD, M. P. (1891). "Une mission commerciale sur le Lahou," Afrique Francais, 8:6-8.

HAY, M. J. (1967). "Coffee and cocoa in the Ivory Coast: A study in the dynamics of economic change." M.A. thesis, University of Wisconsin.

HOPKINS, A. G. (1973). An economic history of West Africa. London.

KÖBBEN, A. (1956). "Le planteur noir." Etudes Eburéennes, V. Abidjan.

LASNET, DR. (1896). "Notes sur le Baoulé." A travers le Monde, 52:409-412.

LESTIDEAU, E. (1907). La question de la main-d'ouvre dans les colonies francaises et spécialement dans celles de l'Afrique Occidentale Francaise. Paris.

MÊMEL-FOTÉ, H. (1969). "Le système politique des Adioukrou: Une société sans état et à classes d'age de Côte d'Ivoire." Paris, thèse de 3e cycle.

MERLIN, M. (1913-1914). "La crise du Caoutchouc." Afrique Francaise, 12:420-428; 1:56.

MORGANTHAU, R. S. (1964). Political parties in French-speaking West Africa. Oxford.

NEBOUT, A. (1900-1901). "Note sur le Baoulé." A travers le Monde, 1900:393-396, 401-404, 409-412; 1901:17-20, 35-36.

NEWBURY, C. W. (1971). "Prices and profitability in early nineteenth century West African Trade." In C. Meillaxxoux (ed.), The development of trade and markets in West Africa. London.

NIANGORAN-BOUAH, G. (1965). "Les Abouré: Une société lagunaire de Côte d'Ivoire." Annales de l'Universite d'Abidjan, Sciences Humaines, I:37-171.

PRIVEY, CAPITAINE (1904). "Aperçu sur la situation politique et militaire de la Côte d'Ivoire." Revue des Troupes Coloniales, 309-33Q.

ROBINSON, R. E. (1972). "Non-European foundations of European imperialism: Sketch for a theory of collaboration." Pp. 117-140 in R. Owen and B. Sutcliffe (eds.), Studies in the theory of imperialism. London.

SCHNAPPER, B. (1961). La politique et le commerce français dans le golfe de Guinée, 1838-1871. Paris.

WALLERSTEIN, I. (1974). The modern world-system: Capitalist agriculture and the origins of the European world economy. New York.

WEISKEL, T. C. (1976). "L'Histoire socio-éonomique des peuples baule: Problèmes et perspectives de recherche." Cahiers d'Etudes africaines, 61-62 (XVI):1-2, 357-395.

———— (1976-1977). "French colonial rule and the Baule peoples: Resistance and collaboration, 1889-1911." Unpublished D. Phil.thesis, Oxford University.

ZOLBERG, A. (1964). One party government in the Ivory Coast. Princeton.

PART 5

CLASS STRUGGLES IN THE
TWENTIETH-CENTURY PERIPHERY

Chapter 10

WITHDRAWING FROM THE WORLD-SYSTEM: SELF-RELIANCE AND CLASS STRUCTURE IN CHINA

Richard Curt Kraus

Such facts as a peasant vice-premier, bureaucrats systematically engaged in manual labor, a massive program of paramedical care in the countryside, and a close connection between eduction and production all set China apart from other third world nations which share with the People's Republic low per capita income, large peasant populations, and public commitment to planned industrialization. What is different about Chinese social structure that has sustained radical policies for the improvement of groups which in other third world societies are more obviously the "lower" classes?

One distinctive element is a low level of interaction with the international political economy. Although the Chinese constitute a quarter of the world's population, the People's Republic accounted for only 0.7% of the total world exports in 1976 (C.I.A., 1977:13). The amount of Chinese foreign trade (exports plus imports) in 1970 was only slightly greater than in 1960, and although it tripled by 1976, this rise did not keep up with the rapid expansion of the world market between 1960 and 1976. The industrial nations of the Organization for

AUTHOR'S NOTE: In writing this paper, I have benefited from the comments of William Maxwell, Mauricio Solaun, Norbert Wiley, Reeve Vanneman, and the participants in the Workshop on the Pursuit of Political Interest in the People's Republic of China (Ann Arbor, August 1977).

Economic Cooperation and Development increased their foreign trade in this period nearly eight-fold, the Soviet Union by nearly seven times, Indonesia by 10 times, and Taiwan by 34 times (C.I.A., 1977:13, 55-56, 60-61; Chen, 1975:645). Other important indications of China's relative isolation from the international political economy are the absence of significant foreign indebtedness and the relative infrequency of institutional links between Chinese and foreign organizations.

Students of the modern world-system have argued from a diversity of approaches that inequality within third world societies is exacerbated by the peripheral status of these nations in the international political economy (Chase-Dunn, 1975; Frank, 1975; Rubinson, 1976; Wallerstein, 1975). Such writers have maintained that the direct influence of powerful core societies and the indirect mechanisms of the world market contribute to an elitist orientation in social policy within the peripheral units of the world-system. Although such analyses bear the implicit suggestion that withdrawal from the world-system might encourage greater egalitarianism within third world societies, there are few negative cases by which world-system theory's association of peripherality and internal inequality can be judged. While many countries have erected barriers to protect themselves against disadvantages in international trade, few have possessed adequate resources and population to attempt more seriously to minimize external influences on domestic development. Indeed, only the Soviet Union and the People's Republic of China have implemented measures of partial withdrawal from the world-system.

In this chapter I will consider the relationship between radical social policies and China's changing position in the international political economy. Cut off from the West after Liberation (1949) and from the Soviet Union after the Great Leap Forward (1958-1959), China's leaders have pursued an economic development strategy of "self-reliance," of constructing an industrial and socialist society with minimal foreign intervention. I will argue that self-reliance has had a significant impact on the cleavages within China's social structure, and that the system of class relationships which has evolved since Liberation generally has reinforced political voices advocating anti-elitist social programs.

Three cautions are necessary from the outset. First, the basis of radical social programs certainly cannot be reduced to the single factor of China's relationship to the world-system. A more detailed analysis of the foundations of Chinese radicalism must draw upon current understanding of the character of China's leadership (Solomon, 1971), and of the protracted and radicalizing nature of China's revolution, which both attracted large numbers of cadres of humble origin and schooled them in techniques of mass mobilization (Selden, 1971; Meisner, 1974). Such an analysis must also consider the resilience of the agrarian society which required such a protracted revolutionary struggle before a new order could be established (Skocpol, forthcoming). None of these perspectives, however, is at odds with the world-system interpretation offered here.

Second, the experience of the Soviet Union makes it clear that there is no direct causal link between withdrawal from the world-system and internal trends toward greater egalitarianism. The Soviet period of "socialism in one country" was characterized both by the terrorist destruction of worker and peasant organizational autonomy and by increasing material differentiation among Soviet citizens (introduced to the accompaniment of Stalinist attacks upon "petty bourgeois equality-mongering"). Thus, a more limited claim for the impact of China's withdrawal from the world-system must be made. Withdrawal has not *caused* radical policies, rather it has created conditions which enhance the possibility that worker and peasant interests can be forcefully expressed.

Third, although the conscious limitation of contacts with the international political economy has been a prominent aspect of Chinese policy since 1960, the slogan of self-reliance has been variously interpreted by Chinese leaders (Oksenberg and Goldstein, 1974). Self-reliance (*tzu-li keng-sheng:* literally, "regeneration through one's own efforts") has been equated by none with autarky, and all have agreed on the need to avoid external domination of China's internal development. But within this broad conception some rather different levels of involvement with the world-system have been advocated, including the expansion of contacts which followed the Cultural Revolution and have intensified since the death of Mao Tse-tung in 1976. Chinese have debated what degree of external involvement may best assure China's long-term independence within the world-system.

PERIPHERALITY, SELF-RELIANCE, AND CLASS STRUCTURE

The emerging world-system perspective begins with a rejection of the nation as an independent unit of analysis (Amin, 1976; de Kadt and Williams, 1974; Foster-Carter, 1974; Meyer et al., 1975; Oxaal et al., 1975; Wallerstein, 1974b, 1974c). In the latter part of the twentieth century, no nation is socially independent, and internal structural changes must be considered in the context of the development of global political economy. An expanding capitalist world-system has resulted in an international division of labor which ranges nations in a global stratification of rich and poor (Chirot, 1977; Chase-Dunn, 1975). Wealthy industrialized nations (the United States, West Europe, Japan) form this social system's core, which dominates poor nations at the system's periphery. Core and periphery are distinguished not by the nature of the commodities they exchange in the international market, but by the level of wages required to produce these commodities (Wallerstein, 1974a). Ranged between these two groups is a set of semi-peripheral nations, attempting to move from periphery to core (Argentina), or which have been displaced from the core (Spain, Portugal).

An important corollary of this theory is that internal social structure is highly influenced by position in the world-economy. From this it is argued that underdevelopment and its attendant problems of poverty, excessive urbanization, poor nutrition, etc., should be seen as an active, rather than a passive event. According to Frank (1969), third world societies are systematically underdeveloped by rich nations which seek to incorporate them into the expanding capitalist division of labor. The decisions that turn peasant laborers into tenders of banana plantations or miners of tin are thus often made ultimately in the capitals of the world social system.

Such underdevelopment is strengthened because each element in the class structure of a peripheral nation has become dependent on the core (Leys, 1974). Landed elites encourage a commercial agriculture to produce agricultural goods (jute, coffee, peanuts) to satisfy the demands of consumers in core nations. Indigenous business groups may well oppose the competition of multinational firms, but their nationalism does not diminish their desire to tap international markets for themselves, their search for foreign capital to aid their own growth, and their cultural fondness for material and intellectual tastes established in the core. Local bureaucrats share a similar ambivalence —fiercely nationalistic in their opposition to colonial rule, yet supportive of the international system after the attainment of political independence (Alavi, 1973).

Workers become dependent on the international order to the extent that their factories are foreign-owned, or that they process imported materials or manufacture goods for export. By contrast, handicraft workers are less dependent, at least until their crafts are turned into the production of tourist trinkets instead of items for internal use. By their sheer numbers, peasants are apt to be least well-integrated into this system, in that most peasant production is for internal consumption. Yet even here the drive to specialize is apparent.

Somewhat extravagantly simplifying the world-system analysis, the political sociology of dependent third world societies may be said to center around shifting alliance and conflicts among these half-dozen social forces:[1]

Foreign Interests
Landowners
Indigenous Bourgeoisie
Bureaucrats
Workers
Peasants

Each of these groups is internally divided and subject to a continuing process of reformation. Their relationships change as the interests of each group are altered, and world-system theorists would point especially to international market forces as sparks which often lead to realignment. Thus, higher coffee prices should enhance the power of landowners, while increased demand for textiles might strengthen the role of local capitalists, and (less directly) the workers in their textile mills. In such a configuration, foreign influences (either the level of market prices, or the more direct intervention of international bodies such as the world bank) reinforce local upper classes: capitalists, landowners, and bureaucrats are alternatively favored in different situations, but peasant and worker interests are only weakly expressed and are infrequently enacted into social policy.

There is obviously considerable variation in the extent to which third world societies fit this stereotypical pattern that I have sketched. Some (Liberia, Bolivia, Thailand) are deeply involved in the international order, and its impact is widely felt upon internal social divisions. At another extreme, some societies have only recently been brought into the still-expanding international system at all (Ethiopia); there a variety of earlier production relationships still strongly influence internal class structure. Certain regions of Republican China fit the world-system model; that more do not is both a function of the size of China and the relatively small scale of the international market in the Republican period.

This image of third world social structures offered is of course a limited one, which can be used insensitively to over-emphasize international influences, not taking adequate note of internal processes of social change. Its great merit, however, is that it compels us to consider the international context which sets the parameters even for internally generated social structural change.

The study of Chinese social structure has not been very well served by past explanations which rely on external factors. Thus, Schurmann's (1968, 1974) efforts to explain the cultural revolution by the American invasion of Vietnam have seemed eccentric, precisely because this movement was so clearly a product of domestic social tensions. The search for direct linkages, acting in a mechanical cause-and-effect manner, is unlikely to satisfy because it ignores the role of self-reliance in helping the Chinese fulfill their own claims to be "makers of their own history."

This does not mean that the world order is irrelevant, but rather that its influence is indirect. China's relationship to the international political economy establishes a set of possibilities within which social conflict must be fought (Friedman, 1975). And if close dependence on the world-system helps shape internal social structure, then the lack of such dependence should also have distinctive consequences.

Although China's self-reliance has been shown to bear multiple, sometimes contradictory meanings in political discussion (Oksenberg and Goldstein, 1974), its central thrust has been to limit Chinese involvement in the international political economy to transactions which offer prospects of reinforcing long-term autonomy. In Wallerstein's terms, self-reliance is a policy of "mercantilist semi-withdrawal" from the world-system (1974c).

Withdrawal from the world-system was not entirely a voluntary choice by China's leaders, but rather the policy of self-reliance was forced on them by Western, and then by Soviet hostility. China's deliberate opening to the West after the Cultural Revolution (and before Mao's death) makes it difficult to ascribe intransigent isolationism to Maoist ideology. Voluntary or not, China's relationship to the world-system has resulted in the progressive elimination of powerful and conservative social forces. This has restructured the cleavages which divide Chinese citizens so that groups favoring radical policies have been strengthened.

The first such realignment of internal class relations was completed shortly after Liberation. The destruction of the landlord class in land reform left the following groups as active participants in Chinese politics:

Foreign Interests
Indigenous Bourgeoisie
Bureaucrats
Workers
Peasants

Without a landed class in the countryside, it was possible for the Communist Party quickly to introduce collective agriculture. And without a rural ally, the urban bourgeoisie was less able to resist the socialization of industry in 1956. Both of these radical structural reforms were eased by the fact that the foreigners active in China had become socialist Russians instead of capitalist Westerners and Japanese, and by the fact that the bureaucrats had been rejuvenated by a massive addition of Communist administrators, especially in leading positions.

It is now apparent, however, that the new Soviet influence was not consistently radical in its policy implications. By the early 1950s, Soviet society was one in which the dominant class was a group of powerful bureaucrats, who advocated policies in China similar to those which underlay their own power at home. Both centralized planning and capital-intensive development threatened to replicate the Soviet experience of leaving the peasantry as a passive (and hostile) force in industrialization. But many of China's bureaucrats found Soviet policies attractive, and they gave Soviet influence many institutional manifestations. Prominent among these was the 1956 civil service reform, which abandoned guerrilla egalitarianism by applying a Soviet model to both civilian and military bureaucratic life, with high salaries and visible status distinctions (Vogel, 1967).

With the socialization of private industry in that same year, still another class was removed from the configuration of forces in Chinese social life:

Foreign Interests
Bureaucrats
Workers
Peasants

This realignment facilitated the radicalism of the Great Leap Forward, which was motivated in large measure by the Communist Party's perception that the Soviet model for social change was not appropriate for a poor and agrarian China. Drawing on lessons from its guerrilla past, the Party emphasized mass mobilization and labor-intensive techniques (Schram, 1975). Soviet displeasure at this strategy, coupled with some basic disagreements about how to treat the capitalist powers, led to a sudden elimination of Soviet influence in China by 1960.

Since that time, the class structure of Chinese society has resembled even less the dependent model outlined above:

Bureaucrats
Workers
Peasants

In dependent societies, bureaucrats have access to several groups which will help them withstand pressures to represent worker and peasant interests (see the discussion of the Mexican Diaz regime in Goldfrank, 1975:422). With the removal of Soviet influence, elitist tendencies among China's cadres were no longer reinforced either by other indigenous privileged groups, or by contact with the international order. In the absence of capitalists, landlords, and foreign interests—each arguing in different ways for elitist policies—Chinese bureaucrats developed an internal dependence on the formerly exploited classes, whose demands (however poorly articulated) cannot easily be defused.

CHINA'S NEW CLASS OF BUREAUCRATS

It is not customary to discuss China's bureaucrats as a "class." Most Marxists have avoided this usage, both because of the difficulty of linking individual bureaucrats to the means of production, and because of a long-standing Marxist tradition of treating bureaucrats as a group in the service of some other class—"feudal" aristocrats, capitalists, or proletarians. Neither have liberals been quick to consider bureaucrats in class terms, preferring instead to regard bureaucracies as neutral administrative structures through which a variety of social groups attempt to influence policy, in the manner of classical interest group analysis.

Neither of these approaches is acceptable, as they both blind us to the reality of China's cadres as a vigorous, expansive, and distinctive social group with material interests of its own. By bureaucrats, I mean to include both civil and military and party and state cadres. As a group they are internally divided vertically and horizontally, much as the category of "capitalist" includes both petty bourgeoisie and corporation executives, and both commercial and industrial entrepreneurs. China's bureaucrats do have a distinctive relationship to the means of production, but it is a collective one, resting on control of the administrative apparatus, rather than individual property rights to discrete commodities. Since the 1956 socialization of Chinese agriculture and industry, the cleavage between the propertied and the propertyless has been supplanted by a new cleavage between those with greater and lesser authority in administration. The power of bureaucrats vis-à-vis other classes has been enhanced by this shift, which is probably reinforced by cultural predispositions derived from China's imperial tradition of patrimonial bureaucracy (Weber, 1968; Balazs, 1964). Although internal differentiation among bureaucrats is obviously important in understanding Chinese politics, here I want to emphasize the common interests of leading cadres, the group which Mao described in saying that: "There are several hundred thousand cadres at the level of the county Party committee and above who hold the destiny of the country in their hands" (quoted in Hua, 1977:48).

Although the bureaucrats still employ Lenin's vanguard theory in which the Communist Party is seen as an advanced agent of the proletariat, this formulation is an inadequately realized ideal. It is also for some a rationalization for privilege by which an increasingly powerful class establishes its ideological hegemony throughout society (much as bourgeois myths of equal opportunity use the promise of limitless upward mobility to foster a false consciousness among subordinate classes in capitalist societies). The vanguard theory possessed considerable reality before Liberation, when involvement in revolutionary activity often entailed personal sacrifices which discouraged careerists from joining the Party. But since Liberation, the

Party and the state apparatus under its influence have become an establishment, membership in which carries far greater rewards than penalties. The massive growth of the Party since Liberation may be seen not as the takeover of Chinese society by the Party, but as the takeover of the Party by society, as ambitious persons from a variety of backgrounds dilute the proportion of revolutionary cadres. Regular political study and systematic rectification can mitigate this problem, but such measures may only retard the trend toward the consolidation of a bureaucratic class.

It is not my intention to apply to China a "new class" interpretation in the manner of Djilas (1957), who argues that bureaucratic privilege has increased in Eastern Europe following the forced removal of former elites. This mode of analysis has never been popular in Chinese studies, and for very obvious reasons: Chinese bureaucrats allow themselves to be subjected to cultural revolutions and sent to May 7th cadre schools, they have not increased their salaries since 1956, and in general they permit the flourishing of antibureaucratic abuse which no truly *ruling* class of bureaucrats would be likely to tolerate. Indeed, a tone of commiseration informs much Western scholarship on contemporary Chinese bureaucrats.

As I have suggested, the relative weakness of Chinese bureaucrats, compared to their Eastern European counterparts, must in part be attributed to the nature of China's revolution, a protracted affair in which vast numbers of lower-class personnel were incorporated into the ranks of the Party's cadres. That the reconstruction of the Chinese bureaucracy has proceeded for only one generation suggests that its cadres should be viewed as a class in formation, one which is only now beginning to confront such critical issues as the transmission of its presently limited privileges to its children.

But self-reliance has also been an important factor in limiting bureaucratic cohesion as a class, because it has encouraged the split which Maoists identify as the two-line struggle. One group of bureaucrats, led by Mao Tse-tung, has since 1958 consciously endeavored to respond to worker and peasant interests against the preferences of more conservative and elitist bureaucrats. This does not imply any saintliness on the part of Maoist politicians, who merely have sought to enhance their own power through the mobilization of the constituency which shares their views. But more conservative bureaucrats, lacking an alternative constituency in the form of business, landlord, and foreign interests, have been hard-pressed to resist radical policy initiatives since the early 1960s.

We all know that a clear-cut split between "Liuists" and "Maoists" has been artificially read back into the precultural revolution history of the People's Republic (Dittmer, 1974). Individual politicians choose policy preferences by issue, rather than by world view, and these preferences often change over time. Yet even if it is difficult to categorize individual political actors neatly into two unchanging camps, there is ample evidence that earlier radical initiatives in social policy had been undermined by conservative bureaucratic resistance. This was true of educational reforms (the establishment of rural schools, the effort to de-emphasize university entrance examinations, and the reform of educational curricula [Seybolt, 1973; Hinton, 1972]), of health care reforms (investments in public health, the utilization of traditional medicine, and the spreading of health benefits from urban areas to the countryside [Sidel and Sidel, 1973; Horn, 1969]), and of reforms in the arts (the introduction of themes glorifying contemporary peasants and workers instead of emperors, courtesans, and intellectuals [Ahn, 1976]).

Maoist politicians are bureaucrats by social position, but by political preference they advocate policies which make them "traitors" to their class. Conservative bureaucrats strongly prefer to implement policies through routine administrative techniques which enhance their control of the outcomes (Oksenberg, 1974a), whereas Maoists regularly opt for applying the mass mobilizing campaign style to a variety of social problems as a way of involving nonbureaucratic classes in the process by which decisions are made.

In this shadowy conflict which has split the bureaucrats since the beginnings of self-reliance, there was a major period of bureaucratic resurgence in the confused aftermath of the Great Leap Forward. But the more conservative administration of Liu Shao-chi could not be sustained in the absence of social groups which would ally themselves with bureaucratic preferences. Without self-reliance and its impact on internal social cleavages, there could have been no Cultural Revolution. In that movement the bureaucrats reaped an ironic harvest: their prior success at destroying domestic and foreign rivals had undermined their capacity to protect their own interests.[2]

A DIVIDED PROLETARIAT

Lack of cohesion limits the capacity of bureaucrats to act as a class in pursuit of its own interests. Bureaucrats are aided, however, by similar tendencies toward fragmentation among China's workers and peasants. Indeed, in this rough three-class model which I am sketching,[3] the divisions within each group are strongly influenced by the tensions among them.

The position of the working class in Marxist social theory and the central role of the proletariat in China's massive industrialization drive help explain why many of the fruits of the revolution have fallen into the hands of workers. These factors do not explain, however, why a stratum of skilled industrial laborers enjoys permanent employment at relatively high wages, in addition to insurance and pension benefits and access to child-care and medical facilities which are denied another group of "contract" and temporary workers (White, 1976; Hoffman, 1974; Riskin, 1975).

This surprisingly rigid internal stratification of the Chinese working class is based on pre-liberation practices which became institutionalized in the Soviet-influenced wage reform of 1956. The maintenance of these distinctions seems anomalous, however, and they were severely criticized (but not abrogated) during the Cultural Revolution. It is likely that in China, as in capitalist societies, an economically divided working class helps managers to depress wages and enjoy considerable flexibility in labor allocation.

But there is another reason why Chinese bureaucrats might find working class division attractive. For one way of reducing the dependence of socially isolated bureaucrats on the working class is to allow the emergence of a privileged stratum of workers which might support the bureaucrats in struggles over power and the distribution of material benefits. Such a stratum forms an intermediate level in conflicts between bureaucrats and the least privileged workers. Wallerstein (1975:368) argues that

> Such a three-tiered format is essentially stabilizing in effect, whereas a two-tiered format is essentially disintegrating. We are not saying that three tiers exist at all moments. We are saying that those on top always seek to ensure the existence of three tiers in order the better to preserve their privilege, whereas those on the bottom conversely seek to reduce the three to two, the better to destroy this same privilege. This fight over the existence of a middle tier goes on continually, both in political terms and in terms of basic ideological constructs (those that are pluralist versus those that are manicheist). This is the core issue around which the class struggle is centered.

This does not imply that worker differentiation is calculated by conservative cadres as a means of protecting their social position. The reshaping of the occupational structure through industrialization brings differentiation as new job categories are introduced. The political issue is whether this process will be relatively isolated from the distribution of rewards.

White (1976) has shown that during the period of bureaucratic resurgence between the Great Leap and the Cultural Revolution, Shanghai's permanent workers were offered increased wages, bonuses, increased labor insurance benefits, and vacations—none of which were extended to other categories of workers. These workers tended to support conservative bureaucrats early in the Cultural Revolution, especially when the beleagured cadres induced additional support by dispersing state funds to the labor aristocracy.

Maoist interest in promoting working class cohesion as a check against the power of conservative cadres has been frustrated by financial and political constraints. It has been politically unfeasible to reduce existing benefits to any group (Kraus, 1976), and too expensive to extend them to all workers (which might also arouse peasant resentment).

Instead, Maoists have attempted to minimize the effects of other divisions among workers, especially distinctions of technique and authority. Under the formula "red and expert," Maoists have argued that specialization should not be treated as the property of any worker, and that even those with technical training should govern their expertise with firmly revolutionary politics (Lee, 1973). Maoists hope thereby to preclude the emergence of a stratum of technical workers, highly paid and supportive of privileges which they might share with administrative cadres. Since the Cultural Revolution, this problem has been attacked institutionally by the introduction of the "three-in-one" combination of workers, technicians, and managers who jointly solve production problems.

By demanding that cadres participate in labor, and that workers be represented on administrative bodies, Maoists have offered the inducement of authority to counter the conservative bureaucrats' blandishment of individual material benefits (Andors, 1974). While many Westerners might regard this as a poor exchange, the status of heavily industrial areas (Shanghai and Liaoning) as centers of radical power suggest that many Chinese workers have found it a good bargain.

A PRECARIOUS WORKER-PEASANT ALLIANCE

In dependent third world societies, peasants are typically passive elements in development strategies, objects, rather than subjects of planned social change. Self-reliance has given the Chinese peasantry a more central role. Because of the United States trade embargo which followed Liberation, and because of the split with the Soviet Union, China's bureaucratic planners have not been able to include foreign aid, international sources of credit, and external investment as developmental techniques. Instead, the Communist Party has been forced to rely consciously and systematically on the peasantry as a source of capital for industrial and agricultural development.

This has resulted in economic planning with a powerful rural emphasis, and the conditions of rural life have improved vastly under Communist rule. China has begun to industrialize without the increasing maldistribution of material benefits typical of the third world (Adelman and Morris, 1973). Nonetheless, it is apparent that rural residents are still on the inferior side of what the Chinese call the "three great differences:" the gaps between worker and peasant, city and country, and mental and manual labor. Although self-reliance alters class relations by limiting the options available to bureaucrats, it does not offer an easy way of redressing class inequalities.

Worker-peasant class distinctions in dependent third world societies often pale into relative insignificance in the presence of a far greater gulf between these two groups and the propertied classes. The existence of a common adversary—typically a ruling combination of landlords, capitalists, bureaucrats, and foreign interests—sustains perceptions of shared suffering, even if the worker-peasant alliance of Communist theory often exists only in latent form. But revolution and self-reliance have altered this set of relationships by destroying several of its elements, and in the absence of massive oppression, worker and peasant interests have tended to diverge.

Neither Maoist nor conservative bureaucrats have fostered open peasant hostility toward the industrial working class, and both have sought to dampen peasant resentment by continually reminding rural residents of the improvement in their living conditions. They have disagreed, however, on other strategies.

As with the working class, increased internal statification of the peasantry tends to dampen class solidarity vis-a-vis the officials. When conservative bureaucrats attempted to revive agricultural production after the Great Leap by encouraging household (rather than collective) production and permitting widespread use of individual incentives and private plots (Baum, 1975), the conditions for a prosperous stratum of peasants were established. This set of policies was terminated in the Cultural Revolution, but its success might have nurtured a new rural gentry, likely to support elitist policies.

In opposition to such rural policies, Maoists have attempted to intensify peasant cohesion. One technique has been to demand participation in labor by leaders, thereby splitting the lowest stratum of rural cadres from the upper levels of the bureaucracy. Another has been to advocate a relative homogenization of income through the emphasis of the radical Ta-chai model of work-point distribution and by stressing collective, instead of household management of subsidiary "sideline" agricultural activities (Riskin, 1973; Crook, 1973). Rather than improve peasant living standards by pitting peasants against one another, Maoist policies have stressed improving collective benefits in the countryside, through the establishment, especially since the Cultural Revolution, of educational and medical facilities.

A new threat to peasant unity has been introduced along with another Maoist reform, the scattering of small-scale, argriculture-related industries throughout the countryside (Sigurdson, 1975). Although this program is intended in large measure to reduce rural-urban inequalities, the employment of 5% of the rural workforce in such enterprises might introduce a new kind of privileged stratum in China's countryside. In order to avoid such a development, cement factory cadres in the model Hsi-yang County reported that (Ehrenreich, 1975:24):

> every three to five years the workers in the factory will go back to be commune members, and different commune members will come to the factory. . . . We are trying to turn out peasant-workers.

But peasant unity might be destructive of national unity in the absence of strong programs to bind different classes more closely together. To this end, Maoists have strongly advocated (against frequent bureaucratic resistance) political criteria for university admissions, rather than standards based solely on prior book learning. Although this reform has been significantly weakened since Mao's death, its intent was partly to open new channels for upward mobility to peasants. Even more impressive is the massive program of sending urban young people to resettle in the countryside. More than ten million persons have become a part of this migration, unique in that it reverses the movement from village to city typical of poor agrarian societies (Chen, 1972; Berstein, 1977; White, 1974). More conservative bureaucrats find this program palatable because of the inability of urban industries to employ the large number of new entrants to the urban labor force. But for Maoists, the down-to-the-villages movement has other attractions: by placing a sophisticated group into rural life, new stimuli for social change may be introduced, and the urban families and friends of these young people now have a personal stake in improving the quality of life in rural areas.

CONCLUSION

There have been two fundamental changes in the class structure of the People's Republic of China. One has been the transformation of property relations and the destruction of the classes which defined themselves by property ownership. Less noticed, but equally radicalizing in its effect has been the restructuring of power relationships made possible by revolution and self-reliance.

The world-system perspective which I have employed here suggests that partial withdrawal from the international political economy has been crucial in engendering a set of class relationships in which bureaucrats have been unable to balance worker and peasant demands with the more conservative policy preferences of propertied and foreign groups. Relationship to the world-system and internal social structure are intimately linked, so that the former should be seen a basic element of the latter.

Although China has severely limited this international dimension of its social structure, no one should presume that self-reliance is a solution open to any third world society whose citizens seek to avoid the distorted growth of dependency. China's size and resource base facilitate self-reliance in ways which are not feasible for Senegal or Ecuador. Moreover, Perkins (1975) and Myers (1975) have identified important cultural resources for economic growth which any third world nations do not possess.

One irony suggested by this analysis is that American policy makers, in their anti-communist zeal, pursued a self-defeating policy in attempting to "contain" the Chinese revolution. The imperialist embargo of the People's Republic was intended to isolate a revolutionary movement until it had outgrown its radicalism. But the joining of our blockade by the withdrawal of Soviet influence actually strengthened the structural bases for radical policies by altering the character of internal class relations in China.

By failing to consider the dramatic change in class relationships, students of China have neglected a potent force for the maintenance of radical social policies. Thus, Oksenberg (1974:112) argues that:

> The bureaucrats' socially beneficial programmes resulted from their attitudes and the pressures upon them from the top. *But, if this pressure ever ceased, few structural impediments exist to prevent bureaucrats from redirecting their efforts, more to the benefit of themselves and privileged sectors of society.* [Emphasis in the original]

But radical policies are not a benevolence bestowed upon a grateful populace by philanthropic rulers; they are the consequence of hard-fought political struggles in which a class of bureaucrats has been too weak to prevent the defection of many of its leading members to voice the aspirations of workers and peasants.

To argue that class tensions form an important context for political life in China does not imply that these tensions equal in severity those found in other societies. Chinese bureaucrats may enjoy privileges unavailable to workers and peasants, but the limited nature of these advantages and the willingness of most cadres to forego increases in personal consumption in favor of greater public investment of China's economic surplus render class exploitation an unhelpful concept. Moreover, the classes are only loosely delineated, as much of the conflict among them centers on the issues of to which class certain intermediate strata will adhere. Indeed, this fluidity is the source of much of the dynamic quality of Chinese politics.

That the death of Mao was followed so quickly by a massive campaign against some of his radical associates might suggest that this discussion of social cleavages and self-reliance is quite beside the point. Does not the purge of the gang of four prove that the primary support for radical policies was not in the social structure after all, but rather in the will and political talent of Chairman Mao?

But it is too crude to read the downfall of the gang of four simply as the successful counterattack of conservative cadres. To be sure, one may imagine that such cadres have eagerly supported the recent campaign, and several radical policies have come into question. Nonetheless, the administration of Hua Kuo-feng has indicated its enthusiasm for many aspects of Maoist policies (including the distribution of material benefits to the countryside, the participation of cadres in physical labor, and the down-to-the-villages program). It seems unlikely that the Maoist package of social policies will soon be discarded, although it is clear that Mao's death has incited tampering with its contents.

The constituency to which Mao appealed, and which inspired his own radicalism, was not dispersed at his death. The disgraced gang of four made the error of pushing its attack too close to the heart of the bureaucrats: among Chiang Ch'ing's unfinished projects was a film glorifying a Cultural Revolution attack upon a conservative provincial cadre. Other radical politicians will have to be more circumspect (as was Mao) in the future.

But the present balance of classes is certainly not immutable. How might it change in the future to create structural impediments to the implementation of radical policies?

One such change would be a greater consolidation of the bureaucratic class, especially its closure to workers and peasants. In the past, Maoists have attempted to keep recruitment into leadership positions open to both of these groups, but now that more than a generation has passed since Liberation there are large numbers of cadres whose personal interests would be served by placing their children, and not the children of workers and peasants, into new bureaucratic positions. Data indicating the social composition of the Party and state apparatus in recent years are unavailable, and an assessment of this issue is difficult.

A second change would be increasing internal stratification among workers and peasants, whereby new privileged strata would be formed which might support bureaucratic attacks on policies to maintain an open and shifting distribution of power and privilege. The increased application of sophisticated technology to both industrial and agricultural production raises the possibility that some workers and peasants may be in a position to appropriate technical skills to their personal material advantage. It remains to be seen whether existing programs to temper occupational specialization can restrain such a development.

Finally, the reintegration of China into the international political economy—either Soviet or capitalist sections—might offer bureaucrats new leverage against worker and peasant demands. But caution is advisable in interpreting the post-Cultural Revolution expansion of Chinese contacts abroad. First, many of these relationships have been supported by Mao and other radicals eager to balance the ascendant force of the Societ Union. Second, although conservative bureaucrats, especially those in trade and diplomatic organizations, may attempt to manipulate international contacts to their advantage, it is unlikely that such significant material resources as foreign investment capital will soon be accepted by the People's Republic. But only massive involvement with the international system would easily counteract the effects of two decades of self-reliance. With characteristic confidence, Mao once put the issue in these terms:

You Americans can go on withholding recognition of our government for one hundred years, but I doubt if you can withhold it in the 101st. One day the United States will have to establish diplomatic relations with us. When the Americans come to China then and look around, they will find it too late for regrets. For this land of China will have become quite different, with its house swept clean and the 'four pests' eliminated, they won't find many friends here and they can't do much even if they spread a few germs. [*Peking Review*, (April 22, 1977), 20:27.]

NOTES

1. A more leisurely paced analysis would take up such groups as the petty bourgeoisie and the unemployed. It would also stress, as I will below, the importance of differentiation within each of these groups.

2. Objections might be raised that the Imperial Chinese bureaucrats were without foreign or capitalist allies, yet managed to avoid succumbing to radical policy demands. The difference, of course, lies in the fact that Imperial China had never joined the international political economy, much less suffered the structural shocks of withdrawing from it. Communist cadres must confront an industrial proletariat which did not previously exist, as well as a transformed peasantry—all without benefit of the land-office tie which sustained their bureaucratic ancestors.

3. Although the alliance of workers, peasants, and bureaucrats destroyed the legal foundations of their capitalist rivals early in the history of the People's Republic, two survivals of the bourgeoisie must be noted.

Self-reliance is not autarky, and even limited involvement with the world-system demands specialists in market transactions. Some of these experts are found today within the banking and foreign trade sections of the bureaucracy. Others, however, are concentrated in Hong Kong, where they continue to own property and behave as capitalists. For China as a social system (if not as a political system), Hong Kong functions as a reservation of capitalists. Geographical isolation permits the People's Republic to benefit from bourgeois skills without sustaining the costs of internal capitalist institutions. This restoration of imperial preference for restricting foreign trade to a single South China port has been given renewed vitality by the realignment of class relationships since Liberation.

The other bourgeois survival assumes the more abstract form of cultural influence. At one level this influence is transmitted primarily through intellectuals. Although most intellectuals on the eve of Liberation were attached to the bourgeoisie either by social origin or by institutional patronage, after socialization they quickly gained bureaucratic affiliations (Schurmann, 1964:83). But bureaucratization did not in itself destroy bourgeois ideology, which has shown remarkable tenacity through several fierce campaigns. Bourgeois ideology also seems to be recreated within the new institutions of a socialism which, in Marx's phrase, is "in every respect, economically, morally and intellectually, still stamped with the birth marks of the old society from whose womb it emerges" (for a discussion, see Bettleheim, 1974).

Radical politicians have accused conservative bureaucrats of seeking to restore capitalism by drawing on its ideology. The charge is wild, but points to an underlying reality: revolutionary cadres once eager to destroy the bourgeoisie have become bureaucrats willing to make their peace with its ghost, borrowing selective elements from its ideology with which to buttress their social position.

REFERENCES

ADELMAN, I., and MORRIS, C.T. (1973). Economic growth and social equity in developing countries. Stanford: Stanford University Press.

AHN, B. (1976). Chinese politics and the Cultural Revolution. Seattle: University of Washington Press.

ALAVI, H. (1973). "The state in postcolonial societies: Pakistan and Bangladesh." In K. Gough and H.P. Sharma (eds.), Imperialism and revolution in South Asia. New York: Monthly Review Press.

AMIN, S. (1976). Unequal development. An essay on the social formations of peripheral capitalism. New York: Monthly Review Press.

ANDORS, S. (1974). "Factory management and political ambiguity, 1961-1963." China Quarterly, 59 (July/September):435-476.

BALAZS, E. (1964). Chinese civilization and bureaucracy. New Haven: Yale University Press.

BAUM, R. (1975). Prelude to revolution. Mao, the Party, and the peasant question, 1962-1966. New York: Columbia University Press.

BERNSTEIN, T.P. (1977). "Urban youth in the countryside: Problems of adaptation and remedies." China Quarterly, 69 (March):75-108.

BETTLEHEIM, C. (1974). Cultural revolution and industrial organization in China. New York: Monthly Review Press.

Central Intelligence Agency (1977). Handbook of economic statistics.

CHASE-DUNN, C. (1975). "The effects of international economic dependence on development and inequality: A cross-national study." American Sociological Review, 40 (December):720-738.

CHEN, N. (1975). "China's foreign trade, 1950-1974." In Joint Economic Committee, Congress of the United States, "China: A reassessment of the economy." Washington, D.C.: U.S. Government Printing Office.

CHEN, P. (1972). "Overurbanization, rustication of urban-educated youths, and politics of rural transformation." Comparative Politics, 4 (April):361-386.

CHIROT, D. (1977). Social change in the twentieth century. New York: Harcourt, Brace, Jovanovich.

CROOK, F.W. (1973). "Chinese Communist agricultural incentive systems and the labor productive contracts to households: 1956-1965." Asian Survey, XII (May): 470-481.

DE KADT, E., and WILLIAMS, G. (1974). Sociology and development. London: Tavistock.

DITTMER, L. (1974). Liu Shao-ch'i and the Chinese cultural revolution. Berkeley: University of California Press.

DJILAS, M. (1957). The new class. New York: Praeger.

EHRENREICH, J. (1975). "The dictatorship of the proletariat in China." Monthly Review, 77 (October):16-28.

FOSTER-CARTER, A. (1974). "Neo-Marxist approaches to development and under-development." In E. de Kadt and G. Williams (eds.), Sociology and development. London: Tavistock.

FRANK, A.G. (1969). Latin America: Underdevelopment or revolution. New York: Monthly Review Press.

———(1975)l On capitalist underdevelopment. Bombay: Oxford University Press.

FRIEDMAN., E. (1975). "The international political economy and Chinese politics." In B.G. Garth et al. (eds.), China's changing role in the world economy. New York: Praeger.

GOLDFRANK, W. (1975). "World system, state structure, and the onset of the Mexican Revolution." Politics and Society, 5:417-439.

HINTON, W. (1972). Hundred Day War: The Cultural Revolution at Tsinghua University. New York: Monthly Review Press.

HOFFMAN, C. (1974). The Chinese worker. Albany: State University of New York Press.

HORN, J. (1969). Away with all pests. New York: Monthly Review Press.

HUA KUO-FENG (1977). "Political report to the 11th National Congress of the Communist Party of China." Peking Review, 20 (August 26):23-57.

KRAUS, R.C. (1976). "The limits of Maoist egalitarianism." Asian Survey, XVI (November):1081-1096.

LEE, R.W., III. (1973). "The politics of technology in Communist China." In C. Johnson (ed.), Ideology and politics in contemporary China. Seattle: University of Washington Press.

LEYS, C. (1974). Underdevelopment in Kenya. Berkeley: University of California Press.

MEISNER, M. (1974). "Utopian socialist themes in Maoism." In J.W. Lewis (ed.), Peasant rebellion and Communist revolution in Asia. Stanford: Stanford University Press.

MEYER, J.W. et al. (1975). "Convergence and divergence in development." In A. Inkeles et al. (eds.), Annual review of sociology, Vol. 1. Palo Alto: Annual Reviews.

MYERS, R.H. (1975). "Cooperation in traditional agriculture and its implications for team farming in the People's Republic of China." In D.H. Perkins (ed.), China's modern economy in historical perspective. Stanford: Stanford University Press.

OKSENBERG, M. (1974a). "The Chinese policy process and the public health issue: An arena approach." Studies in Comparative Communism, VII (Winter):375-408.

_____(1974b). "Political changes and their causes in China, 1949-1972." The Political Quarterly, 45 (January-March):95-114.

_____and GOLDSTEIN, S. (1974). "The Chinese political spectrum." Problems of Communism, XXIII (March-April):1-13.

OXAAL, I. et al. (1975). Beyond the sociology of development. London: Routledge and Kegan Paul.

PERKINS, D.H. (1975). "Growth and changing structure in China's twentieth-century economy." In D.H. Perkins (ed.), China's modern economy in historical perspective. Stanford: Stanford University Press.

RISKIN, C. (1973). "Maoism and motivation: Work incentives in China." Bulletin of Concerned Asian Scholars, 5 (July):10-24.

_____(1975). "Workers' incentives in Chinese industry." In Joint Economic Committee, Congress of the United States, "China: A reassessment of the economy." Washington, D.C.: U.S. Government Printing Office.

RUBINSON, R. (1976). "The world-economy and the distribution of income within states: A cross-national study." American Sociological Review, 41 (August):638-659.

SCHRAM, P. (1975). "On the Yenan origin of current economic policies." Pp. 379-402 in D.H. Perkins (ed.), China's modern economy in historical perspective. Stanford: Stanford University Press.

SCHURMANN, F. (1964). "China's 'new economic policy'—Transition or beginning?" China Quarterly, 17 (January/March):65-91.

_____ (1968). "The attack of the Cultural Revolution on ideology and organization." In Ping-ti Ho and Tang Tsou (eds.), China in crisis, Vol. 1.

_____(1974). The logic of world power. New York: Pantheon.

SELDEN, M. (1971). The Yenan way in revolutionary China. Cambridge: Harvard University Press.

SEYBOLT, P.J. (1973). Revolutionary education in China. White Plains, N.Y.: International Arts and Sciences Press.

SIDEL, V.W., and SIDEL, R. (1973). Serve the people. Boston: Beacon Press.

SIGURDSON, J. (1975). "Rural industrialization in China." In Joint Economic Committee, Congress of the United States, "China: a Reassessment of the economy." Washington, D.C.: U.S. Government Printing Office.

SKOCPOL, T. (1979). States and social revolutions: A comparative analysis of France, Russia, and China. New York and London: Cambridge University Press.

SOLOMON, R.H. (1971). Mao's revolution and the Chinese political culture. Berkeley: University of California Press.

VOGEL, E. (1967). "From revolutionary to semi-bureaucrat: The 'regularization' of cadres." China Quarterly, 29 (January-March):36-60.

WALLERSTEIN, I. (1974a). "Dependence in an interdependent world: The limited possibilities of transformation within the capitalist world economy." African Studies Review, XVII (April):1-26.

_____(1974b). The modern world-system. Capitalist agriculture and the origins of the European world-economy in the sixteenth century. New York: Academic Press.

_____(1974c). "The rise and future demise of the world capitalist system: Concepts for comparative analysis." Comparative Studies in Society and History, 16 (September):387-375.

_____(1975). "Class-formation in the capitalist world-economy." Politics and Society, 5:367-375.

WEBER, M. (1968). The religion of China. New York: Free Press.

WHITE, G. (1974). "The politics of Hsia-Lsiang youth." China Quarterly, 59 (July/September):491-517.

WHITE, L.T., III. (1976). "Workers' politics in Shanghai." Journal of Asian Studies, XXXVI (November):99-116.

Chapter 11

CONTRADICTIONS OF SEMI-PERIPHERAL DEVELOPMENT: THE SOUTH AFRICAN CASE

Ruth Milkman

Until World War II, South Africa's position in the world-economy as a whole was essentially peripheral. It conformed to the classic pattern of a colonial economy, exporting raw materials, most importantly gold, and importing consumer goods. During and after the war, however, manufacturing industry developed rapidly inside South Africa, fueled by massive foreign investment. Imports of consumer goods were restricted in favor of import substitution industry, and capital goods became the main items on an expanded import bill. The result of this process of dependent capitalist development is that South Africa today is no longer peripheral to the capitalist world-economy, but is now part of what Wallerstein calls the semi-periphery, along with a large group of other countries which combine characteristics of both core and peripheral economies.

This chapter explores the causes and consequences of South Africa's economic development and its relationship to the world capitalist system today. The first part of the argument is that South Africa's movement from peripheral to semi-peripheral status in the

AUTHOR'S NOTE: I am grateful to Fred Black, Michael Burawoy, Linda Collins, Stacey Oliker, Robert Price, Steven Schneider, Kay Trimberger, and Judith van Allen for their very helpful criticisms of earlier drafts of this chapter.

postwar period was made possible by two key factors: its unique role in the international division of labor as the capitalist world's main gold producer, and the fact that the white settlers, and not the African natives, acquired control of the state when the country became independent of Britain. South Africa's achievement of semi-peripheral status, while greatly increasing its power vis-a-vis other nations, especially in Africa, also created new contradictions, and it is these with which the second part of this article is concerned. The new problems are most importantly manifested in chronic and severe balance-of-payments crises, ultimately rooted in technological dependence on the advanced capitalist countries. Finally, the third part of the chapter suggests a link between the social structure of apartheid which emerged in postwar South Africa and that country's location within the world-economy. Indeed, there is a striking resemblance between the development of apartheid in South Africa and that of the "dualism" characteristic of dependent development in some Latin American countries—though the racial dimension is less prominent there.

In putting forth this set of arguments, I want to steer a middle course between two modes of discussion about South Africa's relationship to the world-economy. On the one hand, I want to avoid the pitfalls of most of the Africanist literature on this question, which consists almost entirely of debate as to whether the effect of foreign investment on apartheid is destructive or reinforcing. On the other hand, I want to temper the theoretical arguments put forth in the small but growing body of literature about dependent development, subimperialism, and the semi-periphery, which all too often collapse South Africa with a variety of other countries. While the first approach fails to take account of the importance of the constraints imposed on South African social structure by the world-economy, the second tends to liquidate the unique history and development of specific countries.

In the Africanist literature, until quite recently, the notion that industrialization is accompanied by forces which inexorably erode "ascriptively based" modes of social organization such as apartheid was widely accepted among commentators on South African society (van den Berghe, 1965; Horwitz, 1967; Feit and Stokes, 1976; Adam, 1971; Nickel, 1978). This view has been increasingly criticized, however, both for its crude economic determinism and for its inconsistency with the historical fact of the resilience of apartheid over the course of the rapid industrialization South Africa underwent in the postwar period (Johnstone, 1970; Blumer, 1965; Legassick, 1974;

Wolpe, 1972). In regard to the role of foreign investment, which both sides in the debate see as the key force behind South Africa's industrialization, a counterargument has been developed which views the inflow of foreign capital into South Africa as supportive (rather than undermining) of the ability of the white government to enforce apartheid (First et al., 1973; Kramer and Hultman, 1972; Corporate Information Center, 1973; Gervasi, 1975; Rogers, 1976b).

Nevertheless, the "industrialization erodes apartheid" thesis and its corollary asserting the progressive role of foreign investment continue to reemerge from time to time (Lipton, 1976). To be sure, in response to the recent criticism of this view, some of its adherents have retreated from the position that the corrosive effects of industrialization on economic racism are automatic and now put forth a weaker, more voluntaristic version of the same argument. Indeed, Western companies operating in South Africa now claim to be helping the process of eroding apartheid along by providing a model of nonracialism, which means paying their African employees higher wages, introducing training programs, and facilitating Africans' upward mobility in various other ways.[1] The guiding notion is that South African employers and the government will come to see the advantages of such measures and eventually implement them throughout South Africa.

There are serious difficulties with this position as well, of course. One is that since most foreign firms' operations in South Africa are extremely capital-intensive, they employ very few Africans to begin with. The most generous estimates suggest that 100,000 jobs for Africans may have been created by U.S. direct investments of over $1.5 billion (Blashill, 1972; U.S. Senate Committee Report, 1978). Thus, even if all foreign-controlled companies did practice nonracialism in every respect—which has by no means been the typical case—they would have a minuscule impact on the larger social structure of South Africa. In any case, the ability of any employer to implement genuinely nonracial policies is severly limited by the labor laws which are embodied in the apartheid system. Under the Industrial Conciliation Act, for example, certain jobs can be reserved "for whites only." In addition, the Physical Planning Act restricts the expansion of business operations which would involve an increased number of African employees. Another law prohibits Africans from being members of any trade union which is recognized by the government—and the (white) unions monopolize employment in many skilled occupations (Blashill, 1972; U.S. Senate Committee Report, 1978). When all these factors are considered, the argument that foreign firms can be an effective force for progress in the sphere of South African race relations becomes tenuous indeed.

While the debate over this argument has been a necessary one and obviously has considerable political importance, it is far too narrow in scope, and provides no analysis of South Africa's relationship to the international economic system independent of the specific effects of that relationship on apartheid. In fact, South Africa is not only a racially structured society, but also a highly industrialized capitalist one with strong ties to and dependence on the advanced capitalist countries of the world. This has crucial political implications which must be confronted no matter how the conflict between whites and Africans in South Africa is resolved.

It is here that the theoretical discussion about the world-economy as a whole should be useful. Unfortunately, however, South Africa is among the countries least satisfactorily dealt with in this literature, falling uncomfortably in between the dependent, underdeveloped periphery and the dominant development core. Recently more theoretical attention has been devoted to the countries which fit neither of these two categories, notably in Wallerstein's discussion of the semi-periphery. While a long overdue improvement over the two-category schemes still prevalent in much of the theorizing about international relations in both mainstream and Marxist writing, the semi-periphery remains one of the weakest and most ambiguous components of Wallerstein's framework.

Beyond pointing to (1) the rather obvious fact that semi-peripheral countries are exploited by trade with core countries even as their trade with peripheral countries exploits the latter, and (2) the high degree of state involvement in the economies of these countries, Wallerstein (1974, 1976) has done little to specify what is distinctive about a semi-peripheral location in the world-system—and the second feature is far from distinctive! The category seems to serve as a catchall for all of the countries which elude ready classification in the core or the periphery and thus includes such diverse cases as Canada, China, Iran, and Poland, as well as Brazil and South Africa.[2]

The theories of dependent development and subimperialism are somewhat less inclusive, and avoid the problems intrinsic in collapsing state socialist societies like China and Eastern Europe with the extremely polarized social structures of countries like Brazil and

South Africa. Still, there are important variations among the countries classified as cases of dependent capitalist development, a pheno- menon best described for Latin America. Dependent development is conceptualized as partial capitalist industrialization rather than the stagnation predicted by earlier dependency theory, but a form of industrialization which remains heavily dependent on technological expertise and capital goods transferred from core countries, usually through multinational corporations (Cardoso, 1972; McMichael et al., 1974; Evans, 1975-1976). Yet Mexico, Iran, India, Chile,and South Africa, all of which are among the cases commonly grouped together in this category, vary significantly along such dimensions as the extent of the state's repressive apparatus, and the size and distribution of the revenues received from primary product exports.

The grouping of subimperial powers, those which dominate a region of the periphery politically and economically, is a subset of the dependent development category, and also somewhat less proble- matic. But the theory of subimperialism tells us much more about the complex web of core-periphery relations, in which subimperial count- ries, by definition, are often important intermediaries, than about the various internal social structures of the specific countries involved. In short, these three attempts to theorize about countries which combine features of core and periphery have been far too insensitive to the complex variations among different cases. In order for such efforts to have better success in the future, there must be much more work on specific cases which is informed by broader, comparative questions (e.g., Ehrensaft, 1976). It is in that spirit that the present article is presented.

GOLD, SETTLERS, AND CAPITALIST DEVELOPMENT IN SOUTH AFRICA

The relative success of South African capitalism in overcoming the various problems of dependence and underdevelopment which con- front most countries on the periphery of the world-economy—or what might be called South Africa's successful movement from periphery to semi-periphery—was an achievement predicated on two distinctive features of its national economy. The first is South Africa's role as the capitalist world's main producer of gold and the uniquely secure market which existed for that commodity for most of the twentieth century. The second is the presence inside South Africa of a large population of European settlers who had an interest in autonomous, nationalistic economic development and who played an important political role in the country's movement into the semi-periphery. In addition to the independent effects of these two factors, their interaction was quite significant in that the political power of the settlers was used to augment the proportion of the capital accumulated through the development of gold mining which remained inside the country for use in developing the national economy.

The development of gold mining had tremendous importance in South African economic development from the time of the first major discovery of the mineral there in 1886. Gold very quickly displaced agriculture as the country's main export base, and formed 60% of all South Africa's exports over the years from 1909 to 1937. Mineral products (after gold, diamonds were most important) accounted for three-fourths of its exports during this time, with agricultural products composing most of the balance (Frankel, 1938). Although some sheltered light manufacturing industry did develop in South Africa during this period, most of the consumer goods sold to the settler population were still imported from Europe, and the country was heavily dependent on gold-financed foreign trade for its economic well-being.

Much of the capital accumulated through the development of gold mining was exported, of course, and indeed much of the initial capital invested had come from abroad. But even if only a small percentage of the proceeds had remained in South Africa, the country's benefits would have been far greater than from almost any other primary export industry it might have relied on, due to the uniquely secure market for this particular metal. For more than three-quarters of a century, the entire output of the gold mines in South Africa was readily absorbed into the international monetary system, at a guaranteed price and with no marketing difficulties (*Africa Today*, 1970). This meant much higher aggregate revenues than would have been obtained from any other primary export, for agricultural and mineral commodities typically have extremely unstable prices on the world market. South Africa's experience was particularly distinctive from that of other peripheral nations in this regard during the 1920s and 1930s, when most primary product prices fell but the gold market stayed firm. Indeed, the price of gold actually rose during the Great Depression of the 1930s (First et al., 1973).

Throughout South African history, and particularly in the period after World War II, when secondary manufacturing industry began to develop, gold revenues were critical to the process of economic development. Gold underwrote the success of import substitution and other such policies which required vast imports of expensive capital goods from the advanced capitalist countries to be realized. As we shall see, there were limits to this development even for South Africa, but it is clear that the role of gold as its central industry and main export permitted far more extensive economic growth than was possible in other countries with economies centered around export-oriented agriculture or extractive industry.

The proportion of capital accumulated from the gold industry which remained inside South Africa, furthermore, was far greater than it would have been if not for the actions of the white settlers. The provision of cheap African labor for the gold mines was secured for the mining companies by members of the white settler community, made up of the Afrikaners who had come several centuries before from Holland, and of permanent settlers from Great Britain who were attracted by the gold industry itself. Their role in labor recruitment strengthened the bargaining power of the local interests. Some of the British settlers were eventually integrated into the internationally oriented mining capitalist class, but the other settlers, especially the Afrikaners, excluded from direct participation in the industry which had become the main source of wealth in their country of settlement, organized to impose taxes on the mining houses (Bienefeld and Innes, 1976).

The South African gold industry would have developed much more slowly if not for the role of foreign capital. The initial inputs of capital required to develop the minefields were of a scale inaccessible to the white settlers. Not only did a full 60% of all the capital invested in the country's gold mining industry in this period come from abroad (Frankel, 1938), but technology and skilled labor were also imported from Europe.

Gradually, however, the locally based mining companies gained an advantage over the Europe-based firms, which is not surprising given the settlers' advantages in identifying and pursuing new opportunities to develop the industry. Communications and transportation between South Africa and Europe were not yet developed to the point they are today, and local capital may have been somewhat more willing to take risks. In any case, local share ownership in the mining industry increased from 15% in 1913 to about 40% in the 1930s. The most important single development of this kind was the rise of the Anglo-American Corporation in the 1920s, which despite its name was locally controlled (although initially funded by British and American as well as South African capital), and which has since come to dominate the South African mining industry (Legassick, 1974; Bienefeld and Innes, 1976).

However, the transfer of control from the British mining houses to locally based interests did not in itself change the basic tendency of capital to be exported from South Africa as gold was extracted from its mines. Although Anglo-American's rise was predicated on expanding into new goldfields in South Africa, while mining houses based in Europe invested elsewhere in the world, in a later period when opportunities for further investment in South Africa were perceived as more limited, Anglo-American too shifted an increasing proportion of its capital to the metropolitan economies (Legassick, 1974; Bienefeld and Innes, 1976). Locally based capital in an export-oriented economy, in short, is likely to quickly develop an international orientation, and so the presence of local capital in a peripheral economy does not necessarily do much to alleviate balance of payments difficulties or to curtail the export of capital.

It was therefore not "local" mining interests, but other settler interests directly competing with them for economic power who played the key role in diversifying the South African economy. The growth of the mining industry did stimulate some infrastructural developments, most importantly the railways built soon after the first mines opened to transport the gold from the mines, located inland, to the ports. Other backward linkages led to the development of local enterprises to meet the needs of the mining industry in such areas as construction materials, explosives manufacturing, and engineering workshops (Houghton, 1973). Mining capital may have favored this variety of import substitution, partly because of the special technical problems of deep-vein mining the South African minefields presented, problems which could best be dealt with locally, and probably partly because of the high transport costs which were involved in importing mining equipment in this period. But it was the Boer farmers who took the lead, establishing monopolies on dynamite and railroad building, and placing tariffs on imported goods in an effort to obtain some share of the enormous wealth being created in South Africa by the gold industry.[3]

Mining capital was not interested in South African economic development and bitterly opposed the early protectionist measures which nonmining settler capital obtained from the state and which led to the development of some small scale final-stage import substitution manufacturing and other light industry such as food processing in the 1920s. More important was the state sponsorship in the same decade of basic infrastructural enterprises, also against the protests of mining capital, such as electricity generation (ESCOM) and iron and steel production (ISCOR) (Legassick, 1974; Bienefeld and Innes, 1976; First, et al., 1973). Local industries of all sorts were most successful in periods when imports from Europe were curtailed, as was the case during the Great Depression and during both world wars.

The remarkable extent, relatively speaking, to which capital was diverted into secondary and infrastructural industry in this way was due largely to the presence of large numbers of white settlers in the country, numbers far too large to be incorporated by the mining interests into a single, monolithic group. Both local and foreign mining capital sought to minimize the costs of extracting South Africa's mineral wealth for sale on the international market, and therefore opposed protection and diversification. Nonmining (largely Afrikaner) settler capital, originally accumulated from earnings from agricultural exports, however, sought a share in the country's new wealth through imposing taxes on mining and protective tariffs in order to develop consumer goods industries and infrastructural projects inside South Africa. This set of interests was defeated in the Boer War but then gained a new foothold during World War I when there was a temporary scarcity of goods to be imported from Europe. After the war nonmining capital won some concessions from the state for protection and taxes on the mining industry, and in 1924 this group won control of the state (Bienefeld and Innes, 1976).

The very presence of a large settler community and therefore of these competing capitals was, then, a major spur to economic diversification in South Africa. The settlers, especially the Afrikaners whose domination of the country and of its native population was torn asunder by the growth of British influence in the country and the development of the mines, were resolutely opposed to British capital. In this sense they were essentially anti-imperialist—and indeed Lenin supported the Boers in 1900. Not only in South Africa but also in other British and French colonies, settlers have opposed imperial interests at many historical junctures, although the presence of the Afrikaners complicated the situation relative to that in other British colonies. Arghiri Emmanuel (1972:40) has stated this point well:

> The most difficult struggles of the imperialist countries since the 18th century had not been with the natives in their colonies but with their own settlers. And it should not be forgotten that if England is a second-class power today, this is due to her defeat in a conflict of this type and the subsequent founding of the United States.

Of course, South Africa was much less successful than the United States had been in breaking its bonds of dependence on Great Britain. But this was due largely to the fact that South Africa's industrial development began a full century later than that of the United States. In the early twentieth century, developing the technology necessary to manufacture goods which would be competitive on the world market had become much more complicated than smuggling blueprints out of England. Nevertheless, while South Africa's development is a far cry from that of the United States, or even that of Canada and Australia, there are many parallels between these cases which shed some light on South Africa's economic advancement relative to the periphery as a whole, and the presence of settlers is one of the most striking.

Just as American isolation from the British economy before and during the War of 1812 spurred the development of domestic industry, so the temporary suspension of British imports in South Africa during World War I and again in the 1930s and early 1940s paved the way for the political victory of those South Africans committed to national economic autonomy. Since investment opportunities elsewhere in the world were limited, the gold price rise during the Great Depression led to expansion of investment in the South African gold industry and several new gold fields were developed. At the same time the stagnation of international trade impeded the flow of imports into the country, and thanks to the actions of the nonmining settler capitalists, there was substantial growth of the national economy. This was also the case in several Latin American countries in this period (Bienefeld and Innes, 1976; Horwitz, 1967; Frank, 1972; Cochran and Miller, 1942).

World War II had an even more dramatic impact on industrial production than the Great Depression. Foreign supplies of both consumer goods and primary metals were almost completely cut off, due to widespread conversion from consumer goods production to war production in the United States and Western Europe. Nonmining capital pressed successfully for government measures to spur secondary development in these newly favorable conditions. The capture of state power by the Nationalist party in 1948 was followed, after the war ended and foreign investment revived, by such measures as tariff protection, sometimes guaranteed in advance to induce high-risk investments; import-controls compelling foreign manufacturer-exporters to develop franchises or otherwise directly participate in the South African economy; state financial assistance to investors, with a particular focus on strategic (to economic development), capital-intensive enterprises; and the establishment and expansion of state-run industries (Bienefeld and Innes, 1976; Horwitz, 1967). Such policies emerged earlier and have advanced further in South Africa than elsewhere in the periphery.

The presence of settlers also spurred South Africa's economic development in another respect, by providing a substantial internal market for manufactured products. In the postwar period this market, especially in combinations with the availability of cheap African labor, was a magnet for direct foreign investment in manufacturing industry. All commentators on the subject and all of the parties involved agree that the involvement of foreign capital has been absolutely crucial to South Africa's economic growth. For example, the South African Reserve Bank, surely the party least interested in acknowledging such dependency, has stated that (Rogers, 1976:97):

> In the long run, South Africa has to a large extent been dependent on foreign capital for development purposes. . . . It is still highly dependent on foreign capital, particularly risk capital, to achieve a relatively high rate of growth.

> The relatively high rate of growth experienced by the South African economy during the past three years (1969-1971) was, therefore, only achieved with an increase in the relative importance of foreign funds in the financing of gross domestic investment.

Foreign capital was first attracted to South Africa in large quantities in the late nineteenth century, after the discoveries of diamonds and, more importantly, gold. Nearly two-thirds of all the capital invested from abroad in the fifty years after 1886, the year of the first major gold discovery, went into mining, with gold mines absorbing by far the largest share. Of the balance, about two-fifths was invested in agriculture, commerce, and industry and three-fifths in financial and real estate companies (Frankel, 1938). Gold mining alone accounted for half of the total foreign capital present in South Africa in this period, reflecting its centrality as the most dynamic sector of the economy at that time (Frankel, 1938).

But foreign investments were even more important to the development of secondary manufacturing industry in the years after World War II, and at this point South Africa's relatively large internal market was a significant drawing card, along with Nationalist Party policies encouraging investment. The total sum invested from abroad in the postwar period is three times the estimated cumulative total in all of South Africa's previous history (Rogers, 1976). Manufacturing overtook mining's share of Gross Domestic Product in this period and also replaced it as the key magnet for foreign capital. Locally based South African capital, most importantly the Oppenheimer empire controlling the giant De Beers (formerly owned by Cecil Rhodes himself) and Anglo-American corporations, had gradually increased its share of the mining sector, and foreign investors shifted the bulk of their holdings into manufacturing (First, et al., 1973; *The New York Times,* 1977c). Of all the foreign investment in the country (direct and indirect) today, about 40% is in the manufacturing sector of the economy, although less than 25% of the country's gross domestic product is in that sector (*Business Week,* 1976).

Investments in manufacturing industry tended to be direct rather than indirect or portfolio investments, and frequently took the form of subsidiary companies tied to a parent firm in the West. In the South African mining industry, postwar British investment has typically been indirect, but by 1969 direct investment formed 78% of British holdings in South Africa. U.S. investment has generally involved the establishment of wholly owned subsidiaries of American companies inside South Africa, with 80% of foreign investment from the dollar area taking this form in 1969 (First et al., 1973). Nearly 75% of all U.S. direct investments in South Africa, which skyrocketed in the postwar period from only $50 million in 1943 to over $1.6 billion today (U.S. Department of Commerce, 1976), are controlled by only 12 major multinational corporations, although over 300 U.S. firms are involved in the country (Rogers, 1976b).

The massive inflow of foreign capital into South Africa which occurred after World War II was clearly essential to the postwar economic development of that country, and to its movement from the periphery to the semi-periphery. But if not for the historical accident that South Africa became the main source of the capitalist world's gold, and the presence of a large population of European settlers, in all probability foreign investment in secondary manufacturing industry would have been far less extensive, and the transformation of South Africa from a peripheral to a semi-peripheral nation might not have taken place.

CONTRADICTIONS OF SEMI-PERIPHERAL DEVELOPMENT

South Africa's achievement of semi-peripheral status has strengthened its national economy greatly, particularly in relation to the rest of sub-Saharan Africa. But like other semi-peripheral countries, despite its unique advantages, the contemporary South African economy is faced with a number of very serious problems constraining its further development. These have become particularly acute in recent years as a result of the world-wide economic contraction of the 1970s, but their origins lie in a situation which had already taken shape when that contraction began.

The first problem area is trade and the balance of payments. While returns from the export of gold have certainly moderated the country's trade difficulties, as we have seen, the underlying dynamic of trade between South Africa and the West has clearly been detrimental to South Africa's development over the long term. Despite the country's extraordinary ability to attract foreign investment—itself partly attributable to the presence of gold—much more capital has been exported from South Africa than has been invested there from abroad. Gold was extracted from the country at minimal costs by European capitalists, and their profits were reinvested in the metropolitan economies or reinvested to expand their extraction of gold from South Africa for export.

In addition, despite the large-scale growth of manufacturing industry in South Africa during and after World War II, the country continues to be heavily dependent on exports of primary products. In 1972, 60% of its exports consisted of gold, diamonds, and other raw materials, with gold alone accounting for 37%. Agricultural products constituted another 12% of the total. South Africa's dependence on primary exports is significantly less than it was before World War II, however, with finished manufactured goods making up 17% of all exports in 1972.[4] Yet continuing heavy reliance on raw material exports makes the country's balance of payments quite vulnerable to price fluctuations on the world commodity markets. Gold, of course, was until recently an exceptional primary product in this respect.

While its mineral exports go primarily to the industrialized countries of the world, South Africa's manufactured goods are not competitive in those countries' markets. Yet the severely constricted purchasing power of the black majority of its own population drastically limits South Africa's internal market for consumer durables. That the country has developed a large capacity for manufacturing production, which today generates 22% of its gross domestic product (*Business Week,* 1976), makes it quite dependent on exporting manufactured goods to independent black African countries, where they enjoy the natural advantages of low transport costs and shorter delivery times than comparable products from the U.S., Japan, or Western Europe. South Africa supplies about 80% of the trade in the southern Africa region, and exports to African countries account for about 15% of its total exports, so that this trade is clearly an important source of foreign exchange for the country (First et al., 1973; IMF, 1974). Although this arrangement is to some extent a politically volatile one, it is both more extensive and more stable than the rhetoric of most of the independent black African nations involved might lead one to believe.

Imports of consumer goods, once making up the bulk of South Africa's import bill, have gradually diminished in volume as a result of protectionist policies, but at the same time the development of consumer goods industries inside South Africa has required substantial imports of technologically advanced, expensive capital goods from the metropolitan countries. In 1959, 36% of all imports, by value, were made up of machinery and transport equipment and by 1972 the proportion had risen to 48%. In that year, another 24% of imports consisted of mineral products, chemicals, plastics, and base metals (Gervasi, 1975). The capital-intensive nature of most of its imports gives South Africa little flexibility in its trade relations with most industrialized countries of the world. The United States, Western Europe, and Japan provided 80% of South Africa's imports in 1973 (IMF, 1974). The single largest source of the country's imports is now the United States, although until 1976 it was Britain (U.S. Senate, 1978).

South Africa also imports large quantities of oil, one of the few natural resources of which it has no domestic source. Although the country has rich deposits of coal and relies on oil for less than one-fourth of its energy needs, its import bill in 1976 for this commodity alone was $1.2 billion. About 80% of South Africa's oil comes from Iran, a country with which it has developed close political ties. This makes an effective embargo by the oil-exporting countries on South

African sales unlikely, but the government is taking no chances here and has stockpiled oil reserves estimated at a three years' supply (*New York Times*, 1976).

Despite substantial and somewhat successful efforts to reduce import dependency through import substitution policies, South Africa's imports and exports are each worth about one-fourth of the gross domestic product (Rogers, 1976b). Given an increasing import bill due to rising capital goods and oil prices, and such heavy reliance on exports composed largely of primary products, it is not especially surprising that South Africa has a chronic trade deficit. From 1961 to 1969, total imports increased by over 100% in value and exports by only 50% (Rogers, 1976b). And the balance on current account has been negative in every year but one since 1964 (South African Reserve Bank, 1977).

Throughout South Africa's history, gold has played an important role in financing the country's heavy import bill, as we have seen. Exports of the metal, particularly after the price rises of the early 1970s, have substantially lessened the severity of South Africa's balance of payments problem at many points. However, there has been a gradual decline in the adequacy of gold for this purpose as the import bill has skyrocketed. Gold exports financed 50% of South Africa's imports in 1961, but only 40% in 1969 (Rogers, 1976b). Moreover, now that the United States has abandoned the gold standard and its price fluctuates so widly on the world market, gold is a much less reliable source of trade stability. The long-term problem was obscured by the steep price increases which occurred in the immediate aftermath of the abandonment of the gold standard in the early 1970s, but once the windfall period comes to an end a fall in total Southern African gold production is expected. The import bill, however, will continue to grow, so that the long-run prospect is one of a widening gap between gold sales and the import bill.

The new instability in the gold price is likely to aggravate the situation further, as was made painfully obvious when the South African balance of payments deficit grew to crisis proportions as the price of gold fell from a 1975 average of $165 per ounce to $114 in mid-1976, cutting the country's 1976 revenues by over $1 billion. Other factors have also contributed to the present crisis, of course, most importantly a falling off in new capital investment due to the world recession (and probably exacerbated to some extent by the Soweto insurrection of the summer), and the huge rise in the oil import bill. In 1975, South Africa had a trade deficit of $1.7 billion, and in the second quarter of 1976 it was up to an annual rate of $2.4 billion (*New York Times*, 1976). This balance-of-payments crisis is much more serious than any since the crisis of the early 1960s, when the Sharpeville massacre prompted a flight of foreign capital.

The international bank loans which rescued South Africa from that crisis were extended this time as well, but in the 1970s, unlike the 1960s, a revival of investor confidence may not be sufficient to pull the economy out of its slump. This is because of the long-term changes underlying the current crisis, most importantly the increase in import dependency which accompanied the boom in industrialization of the 1960s. The intensity of the current crisis is manifest in the fact that from 1974 to 1976, international loans to South Africa nearly tripled in volume, increasing by $5.5 billion, and nearly doubled as a proportion of total foreign investment. By the end of 1976, South Africa's overseas debt totaled $7.6 billion (U.S. Senate, 1978). There has already been some improvement in the situation, with a relatively satisfactory balance of payments picture for 1977, including some repayments of international loans (*South African Digest*, 1978). But this was achieved by extremely conservative fiscal and monetary policies in conjunction with a fortuitous recovery in the price of gold.

The only viable long-term solution to the balance-of-payments problem, however, is for the country to develop an independent capacity to produce capital goods and to develop technology. South Africa is attempting this in some areas, but the process is extremely difficult today given the sophistication of technology in the metropolitan countries and the fact that the technology upon which the program of import substitution has been based has been supplied by transnational companies.

Indeed, South Africa's need to import specific goods which are required for industrial development and which are unavailable inside the country is closely linked to its heavy dependence on foreign investments. To some extent, of course, capital invested from abroad directly facilitates the securing of such commodities by providing foreign exchange to help finance them (Brand, 1962). In the case of direct investments, moveover, the presence of subsidiaries of Western companies inside the country guarantees access to the technologically advanced goods which comprise such a large part of the total import bill, and which are critical to the future growth and diversification of the economy.

Without foreign investment, indeed, South Africa's industrial sector would be almost nonexistent. Foreign capital was estimated by the Afrikaner Chamber of Commerce in 1971 to control 80% of all industrial production, directly or indirectly (Rogers, 1976b). U.S. investments in South Africa have figured particularly prominently in high-technology sectors which are clearly critical to economic development, such as energy, heavy engineering, computers, and motor vehicles. For example, the "Big Three" American automobile manufacturers produce more than 60% of South Africa's vehicles, and IBM controls half of the computer market (Rogers, 1976b). West European and Japanese firms control the rest of these and other high-technology industries in South Africa, reflecting the monopoly the advanced capitalist countries exercise over these kinds of production.

South Africa's continuing dependence on exports of primary products and the inability of its manufacturing exports to compete in export markets outside the African continent, which has already been discussed, are essentially a product of this technological dependence. Moreover, the desire to increase export competitiveness in manufacturing maintains downward pressure on African wages and thus prevents expansion of the internal market. The high rate of African unemployment, which is made more severe by the importation of advanced capital-intensive industrial technology, also constrains the growth of the internal market. The small internal market and limited opportunities for export in turn make extremely difficult the financing of domestic capital goods manufacturing capability and the research and development infrastructure needed to develop technological autonomy. Thus, South African development remains highly dependent on direct investment from the metropolitan countries, and shows every prospect of continuing dependence.

APARTHEID AND THE CAPITALIST
WORLD-ECONOMY

South Africa's social structure is unique among industrial capitalist countries in its rigid construction of class boundaries almost perfectly correlated with racial boundaries. As was noted earlier in reviewing the Africanist literature on South Africa's relationship to the international economy, its racial structure is often seen as an obstacle to industrialization and thus also to direct foreign investment. But in fact racial segmentation has facilitated the economic development of South Africa and its movement from periphery to semi-periphery, and today, in turn, South Africa's semi-peripheral location in the international economy structurally reinforces the apartheid system.

The availability of "cheap" African labor has been and remains crucial to the profitability of the South African gold mining industry. The price offered for gold on the world market is fixed, so that mining it is only profitable if the total costs of production are significantly lower than this price. Since capital costs are relatively inelastic, there is an imperative toward squeezing wage costs. Given the strong craft union traditions of the white skilled miners who came to South Africa from Britain and continental Europe and militantly resisted the efforts of employers to substitute African labor for their own, the inevitable victims of this imperative were the African miners. Once the white workers had achieved a monopoly over skilled jobs, to maintain the same returns on its investments, mining capital had to keep the real wages of nonwhite workers—still the bulk of the labor force—constant, or to decrease them. The ratio of white to black wages therefore widened from 11:1 in 1926, to 16:1 in 1956, and to 20:1 in 1969 (Wilson, 1972a), although the increases in the price of gold and new difficulties in labor recruitment from neighboring countries have led to some narrowing of the gap in the 1970s.

In order to depress wage costs, the South African mining companies cooperated very early on in setting up a monopsonistic labor recruitment agency, the Chamber of Mines, and in eliminating wage competition among employers (Wilson, 1972a). The industry also pioneered in the use of migrant labor, which has the advantage of lower reproduction costs than permanent, settled workers require. Many other features of what later was called apartheid were first developed in the gold mining industry, including the job reservation system which established certain jobs as "for whites only."

Part of the explanation for all of this is that South Africa's gold-bearing ore is of very low quality, "so low-grade that the mines could never have been opened up if their labour force had had to be paid 'European' rates" (First et al., 1973:117). Thus, the very existence of the gold-mining industry, which, as we have seen, laid the basis for South Africa's economic development, was dependent on the social structure which channeled the bulk of the country's income to the small white population and preserved a "cheap" labor force of Africans.

While mining capital was not the main force behind apartheid, and at times opposed racialist measures in hopes of replacing white workers with cheaper African workers, it ultimately benefitted from the apartheid system as much as the Afrikaner nationalists. Far from being an obstacle to industrialization, then, South Africa's unique racial structure was crucial to the success of the gold industry which, as we have seen, was a key underpinning of its movement from a peripheral to a semi-peripheral position within the world-economy.

In the period of secondary industrialization, too, South Africa's extremely polarized distribution of income has been quite advantageous for capital accumulation, especially by foreign capital, creating as it does a sizeable market for consumer durables with relatively high capital-output ratios (Ehrensaft, 1976). Although there are limits to the growth possible once this market is saturated, as we have seen, it nevertheless can make the difference between partial, dependent industrialization and little or none at all. Indeed, a similar market structure helps account for the Brazilian "economic miracle," another case of successful movement from periphery to semi-periphery (Ehrensaft, 1976).

In fact, there seems to be a striking parallel between South Africa's apartheid system and the social structures, in most cases not racially based, of other semi-peripheral countries at a comparable level of industrialization. Consider, for example, Cardoso's (1972:90-91) description of the effects of dependent industrialization in Latin America:

> . . . there is an internal structural fragmentation, connecting the most "advanced" parts of their economies to the international capitalist system. Separate although subordinated to these advanced sectors, the backward economic and social sectors of the dependent countries then play the role of "internal colonies." The gap between both will probably increase, creating a new type of dualism. . . . It results directly, of course, from capitalist expansion and is functional to that expansion, in so far as it helps to keep wages at a low level and diminishes political pressure inside the "modern" sector, since the social and economic position of those who belong to the latter is always better in comparative terms.

This passage could easily be mistaken for a description of South Africa. That country's economic development has been highly centralized, with most industry concentrated in four main areas—the southern Transvaal, where the mining industry is centered and which has also become a major manufacturing district, and the three port cities of Cape Town, Durban, and Port Elizabeth (Houghton, 1973). Surely the Bantustans are "separate although subordinated to these advanced sectors," both politically and economically, and moreover they have become increasingly impoverished as the economic development of the industrial centers has progressed (Rogers, 1976a). Cardoso's analysis of this "new type of dualism" as resulting from and functional to capitalist expansion is also borne out in the case of Southern Africa in much of the commentary on the relationship of the Bantustans to the economy as a whole (Wolpe, 1972; Wilson, 1972b).

The "dualism" Cardoso describes is characteristically based on an alliance between the semi-peripheral state and international capital. Although historically the interests of the South African government and the foreign companies which have investment there have frequently come into conflict—and indeed the state's economic nationalism was very important in making possible South Africa's successful movement into the semi-periphery, as we have seen—the key conlicts have been over the terms of trade and investments, not over apartheid. In fact, in regard to the latter the interests of the South African state and international capital coincide to a large extent in that the effects of underdevelopment are borne entirely by the African population, whose exploitation enriches both South African whites as a group and the foreign companies. Again there is a strong resemblance to the situation in other countries where a small part of the population enjoys the benefits of economic growth even as the inequality between this minority and the rest of the population increases with economic development (Evans, 1975-1976).

What is critical is that the particular form of racial domination structured so centrally into South African society is of no particular concern to international capital, except in so far as it presents certain practical difficulties for it (e.g., the white labor shortage), and that, on the whole, the repressive capacity of the South African state is very much in the interests of international capital. Again the comparative evidence is important, for most of the other countries in the Third World with high rates of "fragmented industrialization" are police states of one sort or another also. It has in fact been argued that such highly repressive regimes as those governing Iran, Brazil, South Korea, etc., are politically necessary for the stability of the dependent industral economies of such nations (Evans, 1975-1976; McMichael et al., 1974).

Surely in South Africa the shift from indirect to direct investment has given foreign investors an increased stake in the political stability of the country. Portfolio investments can be withdrawn in a crisis much more easily than can a subsidiary plant operation, and so direct investors are likely to be more committed to bolstering the country up when its stability is threatened. This is well illustrated by the events which followed the 1960 Sharpeville massacre. All around the world, foreign investors withdrew large volumes of capital from South Africa in 1961, fearing that a revolution would occur there. Indeed, Sharpeville occurred in a period in which the wave of independence was rapidly sweeping the African continent and after a decade of widespread African resistance to the Nationalist government.

The principal effect of this outflow of foreign capital was on the stock market, and South Africa's foreign reserves were depleted by nearly 50%. During this 1961 panic, however, American corporations increased their direct investments in South Africa by $23 million, and American financiers made emergency loans of $85 million to the South African government. In the next five years, from 1961 to 1966, new U.S. investment averaged over $33 million each year, providing vitally needed capital inflow to the shaky regime and economy. The total inflow of foreign capital revived once the government's strength and the substantial American willingness to underwrite it became clear (Rogers, 1976b).

Looking at the parallels between South Africa and other semiperipheral countries helps make sense out of these actions and the subsequent support of American corporations and the U.S. government for the apartheid regime in South Africa. They are not some quirk or aberration of U.S. policy, but are thoroughly consistent with the interests of international capital, and in this sense it is clear that South Africa's apartheid system is bolstered by its location within the world-economy.

CONCLUSION

South Africa's economic development since the development of the mining industry in the late nineteenth century has followed a highly unusual course. Because of the unique marketability of gold, the country's primary export, and because of the role of nonmining white settler capital in channelling some of the capital accumulated in the mining sector into secondary industry, South Africa has been more successful in developing economically than other peripheral countries, even the most industrialized. Import substitution has been able to proceed further, a modicum of autonomous technological capacity has been developed, and balance of payments difficulties, at least until very recently, have been less severe than elsewhere in the Third World.

On the other hand, there are striking parallels between South Africa's pattern of development and that of other peripheral countries, particularly those which have been able to significantly develop secondary industry. A high degree of dependence on primary exports and capital-intensive imports of metropolitan technology is a serious problem for South Africa, just as it is for Brazil. The incorporation of a small minority of the population into the metropolitan social organization and the concomitant intensification of the exploitation of those excluded from this sector is not a pattern unique to the apartheid system, but one also found in other "developing" countries on the periphery—lacking, however, the racial dimension. It is not possible to determine precisely how much of the resemblance is due to the Nationalist government's policy of apartheid and how much of it is a product of the international context in which South Africa has developed, but connecting South Africa to the pattern of "dependent development" found elsewhere certainly points to the importance of the international context for understanding the internal dynamics of South African society. The persistence of the apartheid system, then, must be understood not simply as a product of the success of Afrikaner Nationalism, but as a structural consequence of South Africa's links to the world-economy.

NOTES

1. *New York Times* (1977a). The most recent expression of this position was the March 1977 announcement by 12 major U.S. corporations, later endorsed by many more firms, of six principles "aimed to end segregation" and "to promote fair employment practices" at their plants and other facilities in South Africa.

2. Wallerstein (1974:9-16). Discussion of the strategies peripheral countries can use to move into the semi-periphery is more fruitful, however. He specifies three possible strategies: "seizing the chance," "promotion by invitation," and "self-reliance." To a large extent, these strategies result in three distinct patterns of development, as he acknowledges. "Seizing the chance," which essentially involves import-substitution during a period of world economic contraction, results in more extensive industrial development than the second path, that of "promotion by invitation," which occurs during periods of world economic expansion and at the "invitation" of core powers. South Africa is cited as a case of the former, while for the latter Wallerstein points to the Ivory Coast after independence as an example. "Self-reliance," the third strategy, is that employed by socialist states such as China. Distinguishing among these three strategies and the particular types of semi-peripheral countries they result in is indeed useful. But it again points to the fact that as a category, the semi-periphery represents an amalgam of countries with a wide variety of development patterns, more diverse than core or periphery.

3. Ehrensaft (1976:74-75). He states, however, that mining capital took the lead in establishing these industries. He presents no evidence that this was the case.

4. State of South Africa (1975). Computed from data therein.

REFERENCES

ADAM, H. (1971). Modernizing racial domination: South Africa's political dynamics. Berkeley: University of California Press.

Africa Research Group (1974). Race to power: The struggle for Southern Africa. New York: Anchor Books.

Africa Today (1970). "A historical study: South Africa's gold industry." Special issue on "Apartheid and imperialism: A study of U.S. corporate involvement in South Africa," 17 (5):30-32.

ARRIGHI, G., and SAUL, J.S. (1973). "Nationalism and revolution is Sub-Saharan Africa." In G. Arrighi and J.S. Saul (eds.), Essays on the political economy of Africa. New York: Monthly Review Press.

BIENEFELD, M., and INNES, D. (1976). "Capital accumulation and South Africa." Review of African Political Economy, 7:40-42.

BLASHILL, J. (1972). "The proper role of U.S. corporations in South Africa." Fortune, July.

BLUMER, H. (1965). "Industrialization and race relations." In G. Hunter (ed.), Industrialization and race relations: A symposium. London: Oxford University Press.

BRAND, S.S. (1962). "The relation between economic growth and external balance in South Africa." South African Journal of Economics, 30:301-309.

Business Week (1976). "Doing business with South Africa." Special Advertising Section, 2459 (November 22):27.

CARDOSO, F. (1972). "Dependency and development in Latin America." New Left Review, 74 (July-August):83-95.

COCHRAN, T.C., and MILLER, W. (1942). The age of enterprise: A social history of industrial America. New York: Macmillan.

Corporate Information Center (1973). Church investments, corporations, and Southern Africa. New York: National Council of Churches.

The Economist (1968). "The green bay tree." 227 (6514):ix-xlvi.

EHRENSAFT, P. (1976). "Polarized accumulation and the theory of economic dependence: The implications of South African semi-industrial capitalism." Pp. 58-89 in P.C.W. Gutkind and I. Wallerstein (eds.), The political economy of contemporary Africa. Beverly Hills, Cal.: Sage.

EMMANUEL, A. (1972). "White-settler colonialism and the myth of investment imperialism." New Left Review, 73 (May-June):35-55.

EVANS, P. (1975-1976). "Industrialization and imperialism: Growth and stagnation on the periphery." Berkeley Journal of Sociology, XX:113-145.

FEIT, E., and STOKES, R.G. (1976). "Racial prejudice and economic pragmatism: A South African case-study." Journal of Modern African Studies, 14 (3):487-506.

FIRST, R. et al. (1973). The South African connection: Western investment in apartheid. Middlesex, England: Penguin.

FRANK, A.G. (1972). "The development of underdevelopment." In J.D. Cockroft et al. (eds.), Dependence and underdevelopment: Latin America's political economy. New York: Anchor.

FRANKEL, S.H. (1938). Capital investment in Africa: Its course and effects. London: Oxford University Press.

GERVASI, S. (1970). Industrialization, foreign capital and forced labour in South Africa. United Nations: Unit on Apartheid.

———(1975). "The politics of 'accelerated economic growth'." In L. Thompson and J. Butler (eds.), Change in contemporary South Africa. Berkeley: University of California Press.

HORWITZ, R. (1967). The political economy of South Africa. New York: Praeger.
HOUGHTON, D.H. (1973). The South African economy. London: Oxford University Press.
International Monetary Fund (1974). Direction of trade. (June).
JOHNSTONE, F.A. (1970). "White prosperity and white supremacy in South Africa today." African Affairs, 69 (275):124-140.
KRAMER, R., and HULTMAN, T. (1972). "The impact of U.S. investment in Southern Africa." Social Action, 38(7):4-11.
LEGASSICK, M. (1974). "South Africa: Capital accumulation and violence." Economy and Society, 3(3):253-291.
LIPTON, M. (1976). "British investment in South Africa: Is constructive engagement possible?" South African Labour Bulletin, 3(3):10-48.
McMICHAEL, P. et al. (1974). "Imperialism and the contradictions of development." New Left Review, 85:83-140.
New York Times (1976). "Flight of capital is a cause for concern in South Africa." October 11:41-42.
_____(1977a). "12 big concerns in South Africa set equality in plants." March 2:45.
_____(1977b). "South Africans converting coal into motor fuel." June 1:1, 49.
_____(1977c). "From Siberia to 47th Street, De Beers is king of diamonds." October 16:1, 43.
NICKEL, H. (1978). "The case for doing business in South Africa." Fortune, 197 (12):60-74.
ROGERS, B. (1976a). Divide and rule: South Africa's Bantustans. London: International Defense and Aid Fund.
_____(1976b). White wealth and black poverty: American investments in Southern Africa. Westport, Conn.: Greenwood.
South African Digest (1978). February 17:8.
South African Reserve Bank (1976). Second census of foreign transactions, liabilities, and assets, 31 December 1973 (supplement to Quarterly Bulletin), 2.
_____(1977). South Africa's balance of payments, 1956-1975 (supplement to Quarterly Bulletin), A-1, A-2.
State of South Africa (1975). State of South Africa: Economic, financial, and statistical yearbook for the Republic of South Africa. Johannesburg: Da Gama.
U.S. Department of Commerce (1976). Survey of current business, August:49.
U.S. Senate (1978). U.S. corporate interests in Africa. A report to Senate Committee on Foreign Relations, January. Washington, D.C.: U.S. Government Printing Office.
VAN DEN BERGHE, P. (1965). South Africa: A study of conflict. Berkeley: University of California Press.
WALLERSTEIN, I. (1974). "Dependence in an interdependent world: The limited possibilities of transformation within the capitalist world economy." African studies review, XVII (1):1-26.
_____(1976). "Semi-peripheral countries and the contemporary world crisis." Theory and Society, 3(4).
WILSON, F. (1972a). Labour in the South African gold mines, 1911-1969. Cambridge: Cambridge University Press.
_____(1972b). Migrant labour in South Africa. Johannesburg: South African Council of Churches and SPRO-CAS.
WOLPE, H. (1972). "Capitalism and cheap labour-power in South Africa: From segregation to apartheid." Economy and Society, 1 (4):425-456.

Chapter 12

THE RUBBER PLANTATIONS OF COLONIAL INDOCHINA: THE COLONIAL STATE AND THE CLASS STRUGGLE BETWEEN WAGE-LABOR AND CAPITAL, 1910-1940[1]

Martin J. Murray

We can be assured that there exists in no part of the world agricultural enterprises better organized, better managed, and better improved than particular great plantations in Cochinchina. [Statement of Auguste Chevalier, Chief of the permanent Mission of Agriculture for the Ministry of Colonies, after having visited the principal plantations of Java, Malaya, and Ceylon.][2]

We are starving. The French have sparkling wine. We eat spoiled rice, the French have roast beef and bread. Our houses are small and smell awful, those of the French are spacious and are at the top of the hill. The family of the proprietor bathes in fresh cow's milk. Kiki, the proprietor's dog, enjoys brandy more than cheese. Our children crawl painfully, the dust-colored and spoiled rice, it is necessary that they force it down! These children are also people who have feelings and rights. Who, after seeing these unfortunate children, is not distressed!

Brothers and sisters! Let us get quickly into step. Let us fight for our dignity, let us destroy this barbarous enterprise.

Rubber has been given more value than human beings. Every time that a rubber tree is sick, it is rested. . . . The foliage of the rubber trees is a

magnificent green, each tree fattens itself on the bodies of dead workers.
[Brocheux, 1975:69]

INTRODUCTION: THE SUBORDINATION OF WAGE-LABOR TO CAPITAL

In colonial Indochina, rubber cultivation became one of the chief
arenas in which metropolitan capital directly organized the actual
labor process. The principal export commodity, rice, was characterized by landlord-tenant production relations. Rubber production was
different. The typical unit of enterprise was the joint-stock concessionary company where the main financial (and administrative) seat of
operations remained in Paris (or any number of other large metropolitan cities). Metropolitan firms mobilized the requisite private
venture capital and converted it into constant capital (equipment,
tools, supplies, transport facilities, rudimentary processing operations, land) and variable capital (unskilled and semiskilled native
wage-labor combined with European senior managerial staffs). The
typical unit of production was the large-scale agricultural plantation
located in the rich rubber-growing regions of northern Cochinchina
and southern Annam. The primary goal of these metropolitan operations was to organize the capitalist labor process in such a manner that
unit costs remained sufficiently lower than the prices which could be
obtained on the world market, thereby guaranteeing at least normal
rates of profit.

The essence of capitalist exploitation in colonial rubber production
rested on the ability of plantation owners to compel wage-laborers to
perform surplus-labor. Capital accumulation remained subject to the
particular historical conditions of the struggle where wage-laborers
(either collectively or individually) attempted to set definite limits to
the self-expansion of value. In the period between 1910-1940,
colonial rubber production enterprises first originated, then developed, and matured. The capitalist labor process during this specific
historical conjuncture became the site of spontaneous and intense
class struggles. Yet from the point of view of wage-labor, these class

struggles at the point of production operated within definite limits. These struggles where wage-labor resisted concrete developments or operations of the capitalist labor process suffered from the very fact that their origins were more or less defensive. The class struggles of the rubber plantation workers during the turbulent 1920s and 1930s did not reach the level of action, organization, or strategy which would have allowed them to form the basis for general class unification at the level of politics. Nevertheless, these struggles formed the basis for the political struggle that emerged during the 1940s and which eventually did overturn the double yoke of colonial domination and capitalist property relations.

CAPITALIST PRODUCTION AND THE IDEOLOGY OF COLONIAL RULE

The formation of the European rubber plantations in colonial Indochina coincided with the growth of the world demand for rubber. As world demand outstretched the available supply, metropolitan capital poured into the fertile rubber-cultivating regions of Indochina in search of profitable investments. Metropolitan rubber production in colonial Indochina was organized along strict capitalist lines, i.e., it involved, first, the evolution of specific *production relations* where the mode of appropriation of surplus-labor took place exclusively through the circulation of commodities; and second, the formation of a particular *labor process* where capital took command of the organization of the relations of the direct producers to one another and to their instruments and tools of production within the immediate activity or producing commodities. Seen from a broader scale, metropolitan capital was compelled to operate within certain structural constraints which were independent of the will of individual entrepreneurs, that is, in order to ensure the profitability of rubber cultivation in Indochina, the price of production had to remain below the price which could be obtained on the world market. It was in this respect that metropolitan capital worked hand-in-hand with the colonial state administration. Private capital accumulation in rubber production required state aid in four crucial areas: first, the provision of land concessions free-of-charge in order to get rubber cultivation initially underway and also to encourage its further extension; second, the elimination of capital's recurrent difficulties with labor shortages by sanctioning the system of private labor recruitment, by enforcing the semi-servile terms of the three-year contract, and by restricting the geographical mobility of labor-power through the adoption of modified pass laws; third, the payment of production premiums to threatened planters during the 1930s when production costs exceeded world market prices; and fourth, the concerted efforts to short-circuit the emergence of a widespread and coordinated workers' movement by suffocating the traditional instruments through which workers have historically responded to capitalist exploitation, through collective bargaining, trade unions, and public gatherings designed to express demands and petition for the redress of grievances.

Correlatively, a certain ideological perspective buttressed the colonial system in general and capitalist production in particular. European planters, their local agents, and colonial administrators maintained a particularly exclusive and narrow view of the European mission and their own obligations and privileges within it. The following statement by Hervé Bazin, the owner-supervisor of the largest recruitment agency in Tonkin, illustrates what emerged as the dominant values of the colonial environment: "It is truly necessary to be the father and mother to the individual (the Tonkinese *coolie*) who thinks and acts again and again with the thoughtlessness of an infant."[3] Europeans commonly viewed plantation inhabitants as innate liars and gamblers who lacked initiative, resourcefulness, and thrift. These opinions produced a quasi-uniform code of behavior and widespread sense of camaraderie among the European inhabitants of Indochina. The high degree of European consensus reinforced the paternalistic outlook toward the native population. These attitudes in turn provided the colonial justification for the ruthless discipline, appalling working conditions, and maintenance of the type of guardianship associated with the plantation compound system.

THE WORKERS' RESPONSE: SINGULAR AND COLLECTIVE

In order to understand the way in which native wage-laborers responded to the conditions they encountered on the European rubber plantations, it is necessary first to recount the socio-economic situation from whence they came. Contract workers emigrated from closed corporate villages in Tonkin and northern Annam which were characterized by a certain degree of communal solidarity, despite the internal tensions and developing class antagonisms. Most workers who left the relative security of village life were young, able-bodied, male, and virtually landless. They nearly always left behind their wives, children, and parents. The overwhelming majority of recruited workers were preoccupied with the longing to return to their natal villages at the expiration of their contract as soon as they had acquired sufficient cash savings to meet their yearly colonial tax obligations and to service village debts. These so-called "target workers" had little or no intention of remaining in the position of full-time proletarians. Put in another way, without the combination of social differentiation in the northern villages (resulting in the formation of a class of landless—or virtually landless—subsistence cultivators) and administrative compulsion (colonial tax obligations backed by state sanctions such as fines, imprisonment, or the *corvée*), the native population would have had no reason to seek employment on the rubber plantations.

However, once they reached the plantations, workers tended to group themselves into various socio-cultural associations, mutual aid societies, and sport and dance clubs. These somewhat informal and voluntary organizations were obstensibly formed at least partially to compensate for the absence of the twin pillars of native social life around which all socio-cultural events and activities took place: the village commune and the extended family. These organizations had considerable appeal to young workers just recently uprooted from the fortified and insular social matrix of traditional family and village life. Yet, at the same time, the primary function of most of these workers' associations was collective protection against the fear of mistreatment and extortion often practiced by malevolent supervisors. In specific, various mutual aid societies provided at least rudimentary social insurance against destitution and indebtedness frequently resulting from prolonged sickness or work-related injuries. The plantation management found itself hard-pressed to object to many of these forms of workers' self-organization, particularly when they provided the type of social-security services which the plantation owners were unwilling to offer themselves. Nevertheless, the long-term effect of these autonomous workers' activities was to enlarge the horizon of the *coolies* because they transcended the traditional village and provincial affinities. Most importantly, the practical experience gained by the plantation workers who experimented with new organizational forms and patterns of leadership proved invaluable in the clandestine planning for the major strikes which took place on a number of plantations during the late 1920s and 1930s.

The most rudimentary forms of workers' resistance were individualized acts of sabotage of company property, self-mutilation, and desertion. The first two forms are mentioned only infrequently in the literature on the rubber plantations. However, there is no doubt that these activites occurred frequently enough that the colonial administration specifically listed them as criminal offenses punishable by heavy fines, hard labor, or imprisonment. Yet perhaps the clearest indication of the overall state of mind of plantation workers for which ample evidence is available was the number of desertions. Table 1 provides figures (whenever possible) for the number of cases of breach of contract, the number of deserters recaptured, and the number of reported sicknesses and deaths on rubber plantations between 1923 and 1940. Desertion became the most widespread and most successful native response to the oppressive realities of working class life on the rubber plantations. For example, in both 1925 and 1926, when more than one-third of the total number of coolies employed were disabled due to sickness or death, an estimated one out of every ten plantation workers deserted (Lasker, 1972:258). As an index of discontent, these figures do not seem exaggerated: in 1929, according to Goudal (1938:84), approximately 11.2% of the native workforce deserted; and in 1930, approximately 8.3% did the same.

The official explanation for the high desertion rates was that most deserters were enticed away by special recruitment agents and were hired as noncontract workers on plantations which officially did not employ contract labor.[4] To the extent to which this explanation is sufficient, it appears to indicate the coolies pragmatically sought to reach a market where their labor-power would obtain the highest price. This worker strategy was in direct opposition to the combined efforts of European planters and colonial administrators, both of whom attempted to use coercive labor legislation to greatly reduce the bargaining power of native workers.

European planters also complained that numerous desertions occurred among newly recruited workers. Besides the reasons already offered, there was one significant additional explanation why workers often seized upon the earliest opportunity to desert. As one means of encouraging labor recruitment, European planters presented prospec-

Table 1. General Statistics on Breaches of Contract, Captured Deserters, Sickness, and Deaths

Year	Breaches of Contract (in %) a	Breaches of Contract (in absolute figures)	Captured Deserters (in absolute figures)	Hospitalization (in %)	Malaria Cases (in %)	Deaths (in %)
1922b	na	1,462	355	na	na	na
1923	—	730	133	—	—	—
1924	—	847	216	—	—	—
1925	—	1,081	208	—	—	—
1926	—	1,653	558	—	—	—
1927	17.1	3,824	1,070	—	12.0d	5.4e
1928	14.1	4,484	1,446	—	12.0	4.5e
1929	15.0	4,301	1,961	—	12.0	2.8e
1930	9.4	2,973	680	—	12.0	2.4
1931	8.0	743	321	—	12.0	2.0
1932	5.7	487	337	5.1	2.9	1.7
1933	13.4	562	321	7.3	3.1	2.0
1934	8.7	860c	353c	9.6	6.2	2.2
1935	4.6	na	na	8.0	3.0	1.9
1936	2.5	—	—	6.0	2.9	0.5
1937	4.5	—	—	4.0	1.4	1.0
1938	3.9	—	—	2.7	.9	0.7
1939	9.0	—	—	2.8	.9	0.7
1940	na	—	—	4.9	1.0	1.2

na = not available

a = Percentages are given as a proportion of the contract labor-force.
b = From January 1, 1919, to December 31, 1922.
c = Does not include November and December 1934.
d = Between 1927 and 1931 the percentage ranged from 12.0% to 15.0%. Estimated in Mingot and Canet (1937).
e = Estimated by E. Demalarre (1931:20).

SOURCES: Goudal (1938); Le Minor (1944).

tive coolies an "engagement bonus" of 10 piastres (an equivalent of one month's money-wages) at the time of the signing of the three-year contract. Plantation workers were rarely if ever forewarned that certain monthly sums were to be deducted from their cash-wages during the first few months of employment in order to repay this original advance. Numerous workers just simply left the plantation once they realized that they would be forced into indebtedness in order to sustain themselves from the very outset of their contract period. In order to conteract high desertion rates, the colonial administration introduced specific legislative measures designed to curtail what the planters considered the fraudulent retention of advances. For example, the colonial decree of June 1932 stipulated that contract workers who failed to repay their engagement bonuses were liable to imprisonment for not less than two months and not more than two years and a fine of 25 to 3,000 frances, or to either of these penalties singly (Goudal, 1938:82). The annual report of the Labour Inspectorate in Tonkin for 1933-1934 described the new repressive machinery designed to contain breach of contract and which was incorporated into the colonial decree of June 1932:

> Hitherto deserters who returned to Tonkin were practically safe from pursuit. In the future any worker reported as a deserter in the *Bulletin de Police Crimenelle* will, when discovered, be summarily arrested for breach of trust. Notice of his arrest will be given by telegram to the court of the place where the offense was committed, which will then hand over the case to the court of the place of arrest and transmit the file by the most rapid means. [Goudal, 1938:83]

As a consequence of the application of this 1932 decree in Cochinchina, the local magistrates of Bien Hoa and Baria passed sentences of from 15 days to six months' imprisonment in 34 cases and 25 cases, respectively, during 1933-1934.

THE STRIKE: THE OFFENSIVE WEAPON OF PLANTATION WORKERS

Plantation workers forged creative and sophisticated responses to the dictatorship of metropolitan capital. Coolies seized on such diverse measures as desertion, self-multilation (including suicide), sabotage, theft of plantation property, and "loafing" in order to demonstrate their discontent with the appalling working conditions. On the one hand, the inventiveness and sheer bravery of these forms of protest offer distinctive testimony to the existence of a worker consciousness which instinctively uncovered the nature of capitalist exploitation. On the other hand, the fact that these tactics were characteristically reactive responses reveals their definite limits as sufficient methods of challenging the rule of capital.

In contrast, the workers' strike was an economic weapon of a different magnitude. While it involved a much greater calculated risk for the participants, the collective decision to stop work altogether—whether premeditated or spontaneous—represented an offensive defiance directed toward a frontal assault on the prerogatives of capital. While "loafing," pilfering, and willful destruction of plantation property had the effect of keeping the plantation management off balance, workers' strikes actually brought the machinery of exploitation to a halt and, simultaneously, demonstrated in dramatic fashion the collective power of the working class.

Between 1930 and 1937, accounts of at least eight significant strikes on the rubber plantations can be found in official colonial records. Some highlights from these strikes are considered below. The purpose of these illustrations is to attempt, first, to undercover the primary factors which contributed to the cohesion among plantation workers and their collective willingness to bring the production process to a halt, and second, to examine the relationship between the strategies and tactics of communist militants and the formation of workers' consciousness on the rubber plantations.

THE PHU-RIENG STRIKE: FEBRUARY 4-11, 1930

The development of the workers' movement in colonial Indochina was inseparable from the formation of communist organizations. Vietnamese communists first infiltrated the Phu-Rieng plantation (located about 100 kilometers almost directly north of Saigon) in the late 1920s, following the internal decision of the Revolutionary Youth League (Association de la jeunesse revolutionnaire) to win over the relatively small but growing proletariat to the revolutionary cause.[5] Communist infiltration of the Phu Rieng plantation took place in three separate stages. First, in the beginning of 1928, Ngo Gia Tu (one of the pioneers of the communist movement under the leadership of the Revolutionary Youth League) dispatched Nguyen Xuan Cu to the Michelin plantations with the purpose of establishing propaganda cells. Nguyen Xuan Cu enlisted the support of three other coolies, among them Tran Tu Binh, a worker who was assigned to the Phu-Rieng plantation health clinic as an orderly.[6] Second, members of the Revolutionary League in October 1929 formed the nucleus of the first cell of the recently established Indochinese Communist Party, with six members on the Phu-Rieng plantation. Third, communist militants on the plantation engaged in the formation of underground organizations, such as a workers' union (which published a monthly broadsheet called *L'Emancipation* and which coordinated workers' struggles on the plantation) and trained self-defense groups (Brocheux, 1975).

Forced into a clandestine existence, the communist party members used available legal forms of organization as a method of systematically penetrating the various plantation "mutual aid" societies, the theater groups, the dance troupes, and the sports clubs. For example, the dance troupes provided convenient camouflage for self-defense training. In particular, members of the various dance troupes openly practiced the seemingly innocent traditional art of *vo* (boxing and fencing) (Brocheux, 1975). Similarly, the sport clubs regularly involved themselves in physical fitness and the martial arts. For the communists, the most important advantage of these plantation organizations was that members met on a regular basis, thereby permitting numerous opportunities to discuss mutual dissatisfactions in an apparently innocent setting.

A number of factors contributed to the mounting tensions of the Phu-Rieng plantation during the late 1920s. On September 26, 1927, a contingent of coolies (who had only just arrived from Tonkin) refused to proceed to the rubber lots as they were accustomed to after the morning roll-call. Instead, they "attacked their overseer, M. Monteil, and killed him; then, invading the plantation, they indulged themselves in acts of hostility against the director and his European assistants." The immediate response of Governor-General Varenne was to declare that "this extremely regrettable incident confirmed the usefulness of the regulation of employment concerning the main work-force sufficient for the real development of the colonization of Indochina."[7] After an intense official investigation, Governor-General Varenne announced that Monteil's death was not politically motivated but merely concerned a simple act of personal vengeance. Nevertheless,

Varenne's report hinted at the alleged brutality of Triaire, the European *directeur* of the plantation.[8] Another colonial report even ventured so far as to acknowledge that Monteil's assassination "has been the direct response to the abuse committed within the plantations."[9]

It is fortunate that a second account of these events also exists. Tran Tu Binh was an eyewitness to the affair and described it, and the circumstances preceding it, in his memoirs. According to Tran Tu Binh, Monteil was well-known for his ill-treatment of the coolies. One worker who had recently disembarked from Tonkin, Nguyen Dinh Tu, refused to submit to Monteil's frequent beatings. He persuaded some of his companions to join with him in a conspiracy to assassinate Monteil. One night, these coolies ventured into the forest where they took an oath of brotherhood, a rite designed to secure their unity and their determination: each coolie cut his finger and mixed his blood in a bowl of alcohol. Upon sharing this drink, the coolies vowed to remain bound to the others through an oath of silence. The next morning, Nguyen Dinh Tu and his fellow-conspirators killed Monteil with a blow of a hatchet (Brocheux, 1975). Most of the coolies involved in these events were quickly captured and imprisoned. In February 1928, the criminal court of Saigon pronounced the following penalties: one coolie was condemned to death, two were condemned to a life-time of hard labor, and three received a punishment of 20 years of hard labor.[10]

This so-called "Monteil Affair" surfaced as a *cause célèbre* for frightened European planters; they sought to counteract the intensified resistance of plantation workers with concerted demands for not only tighter controls over the contract labor system, but also more stringent penalties for alleged breaches of plantation discipline. Despite the colonial administration's efforts to force plantation managers to curb some of the more obvious sources of tension, the working and living conditions on the rubber plantations continued to deteriorate. One clear indication of these appalling conditions can be demonstrated by a survey of the morbidity and mortality rates on selected plantations. One official colonial report, for example, mentioned a mortality rate of 17% on the Phu-Rieng plantation in 1928.[11] Another colonial report attributed the 123 deaths and 242 hospitalizations on the An-Vinh and An-Loc plantations in 11 months (out of a total 659 employees) to malarial conditions and the lack of infirmaries. This same report referred to the malarial conditions, the extremely difficult work, and the workers' complaint of ill-treatment on the Phu-Rieng plantation. In addition, the report announced that unchecked malarial conditions had resulted in 61 deaths in three months out of less than 1,000 coolies on the Budop plantation in Thudamot province in 1927.[12]

Plantation workers fought back. Brocheux (1975) mentions the occurrence of 12 separate incidents which involved the assassination of native *cais* on the plantations of Loc-Ninh and Cam-Tien alone during the course of 1928. While the assassination of the European, Monteil, was the object of an intense colonial investigation, the increasingly frequent physical assaults on native overseers received little if any official attention. The combination of harsh discipline, inadequate food rations, frequent mistreatment, unhygienic conditions, and a host of other equally persistent vexations contributed to the Phu-Rieng strike of February 4-11, 1930. Within the context of the historical unfolding of the Vietnamese workers' movement, this particular strike was notable for two major reasons: first, its intensity and duration (the strike lasted nearly one week and involved an estimated 1,300 coolies); and second, the fact that the Indochinese Communist Party deliberately and painstakingly prepared the strike for February 1930, the date of *tet*—the new year of the lunar calendar (Brocheux, 1975).

The management of the Phu-Rieng plantation placed the blame for this "workers' mutiny" on a small number of "communist agitators" who had manipulated their fellow-workers.[13] However, within colonial administrative circles, the official opinions were more heterogeneous. On the one hand, Governor-General Pasquier accepted the Michelin version of events, although in clearly more prudent terms. According to one official report, Pasquier held the view that:

> it did not appear. . .that the regime of labor or the conditions of food rationing or hygiene should have dissatisfied the *coolies* and the movement had been plainly of revolutionary inspiration.[14]

On the other hand, a more detailed report admitted that the propaganda which was used to take advantage of the dissatisfaction of the plantation workers "has been in part justified by the mistreatment, at times the brutalities, of the agents of exploitation."[15]

On February, 4, 1930, under the pretext of assisting in the burial of a fellow-worker, an estimated 300 coolies ceased to work. With the arrest of a *cai* whom the plantation management accused of stealing, 1,300 coolies decided to strike. They presented the plantation manager with the following demands: the release of the imprisoned *cai*; the suspension of physical punishment; the suppression of salary reduction as payment for alleged fines; exemption from colonial taxes; payment of salaries to workers on leave for maternity; an eight-hour working-day—including the time required to proceed to and from the rubber lots; an indemnity payment for work-related accidents; the repatriation to Tonkin of workers who reached the end of their terms of contract of three years; and, finally, the removal of two European assistants accused of excessive brutality.[16]

According to Tran Tu Binh, the strike had been meticulously prepared over a period of many months. Rice had been set aside in secret storehouses hidden in the forest and knives and staves had been accumulated. An executive union committee decided on the exact date for the strike. On the first day of the *tet* holidays, the representative of the workers' union took advantage of a public performance of the plantation dance troupe in front of the bungalow of the manager, Soumangnac, to present the workers' demands. The strike itself only got underway with the arrest of the *cai*, Tran Van Cung, who was actually a member of the cell of the Communist Party. The workers quickly routed a section of the *Garde indigène* (local militia stationed on the plantation) and captured a few weapons. After driving off the "compound police with knives and staves," they became masters of the plantation and its installations. They hoisted the red flag embellished with the hammer-and-sickle insignia. The plantation occupation became a great festival: the workers burned the plantation's registries which listed their names and serial numbers. In Broucheux's words, (1975:81) "[the workers] took possession of their lives within the reserves and they indulged in a great collective feast: it is a *tet* without precedent."

The repression was very severe: the communists and organizers of the strike who had openly presented themselves were identified and arrested. Phan Van Phu—alias Tran Tu Binh—was condemned to five years in the prison at Poulo-Condore along with many of his comrades. While pointing out possible reforms that could be established in the contract labor system, the official Herisson report completely exonerated Michelin from any responsibility:

> . . .on the *Michelin* plantations the *coolies* are nourished and housed as well as possible; no act of brutality has been taken up against the assistants capable of motivating a strike. If a blunder has been

committed, it has been the excuse, not the cause of the rebellion. . . . The
Directeurs and the French assistants of the great plantations understand
themselves well. They are all, without exception, brave people.[17]

The workers' occupations and the ensuing military-like reinstatement
of colonial power resulted in considerable physical destruction of
plantation installations. In fact, the damage was so substantial and
costly that Michelin at first considered returning the contract workers
to Tonkin and abandoning the plantation altogether.[18] During the
course of the Phu-Rieng strike, the Michelin management found that
the local police forces proved to be totally ineffective in restoring order
and that reinforcements had to be brought from as far away as Saigon
and Bien Hoa. As a consequence, Michelin requested—and even
agreed to contribute to the cost of—the installation of more police
stations and an outpost of local militia in the vicinity of the Phu-Rieng
plantations.[19]

The Phu-Rieng strike preceded by three months the outbreak of the
massive rural insurrection in Ha-Tinh and Nghe-An provinces in
Annam, the period of the so-called "Red Soviets" of 1930-1931.
These two events demonstrate the actual anchoring of the Indochinese
Communist Party within the mass struggles of the popular classes. In
the course of the Nghe-Tinh rural rebellion, the village commune
served as a natural base for the substitution of popular power for the
autocratic rule of local notables. In contrast, once the coolies had
seized total mastery over the plantation, they found themselves at a
loss as to how to consolidate and extent their control beyond the
boundaries of the plantation itself.

While the great strike at Phu-Rieng represented the convergence of
the immediate aspirations of the coolies and the political goals of the
communist militants, the 1932 Dau-Tieng strike symbolized the
spontaneous and effective actions of plantation workers in order to
prevent an arbitrary reduction of their wage-bill. The 1932 Dau-Tieng
strike will be considered below.

THE DAU-TIENG STRIKE, DECEMBER 16, 1932

For the rubber companies, workers' salaries represented approximately 65% to 75% of their total capital outlay. Beginning in 1930-
1931, European planters attempted to offset the downward spiral of
world rubber prices through the reduction of the salaries of their

coolies and by discharging an estimated 11% of the total plantation workforce (Brocheux, 1975). These actions affected almost entirely noncontract laborers who served as a *disposable contingent* of the plantation labor force. The salaries and conditions of employment for noncontract laborers fluctuated wildly because of the laws of supply and demand. In contrast, contract workers benefitted from the relative stability of employment.

In 1932, European planters—through the agency of the *Union des Planteurs de Caoutchouc*—began negotiations with the colonial administration over the issue of the reduction of salaries of contract coolies. The European planters justified their desire to reduce these salaries in two principal ways. First, they argued that the French government's decision to gradually reduce state subsidies for colonial rubber plantations meant that profitable production could only be maintained if production costs could somehow be lowered. Second, they argued that British planters in Malaya and Dutch planters in Sumatra had recently acquired a competitive advantage in world rubber production. In British Malaya, planters (in November 1930) had reduced workers' salaries on the plantations by 20%. Furthermore, the devaluation of the pound-sterling in the same year had the effect of further lowering production costs on the British rubber plantations. In Sumatra, Dutch planters reduced workers' salaries on the plantations by 10%.[20]

In June 1932, Governor-General Pasquier agreed to the salary reduction proposed by the *Union des planteurs de caoutchouc*. The Governor-General accepted the *Union's* claim that plantation workers in Indochina, despite the cash-wage reductions, would still receive a total wage-bill 50% higher than Malayan rubber workers because of payments-in-kind (daily rice rations) and the *pecule* (i.e., forced savings supposedly returned to coolies at the termination of their contract period). Pasquier also argued that these salary reductions would not only aid in the recovery of the profitability of the rubber plantations (which was in the economic interests of France), but also relieve the French Treasury of the tremendous financial burden of continued state subsidies. Nevertheless, the colonial administration only accepted the proposal of the *Union des planteurs de caoutchouc* on two conditions: first, that the planters maintain the present wage rates for noncontract coolies (which by this time had dropped considerably lower than those of contract coolies); and second, that the planters only apply these salary reductions to individual coolies who had either renewed their former contract or contracted labor for the first time. It was the noncompliance with this second condition by the Michelin plantation which brought about the Dau-Tieng strike of December 16, 1932.[21]

On December 16, 1932, the Michelin management at the Dau-Tieng plantation announced through posted placards that—effective immediately—daily money-wages were reduced from $.40 to $.30 (from $.30 to $.23 for women workers) and that the daily rice ration was reduced by 100 grams (or approximately 12%).[22] The enraged coolies quickly gathered together and demanded that the plantation management reverse its decision. At midnight, when it was evident that these negotiations had collapsed, the coolies decided to leave the plantation and proceed to Thudamot to present their grievances to the *Chef de la Province*. An estimated 1,500 coolies formed themselves into a column and marched off the plantation. About one kilometer from the plantation, the column came across a local militia station. The militia fired into the crowd, killing three workers and seriously wounding four.

A subsequent judicial inquiry concluded that the management of the plantation at Dau-Tieng had provided the workers with false information about the proposed salary reductions.[23] In a separate report, Governor-General Pasquier noted the apparent contradiction between Michelin's "rational and humane treatment of the labor-force" and the incidents "which are not the first . . . caused by the maltreatment of [plantation] agents."[24] Nevertheless, the workers' actions prevented the Michelin plantation management from carrying out their desire to reduce salaries arbitrarily.

THE DAU-TIENG STRIKE, MAY 23-24, 1937

Between 1932 and 1936, the *Syndicat des planteurs* and the *Union des planteurs* continued to pressure the colonial administration to approve their demands for salary reductions (retroactively to the lowest for 1932), the elimination of the forced savings plan (the *pecule*), the maintenance of state subsidies, and the curtailment of the head-tax for contract laborers (because planters were obliged to pay the tax). In 1936, the prevailing economic and political climate in Indochina changed considerably. After the realignment of the piastre with the devalued franc, the rubber planters experienced renewed prosperity. But these rejuvenated economic activites were accompanied by a drastic increase in the cost of living for the working population of Indochina. In France, the *Front populaire* held the reins of government, thereby serving as an inspirational focal point for the intensified political struggles of the popular masses in Indochina (Brocheux, 1975).

Put briefly, with these new political and economic developments, a significant shift in the terrain of the class struggle in Indochina ensued. The accelerated strike wave which hit Indochina during the last six months of 1936 demonstrated the widespread restlessness and discontent among wage-laborers in Indochina.

> The strike begins to snowball: 9 enterprises on strike in September, 17 in October, 29 in November, 51 in December, 112 in January (140 according to the political report of the same month, with 4,000 strikers), 19 in February. The same scale is recorded within the very provisional statistics on the total strength of the strikers and the number of strike days: at a minimum, 15,000 strikers, 69,000 work-days lost in 6 months. We recall, in virtue of comparison, that the strike movement has a second home particularly active in the North. The strikes there are more spectacular than in the South, also longer. [Hemery, 1975:347]

In specific, after a four-year period of respite, wage-laborers on the rubber plantations engaged in a renewed wave of strikes: Dau-Tieng (August 1936), Quan-Loi (August 1936), Dau-Tieng (October 1936), Ben-Cui (November 1936), and Long-Thanh (January 1937).

Beginning in late 1936, the Governor of Cochinchina, Pagês, publicly urged the rubber planters to increase workers' salaries if they wished to avoid strikes and demonstratons on the plantations. Despite the agreements of planters in the province of Bien-Hoa to increase salaries, the *Syndicat des planteurs* rejected the colonial administration's proposal to uniformly increase salaries on April 1, 1937, from $.27 to $.32 per day for male contract workers. Michelin, "which did not belong to the *Syndicat* and readily considered itself as sovereign power within this territory," also refused to apply the proposed salary scale (Hemery, 1975). At Michelin's Dau-Tineg plantation, tensions mounted rapidly. On April 15, and again on May 2, Tonkinese coolies attacked Cochinchinese *cais* who were regarded as particularly brutal. On May 8, a column of 800 coolies marched to the local police-post at Dau-Tieng to protest the ill-treatment of a fellow-worker by local militia stationed near the plantation. On May 23, the plantation coolies refused to work and presented the following demands to the *directeur*: salary increases from $.32 to $.40 per day, rice rations of 800 grams per day, water rations in sufficient quantities both for personal use and household chores, the diminution of the daily tasks required under the piece-work system, and more humane and gentle treatment on the part of European superintendents and *cais*.[25] After a coolie was beated by a *cai*, the workers surrounded the plantation headquarters where they remained all night. When it became obvious that the plantation management had no intentions of negotiating these demands, the workers turned—as they had in 1932—to their principal weapon, the abandonment of the plantation and a march of protest toward Saigon. In order to break the isolation of the plantation, 1,500 coolies began their 80-kilometer march to Saigon along the Ben Suc road on the morning of May 24. Along the route, they were stopped by five truckloads of civil guards who had been hastily dispatched by Pagès. After a long discussion, and the promise of an official inquiry, the workers were given an ultimatum: either be dispersed or return to the Dau-Tieng plantation. After having received vague assurance that their salaries would be increased to the proposed official scale, the workers boarded the trucks and returned to the plantation. But, on June 24, 1937, when the coolies organized a new protest meeting and chose their delegates, the plantation management used three truckloads of civil guards to break up the demonstration and arrest a number of workers' delegates. A column of 600 coolies attempted to free their imprisoned fellow-workers, but this effort was unsuccessful. All in all, 60 coolies were repatriated to Tonkin and seven were condemned to prison terms.[26]

EUROPEAN CONTROL OVER THE CAPITALIST LABOR PROCESS

In colonial Indochina, rubber cultivation took place within the framework of capitalist production relations (i.e., wage-labor and capital) and the capitalist labor process. European investments permitted private entrepreneurs to assume direct control over not only the exchange of the commodity (rubber) on the world market, but also the actual process of prodution. The willingness of these owners of money-capital to invest (i.e., to exchange money-capital for constant capital and variable capital) depended exclusively on the expected rates of return. The continuous struggle of metropolitan capital against native labor-power centered on capital's efforts not only to increase the rate of exploitation (through direct control over the capitalist labor process), but also to maintain a politically docile labor-force. From metropolitan capital's point of view, the class struggle assumed multiple forms. The main elements can be summarized as follows. First, the combination of social differentiation in the rural zones (Tonkin and Annam in particular) and colonial state pressures (e.g., authorization of the contract labor system) brought about the formation of a class of immediate producers who (1) were formally separated from effective ownership and control of the materials and instruments of prodution, and (2) were compelled by economic necessity to negotiate the exchange of their labor-power on the market. Because of the over-abundance of available supplies of labor-power, metropolitan capital was able to use the pressure of unemployment to force a reduction in the value of the commodity of labor-power (thereby increasing the rate of exploitation). Second, metropolitan capital—through its direct control over the capitalist labor process—was able to achieve a relatively high rate of social intensity of labor and given a relatively prolonged working day through the extensive use of various coercive and manipulative tactics. The development of the closed plantation system created a social environment that limited the forms of struggle available to the working population. Third, metropolitan capital gradually broadened and deepened its capacity to organize the labor process. The increased capitalist domination and penetration of the actual laboring activity of immediate producers simply multiplied the ways and means to increase the rate of exploitation through increased division of labor, specialization and reorganization of work functions, routinization and standardization of work-tasks with the aim of expanding output through the utilization of less laboring time, increasing efficiency through the introduction of norms for job performance, and the minimization of unproductive social overhead costs. Fourth, and finally, metropolitan capital used the political support of the colonial state administration to weaken decisively the political organization of plantation workers. Colonial legislation did not recognize trade unions and effectively outlawed work stoppages through the threat of long-term imprisonment and extensive fines. Metropolitan capital attempted to atomize and intimidate the plantation proletariat in order to minimize the forms of struggle through which the workers could effectively counter—through collective action—capitalist power at the point of production.

THE PRODUCTION OF LATEX: "WHITE GOLD" OR "WHITE BLOOD"?

For the European capitalists who sought easy profits through investments in colonial rubber production, the latex which oozed from the rubber trees became known as "white gold." From metropolitan capital's point of view, the capitalist labor process was the specific site of the production process of capital, i.e., the production of "white gold." Plantation owners and the colonial state administration worked hand-in-hand. Whenever the collective power of the working class threatened to disrupt production schedules, the state administration cooperated fully with the plantation management by dispatching civil guards, establishing local militia posts, and supplying police spies (from the *Sureté*, the French secret police). For example, after the Quan-Loi strike of August 1936, M. Erard (Chief of the First Bureau of Management for Economic and Administrative Affairs) offered the following suggestions as one method of preventing the spread of workers' unrest:

> It seems without doubt that the *coolies* of the large plantations are increasingly influenced by communist propaganda and I fear strongly that we are moving towards a generalization of these conflicts if strict measures are not taken to establish a protective cordon around the plantations . . . [and] to proceed immediately to a complete [political] purge of the [plantation] villages. In this work, it is important that the *Sureté* collaborate with the managers of the plantations, the *Inspecteur du Travail*, and the *Chef de province*.[27]

The frequent use of state power to break strikes and settle industrial disputes formed an integral part of crushing workers' resistance.

Following the first wave of labor unrest which occurred in the early 1930s, a number of rubber companies initiated improvements in both the living and working conditions on the plantations. The colonial administration placed considerable pressure on the plantation owners to build day-nurseries and schools, to construct hospitals and clinics, to substitute "model villages" (designed for family habitation) for the original barracks-like accommodations, to introduce market places and competitive shops, and to encourage the formation of sports clubs and cultural associations. On the one hand, the colonial administration assumed the task of formulating state policies designed to undermine workers' mounting tensions on the plantations, thereby maintaining sufficient class harmony to ensure the continued accumulation of capital. Situated outside the "economic space" occupied by individual capital units with investments in Indochina, the state administration enjoyed a favorable vantage point from which to view the terrain of the class struggle. On the other hand, individual rubber-producing companies were forced to operate within the constraints of costs of production and the prices which could be obtained on the world market. Plantation managers were under continuous pressure to maximize rubber output and minimize production costs. Under these circumstances, these European managers considered state regulations and reformist-minded policies as a nagging inconvenience and treated workers' grievances as the consequence of an inherent native laziness and ingratitude.

If the European capitalists called the latex "white gold," the plantation workers found a different name to describe it: "white blood." This expression symbolized the way in which workers experienced the relations of exploitation and domination at the point of production. Despite the state administration's efforts to prevent class polarization by forcing the plantations to make at least superficial improvements, the actual living and working conditions for most plantation workers deteriorated greatly during the 1930s. The following statement, taken from a confidential report prepared after the 1937 Dau-Tieng strike, offers a telling commentary on the impoverished conditions on the Michelin plantations:

> It is necessary to have the courage to say it, there unfortunately exists on the *Michelin* plantations a "planter" spirit which is absolutely lamentable. . . . Besides a magnificent hospital and remarkable industrial installation, the [*Michelin*] company has completely neglected to proceed to the installations which would provide a minimum of comfort for the *coolies*. *Michelin* has been the last to transform barracks-like accommodations [*campements collectifs d'habitations*] of the workforce into small individual houses, but the former have become a filthy saving.

> The arrogance and the feudal spirit of two successive directors . . . has contributed, besides, to make the *Michelin* plantation [a place of] exploitation in a vast enclosure, ignoring the actual life of the Annamites, under the direction of condescending French assistants, far away and without railway branchlines. . . .

> I wish to imply that at all times the *coolies* of *Dau-Tieng* have appeared to be treated as prisoners, as wretched ones in tattered clothing whom

the assistants overpower through contempt and insults instead of physical beatings.[28]

For plantation workers, the limits of the scope of class struggle followed primarily from one condition: the site of the direct confrontation between wage-labor and capital was confined almost exclusively to the plantation itself. The plantation system presented metropolitan capital with numerous advantages from the point of view of the suppression of workers' united action. Coolies were isolated from the most part from outside social and political contacts and influences. They were subject to brutal treatment at the hands of native overseers and European superintendants; and they were bound by long-term contracts, thereby greatly hindering their individual capacity to negotiate a higher price for the sale of their labor-power.

Nevertheless, despite these enormous obstacles, plantation workers demonstrated a remarkable capacity to engage in united action and to formulate collective demands. One cannot help but be struck by the lasting quality of the workers' demand for human dignity. Ngyyen Dinh Tu, collaborator in the assassination plot against the French overseer Monteil, remarked to his comrades: "They are men. So are we. How can we accept that they continually beat us?" (Brocheux, 1975:84).

On the eve of World War II, the proletariat of the rubber plantations of southern Indochina had established its place within the country-wide workers' movement. Unlike the plantation system in British Malaya and Sumatra-Borneo which contributed to the creation of a "plural-ethnic" consciousness, the plantation system in Indochina served as a primary factor of nationalist integration. French labor recruiters were responsible for transferring literally tens of thousands of coolies from the impoverished rural zones of Tonkin and Annam to the southern plantations and back again. By all indications, this migrant labor system (which emerged in other branches of industry as well) was a key factor in overcoming ethnic and regional suspicions and provided the foundation for the eventual political solidarity among the popular masses (wage-laborers, landless tenants situated primarily in Cochinchina, and small-scale subsistence cultivators situated in Tonkin and Annam).

One final point can be made: the process of proletarianization that took place in Indochina during the colonial period was accomplished by the development of new and varied forms of workers' struggles against the despotism of capital. The plantations—just like the mines and urban enterprises—served as schools for the maturation of the first workers' militants and communists. The experimentation with different strategies and tactics at the point of production added to the overall experience of the workers' movement. Nevertheless, the workers' struggles conducted during the 1920s and 1930s were confined for the most part to wages-and-hours demands. It was the communist militants who were instrumental in providing another dimension to the workers' struggle. Despite tactical shifts and internal differences, they operated from one cardinal principle: unify patriotism and communism within the crucible of the anticolonial struggle (Brocheux, 1975). Thus, communist strategy moved beyond the economistic struggle—which centered on merely altering the terms of the rate of exploitation—to the political class struggle, i.e., the overthrow of the colonial regime and the seizure of state power. Eventually, under the leadership of a communist party, the popular masses did accomplish forcible entrance into the realm of rulership over their own destiny. The class resistance of plantation coolies was an important building-block in the historical conjuncture of the anticolonial and the anticapitalist struggle.

NOTES

1. A considerable portion of the research for this project was conducted at the Archives nationales, section d'outre-mer (Paris). The following abbreviations will be used throughout this study:

AOM—Archives nationales, section d'outre-mer;

NF Indochine—Nouveau Fonds Indochine;

SLOTFOM—Service de liaison entre les originaires de la France d'outre-mer;

Agence FOM—Fonds de l'Agence de la France d'outre-mer.

2. AOM, Agence FOM, carton 190, dossier 106, "Rapport de Inspecteur des Colonies, Rheinhart (sur la Cochinchine, 2 Decembre, 1920): Caoutchouc."

3. Hervé Bazin, a graduate of the *Ecole Coloniale* in Paris, was assassinated outside the home of his mistress on February 9, 1929, in Hanoi. Those who accomplished this deed were a break-away faction of the Vietnamese Nationalist Party (VNQDD). A note was pinned to Bazin's body which listed his crimes against the Vietnamese people. See AOM, SLOTFOM, Series III, carton 39, dossier 2, telegram of February 10, 1929.

4. The colonial Labour Inspectorate also reported that "the undertakings from which desertions are abnormally numerous are generally those with an excessively high

mortality rate; while admitting that certain agents entice the workers away, there can be no doubt that their work is greatly facilitated by the bad hygienic conditions on some plantations and the resulting demoralisation of the workers' (Compte rendu sur le fonctionnement de l'Inspection Générale du Travail, 1927-1928, p. 35, cited in Goudal, 1938:84).

5. The Revolutionary Youth League was established by Vietnamese exiles in southern China in 1925. The political aims of the organization were purposely kept very broad in order to appeal to a wide popular audience. The organization's expressed goals were "national revolution," overthrow of the French colonial regime, and the restoration of "national independence through formation of a "united front" of all anticolonial political tendencies in Indochina (Duiker, 1976:191).

6. The memoirs of Tran Tu Binh (worker and communist militant on the Phu-Rieng plantation between 1928 and 1930) provide perhaps the most complete record of communist strategy and tactics in their efforts to organize plantation workers during this period. Brocheux (1975) relies heavily on these memoirs.

7. AOM, NF Indochine 2616, "Note pour le Ministre sur deux incidents survenus sur la plantation Michelin, dans la region du Phu-Rieng," Ministère des Colonies, Direction des Affairs Economiques, 2ème Bureau, 5 juin, 1930.

8. AOM, SLOTFOM, Series III, carton 125, dossier 2.

9. AOM, NF Indochine 2614 (Telegram par M. Pietri, au Ministère des Colonies, Direction des Affairs Economiques, 7 juin, 1930.)

10. AOM, NF Indochine 2616, "Note pour le Ministre sur deux incidents survenus sur la plantation Michelin, dans la region de Phu-Rieng," Ministère des Colonies, Direction des Affairs Economiques, 2ème Bureau, 5 juin, 1930.

11. AOM, NF Indochine 2614 (Telegram N^O 64, Ministère des Colonies, par Gouveneur-General Pasquier, 10 juin, 1930).

12. AOM, NF Indochine 2614 (Telegram par M. Pietre au Ministère des Colonies, Direction des Affairs Economiques, 7 juin, 1930).

13. AOM, NF Indochine 1839 (Lettre de la direction de Michelin & Cie (Clermont-Ferrand—au Ministère des Colonies, Direction des Affairs politiques, 31 mars, 1930).

14. AOM, NF Indochine 2616 ("Note au sujet du mouvement greviste sur les plantations Michelin en Cochinchine," Ministère des Colonies, Direction Politique, 5 juin, 1930).

15. AOM, SLOTFOM, Series III, carton 48.

16. See AOM, NF Indochine 2616 (M. Hérisson: "Rapport sur les plantations d'hévéas à la suite des évènements de Phu-Rieng," Saigon, 28 fevrier 1930); AOM, NF Indochine 2616, "Note pour le Ministère des Colonies, Direction des Affaires Economique, 2ème bureau, 5 juin, 1930. See also Brocheux (1975:80).

17. AOM, NF Indochine 2616 (M. Hérisson: "Rapport sur les plantations d'hévéas a la suite dans évènements de Phu-Rieng," Saigon, 26 fevrier 1930).

18. AOM, NF Indochine 2616.

19. AOM, NF Indochine 1839 (Lettre de la direction de Michelin & Cie— Clermont-Ferrand—au Ministère des Colonies, Direction des Affairs politiques, 31 mars, 1930).

20. AOM, NF Indochine 2616 (Lettre par l'Union des Planteurs de caoutchouc en Indochine au Gouverneur-Général Pasquier, 26 ai, 1932).

21. AOM, NF Indochine 2616 (Rapport par Gouverneur-Général Pasquier au Ministère des Colonies, 9 fevrier, 1933).

22. AOM, NF Indochine 2616 ("Note pour le Ministre," 16-17 Decembre, 1932).

23. AOM, NF Indochine 1839 (Note pour le Ministre, "Incidents des 16 et 17 décembre 1932 survenus sur la plantation Michelin à Dau Tien).

24. AOM, NF Indochine 2616 (Rapport au Ministère des Colonies par Gouverneur-Général Pasquier, 9 fevrier, 1933).

25. AOM, NF Indochine 2404 (Rapport au Ministère des Colonies, Direction des Affairs politiques, par Gouverneur-Général Brevie, 24 juin, 1937). This report mentioned a new tactic devised by the workers: delegates chosen to negotiate with the plantation management were continually replaced and granted no discretionary authority to make binding decisions. Hence, the plantation workers minimized European efforts to break the strike by identifying and arresting the leadership of the workers' movement.

26. See also AOM, NF Indochine 2404 (Rapport au Ministère des Colonies, Direction des Affairs politiques, par Gouverneur-Général Brevie, 24 juin, 1937).

27. AOM, NF Indochine 2404 (Rapport par M. Erard, Le Chef du ler Bureau de la Direction des Affairs Economiques et Administratives, 28 aout, 1936).

28. Rapport confidential au Gougal, date du 27 mai 1937, archives personnelles de M. Pages, cited in Brocheux (1975:75).

REFERENCES

BROCHEUX, P. (1975). "Le proletariat des plantations d'hévéas au Vietnam meridional: Aspects sociaux et politiques (1927-1937)." Le Mouvement Social, 90(Janvier-Mars):69-85.

DELAMARRE, E. (1931). Inspecteur Général du Travail en Indochine. L'Emigration et l'immigration ouvrière en Indochine. Hanoi: I.D.E.O.

DUIKER, W. (1976). The rise of nationalism in Vietnam, 1920-1941. Ithaca and London: Cornell University Press.

GOUDAL, J. (1938). Labour conditions in Indo-China. Geneva: League of Nations International Labour Office, Studies and Reports, Series B, No. 26, appendix II.

HEMERY, D. (1975). Revolutionnaires Vietnamiens et pouvoir colonial en Indochine: Communistes, Trotskystes, nationalistes á Saigon de 1932 á 1937. Paris: Francois Maspéro.

LASKER, B. (1972). Human bondage in Southest Asia. Westport, Conn.: Greenwood.

LE MINOR (1944). Le problème de la main d'oeuvre indigène sur les chantiers des enterprises agricoles Européenes en Indochine. Paris: Ecole Supérieure Coloniale.

MINGOT, R., and CANET, J. (1937). L'Héveauculture en Indochine. Paris: I.F.C.

NOTES ON THE CONTRIBUTORS

DILIP K. BASU is Associate Professor of History at the University of California, Santa Cruz. He has edited a volume on *Colonial Port Cities in Asia* (forthcoming), and is the author of several studies on the nineteenth-century Chinese and Indian economy.

WALTER L. GOLDFRANK is Associate Professor of Sociology and Director of the Interdisciplinary Graduate Program in Sociology at the University of California, Santa Cruz. He has written extensively on the Mexican revolution and is the author of "Fascism and World Economy," which appeared in the 1978 PEWS annual, *Social Change in the Capitalist World Economy.*

MICHAEL HECHTER is Associate Professor of Sociology at the University of Washington, and is the author of *Internal Colonialism: The Celtic Fringe in British National Development* (1975).

TERENCE K. HOPKINS is Director of Graduate Studies in Sociology and an Associate Director of the Fernand Braudel Center for the Study of Economies, Historical Systems, and Civilizations at the State University of New York, Binghamton. He has a work in progress on issues of method in the study of historical change.

MICHAEL S. KIMMEL is a Ph.D. candidate in sociology at the University of California, Berkeley. He is preparing a comparative structural analysis of the English Revolution and the Fronde, of which the paper in this volume is a preview.

RICHARD CURT KRAUS is Assistant Professor of Sociology at the University of Illinois, Urbana. His research focuses on the relationship of class and politics in contemporary China and has appeared in *China Quarterly* (1977) and the *American Journal of Sociology* (1979, with W. Maxwell and R. Vanneman).

PAUL LUBECK is Assistant Professor of Sociology at the University of California, Santa Cruz. He has written extensively on Nigeria and is completing a book entitled: *The Political Economy of Urban Labor: Islamic Nationalism and Class Formation in Northern Nigeria.*

RUTH MILKMAN is a graduate student in sociology at the University of California, Berkeley. She has been active in the movement against apartheid and U.S. involvment in southern Africa.

DAVID MONTEJANO is Assistant Professor of Sociology at the University of California, Berkeley. He has written extensively on race and class with particular reference to the U.S. Southwest.

MARTIN J. MURRAY is Assistant Professor of Sociology, State University of New York, Binghamton. He has completed a monograph entitled *The Development of Capitalism in Colonial Indochina, 1870-1940,* and is presently engaged in research on capitalist development and class struggle in South Africa.

IMMANUEL WALLERSTEIN is Distinguished Professor of Sociology, and Director of the Fernand Braudel Center for Study of Economies, Historical Systems, and Civilizations, State University of New York, Binghamton. He is the author of *The Modern World-System: Capitalist Agriculture and the Origins of the European World-Economy in the Sixteenth Century* (1974).

TIMOTHY C. WEISKEL is currently teaching African history as a Visiting Assistant Professor at Yale University. Combining history and social anthropology, his work focuses on the former French colonies in West Africa.

EDWIN A. WINCKLER is Assistant Professor of Sociology at Columbia University and managing editor of *Contemporary China.* He is currently completing two books about dependent modernization on Taiwan, one dealing with political participation in an authoritarian regime, and the other with the political management of regional development.